Data Munging with Perl

Data Munging
with Perl

DAVID CROSS

MANNING

Greenwich
(74° w. long.)

For electronic information and ordering of this and other Manning books,
go to www.manning.com. The publisher offers discounts on this book
when ordered in quantity. For more information, please contact:

Special Sales Department
Manning Publications Co.
32 Lafayette Place   Fax: (203) 661-9018
Greenwich, CT 06830   email: orders@manning.com

⊗ Recognizing the importance of preserving what has been written, it is Manning's policy to have
the books they publish printed on acid-free paper, and we exert our best efforts to that end.

Library of Congress Cataloging-in-Publication Data
Cross, David, 1962-
    Data munging with Perl / David Cross.
       p.   cm.
    Includes bibliographical references and index.
    ISBN 1-930110-00-6 (alk. paper)
    1. Perl (Computer program language) 2. Data structures (Computer science)
    3. Data transmission systems. I. Title.
    QA76.73.P22 C39 20001998
005.7'2—dc21
                                00-050009
                                CIP

 Manning Publications Co.   Copyeditor: Elizabeth Martin
32 Lafayette Place   Typesetter: Dottie Marsico
Greenwich, CT 06830   Cover designer: Leslie Haimes

Second, corrected printing, August 2001
Printed in the United States of America

2 3 4 5 6 7 8 9 10 – VHG – 04 03 02 01

contents

foreword

Perl is something of a weekend warrior. Outside of business hours you'll find it indulging in all kinds of extreme sports: writing haiku; driving GUIs; reviving Lisp, Prolog, Forth, Latin, and other dead languages; playing psychologist; shovelling MUDs; inflecting English; controlling neural nets; bringing you the weather; playing with Lego; even running quantum computations.

But that's not its day job.

Nine-to-five it earns its keep far more prosaically: storing information in databases, extracting it from files, reorganizing rows and columns, converting to and from bizarre formats, summarizing documents, tracking data in real time, creating statistics, doing back-up and recovery, merging and splitting data streams, logging and checkpointing computations.

In other words, munging data. It's a dirty job, but *someone* has to do it.

If that someone is you, you're definitely holding the right book. In the following pages, Dave will show you dozens of useful ways to get those everyday data manipulation chores done better, faster, and more reliably. Whether you deal with fixed-format data, or binary, or SQL databases, or CSV, or HTML/XML, or some bizarre proprietary format that was obviously made up on a drunken bet, there's help right here.

Perl is so good for the extreme stuff, that we sometimes forget how powerful it is for mundane data manipulation as well. As this book so ably demonstrates, in addition to the hundreds of esoteric tools it offers, our favourite Swiss Army Chainsaw also sports a set of simple blades that are ideal for slicing and dicing ordinary data.

Now *that's* a knife!

DAMIAN CONWAY

preface

Over the last five years there has been an explosion of interest in Perl. This is largely because of the huge boost that Perl received when it was adopted as the de facto language for creating content on the World Wide Web. Perl's powerful text manipulation facilities made it an obvious choice for writing Common Gateway Interface (CGI) scripts. In the wake of the web's popularity, Perl has become one of the hottest programming languages currently in use.

Unfortunately, a side effect of this association with CGI programming has been the popular misconception that this is Perl's sole function. Some people even believe that Perl was designed for use in CGI programming. This is clearly wrong as Perl was, in fact, written long before the design of the CGI protocol.

This book, then, is not about writing CGI scripts, but about another of the computing tasks for which Perl is particularly well suited—data munging.

Data munging encompasses all of those boring, everyday tasks to which most programmers devote a good deal of their time—the tasks of converting data from one format into another. This comes close to being a definitive statement of what programming is: taking input data, processing (or "munging") it, and producing output data. This is what most programmers do most of the time.

Perl is particularly good at these kinds of tasks. It helps programmers write data conversion programs quickly. In fact, the same characteristics that make Perl ideal for CGI programming also make it ideal for data munging. (CGI programs are really data munging programs in flashy disguise.)

In keeping with the Perl community slogan, "There's more than one way to do it," this book examines a number of ways of dealing with various types of data. Hopefully, this book will provide some new "ways to do it" that will make your programming life more productive and more enjoyable.

Another Perl community slogan is, "Perl makes easy jobs easy and hard jobs possible." It is my hope that by the time you have reached the end of this book, you will see that "Perl makes fun jobs fun and boring jobs bearable."

Intended audience

This book is aimed primarily at programmers who munge data as a regular part of their job and who want to write more efficient data-munging code. I will discuss techniques for data munging, introducing new techniques, as well as novel uses for familiar methods. While some approaches can be applied using any language, I use Perl here to demonstrate the ease of applying these techniques in this versatile language. In this way I hope to persuade data mungers that Perl is a flexible and vital tool for their day-to-day work.

Throughout the book, I assume a rudimentary knowledge of Perl on the part of the reader. Anyone who has read and understood an introductory Perl text should have no problem following the code here, but for the benefit of readers brand new to Perl, I've included both my suggestions for Perl primers (see chapter 1) as well as a brief introduction to Perl (see appendix B).

About this book

The book begins by addressing introductory and general topics, before gradually exploring more complex types of data munging.

PART I sets the scene for the rest of the book.

Chapter 1 introduces data munging and Perl. I discuss why Perl is particularly well suited to data munging and survey the types of data that you might meet, along with the mechanisms for receiving and sending data.

Chapter 2 contains general methods that can be used to make data munging programs more efficient. A particularly important part of this chapter is the discussion of the UNIX filter model for program input and output.

Chapter 3 discusses a number of Perl idioms that will be useful across a number of different data munging tasks, including sorting data and accessing databases.

Chapter 4 introduces Perl's pattern-matching facilities, a fundamental part of many data munging programs.

PART II begins our survey of data formats by looking at unstructured and record-structured data.

Chapter 5 surveys unstructured data. We concentrate on processing free text and producing statistics from a text file. We also go over a couple of techniques for converting numbers between formats.

Chapter 6 considers record-oriented data. We look at reading and writing data one record at a time and consider the best ways to split records into individual fields. In this chapter, we also take a closer glance at one common record-oriented file format: comma-separated values (CSV) files, view more complex record types, and examine Perl's data handling facilities.

Chapter 7 discusses fixed-width and binary data. We compare several techniques for splitting apart fixed-width records and for writing results into a fixed-width format. Then, using the example of a couple of popular binary file formats, we examine binary data.

PART III moves beyond the limits of the simple data formats into the realms of hierarchical data structures and parsers.

Chapter 8 investigates the limitations of the data formats that we have seen previously and suggests good reasons for wanting more complex formats. We then see how the methods we have used so far start to break down on more complex data like HTML. We also take a brief look at an introduction to parsing theory.

Chapter 9 explores how to extract useful information from documents marked up with HTML. We cover a number of HTML parsing tools available for Perl and discuss their suitability to particular tasks.

Chapter 10 discusses XML. First, we consider the limitations of HTML and the advantages of XML. Then, we look at XML parsers available for use with Perl.

Chapter 11 demonstrates how to write parsers for your own data structures using a parser-building tool available for Perl.

PART IV concludes our tour with a brief review as well as suggestions for further study.

Appendix A is a guide to many of the Perl modules covered in the book.

Appendix B provides a rudimentary introduction to Perl.

Typographical conventions

The following conventions are used in the book:

- Technical terms are introduced in an *italic font.*
- The names of functions, files, and modules appear in a `fixed-width font`.

- All code examples are also in a `fixed-width font`.
- Program output is in a **`bold fixed-width font`**.

The following conventions are followed in diagrams of data structures:

0	element zero
1	element one

- An array is shown as a rectangle. Each row within the rectangle represents one element of the array. The element index is shown on the left of the row, and the element value is shown on the right of the row.

key1	value one
key2	value two

- A hash is shown as a rounded rectangle. Each row within the rectangle represents a key/value pair. The key is shown on the left of the row, and the value is shown on the right of the row.

key	arrayref ●	→	0	element zero
			1	element one

- A reference is shown as a black disk with an arrow pointing to the referenced variable. The type of the reference appears to the left of the disk.

Source code downloads

All source code for the examples presented in this book is available to purchasers from the Manning web site. The URL www.manning.com/cross/ includes a link to the source code files.

Author Online

Purchase of *Data Munging with Perl* includes free access to a private web forum run by Manning Publications where you can make comments about the book, ask technical questions, and receive help from the author and from other users. To access the forum and subscribe to it, point your web browser to www.manning.com/cross/. This page provides information on how to get on the forum once you are registered, what kind of help is available, and the rules of conduct on the forum.

Manning's commitment to our readers is to provide a venue where a meaningful dialog between individual readers and between readers and the author can take place. It is not a commitment to any specific amount of participation on the part of the author, whose contribution to the AO remains voluntary (and unpaid). We suggest you try asking the author some challenging questions lest his interest stray!

The Author Online forum and the archives of previous discussions will be accessible from the publisher's website as long as the book is in print.

Acknowledgments

My heartfelt thanks to the people who have made this book possible (and, who, for reasons I'll never understand, don't insist on having their names appear on the cover).

Larry Wall designed and wrote Perl, and without him this book would have been very short.

Marjan Bace and his staff at Manning must have wondered at times if they would ever get a finished book out of me. I'd like to specifically mention Ted Kennedy for organizing the review process; Mary Piergies for steering the manuscript through production; Syd Brown for answering my technical questions; Sharon Mullins and Lianna Wlasiuk for editing; Dottie Marsico for typesetting the manuscript and turning my original diagrams into something understandable; and Elizabeth Martin for copyediting.

I was lucky enough to have a number of the brightest minds in the Perl community review my manuscript. Without these people the book would have been riddled with errors, so I owe a great debt of thanks to Adam Turoff, David Adler, Greg McCarroll, D.J. Adams, Leon Brocard, Andrew Johnson, Mike Stok, Richard Wherry, Andy Jones, Sterling Hughes, David Cantrell, Jo Walsh, John Wiegley, Eric Winter, and George Entenman.

Other Perl people were involved (either knowingly or unknowingly) in conversations that inspired sections of the book. Many members of the London Perl Mongers mailing list have contributed in some way, as have inhabitants of the Perl Monks Monastery. I'd particularly like to thank Robin Houston, Marcel Grünauer, Richard Clamp, Rob Partington, and Ann Barcomb.

Thank you to Sean Burke for correcting many technical inaccuracies and also improving my prose considerably.

Many thanks to Damian Conway for reading through the manuscript at the last minute and writing the foreword.

A project of this size can't be undertaken without substantial support from friends and family. I must thank Jules and Crispin Leyser for ensuring that I took enough time off from the book to enjoy myself drinking beer and playing poker or Perudo.

Thank you, Jordan, for not complaining too much when I was too busy to fix your computer.

And lastly, thanks and love to Gill without whose support, encouragement, and love I would never have got to the end of this. I know that at times over the last year she must have wondered if she still had a husband, but I can only apologize (again) and promise that she'll see much more of me now that the book is finished.

about the cover illustration

The important-looking man on the cover of *Data Munging with Perl* is a Turkish First Secretary of State. While the exact meaning of his title is for us shrouded in historical fog, there is no doubt that we are facing a man of prestige and power. The illustration is taken from a Spanish compendium of regional dress customs first published in Madrid in 1799. The book's title page informs us:

> Coleccion general de los Trages que usan actualmente todas las Nacionas del Mundo desubierto, dibujados y grabados con la mayor exactitud por R.M.V.A.R. Obra muy util y en special para los que tienen la del viajero universal

Which we loosely translate as:

> General Collection of Costumes currently used in the Nations of the Known World, designed and printed with great exactitude by R.M.V.A.R. This work is very useful especially for those who hold themselves to be universal travelers

Although nothing is known of the designers, engravers and artists who colored this illustration by hand, the "exactitude" of their execution is evident in this drawing. The figure on the cover is a "Res Efendi," a Turkish government official which the Madrid editor renders as "Primer Secretario di Estado." The Res Efendi is just one of a colorful variety of figures in this collection which reminds us vividly of how distant and isolated from each other the world's towns and regions were just 200 years ago. Dress codes have changed since then and the diversity by region, so rich at the time, has faded away. It is now often hard to tell the inhabitant of one continent from another. Perhaps we have traded a cultural and visual diversity for a more varied personal life—certainly a more varied and interesting world of technology.

At a time when it can be hard to tell one computer book from another, Manning celebrates the inventiveness and initiative of the computer business with book covers based on the rich diversity of regional life of two centuries ago—brought back to life by the picture from this collection.

Part I

Foundations

In which our heroes learn a great deal about the background of the data munging beast in all its forms and habitats. Fortunately, they are also told of the great power of the mystical Perl which can be used to tame the savage beast.

Our heroes are then taught a number of techniques for fighting the beast *without* using the Perl. These techniques are useful when fighting with any weapon, and once learned, can be combined with the power of the Perl to make them even more effective.

Later, our heroes are introduced to additional techniques for using the Perl—all of which prove useful as their journey continues.

Data, data munging, and Perl

1

What this chapter covers:

- The process of munging data
- Sources and sinks of data
- Forms data takes
- Perl and why it is perfect for data munging

1.1   *What is data munging?*

> **munge** (muhnj) vt. **1.** [derogatory] To imperfectly transform information. **2.** A comprehensive rewrite of a routine, a data structure, or the whole program. **3.** To modify data in some way the speaker doesn't need to go into right now or cannot describe succinctly (compare mumble).
>
> The Jargon File <http://www.tuxedo.org/~esr/jargon/html/entry/munge.html>

Data munging is all about taking data that is in one format and converting it into another. You will often hear the term being used when the speaker doesn't really know exactly what needs to be done to the data.

"We'll take the data that's exported by this system, munge it around a bit, and import it into that system."

When you think about it, this is a fundamental part of what many (if not most) computer systems do all day. Examples of data munging include:

- The payroll process that takes your pay rate and the hours you work and creates a monthly payslip
- The process that iterates across census returns to produce statistics about the population
- A process that examines a database of sports scores and produces a league table
- A publisher who needs to convert manuscripts between many different text formats

1.1.1   *Data munging processes*

More specifically, data munging consists of a number of processes that are applied to an initial data set to convert it into a different, but related data set. These processes will fall into a number of categories: recognition, parsing, filtering, and transformation.

Example data: the CD file

To discuss these processes, let's assume that we have a text file containing a description of my CD collection. For each CD, we'll list the artist, title, recording label, and year of release. Additionally the file will contain information on the date on which it was generated and the number of records in the file. Figure 1.1 shows what this file looks like with the various parts labeled.

Each row of data in the file (i.e., the information about one CD) is called a data *record*. Each individual item of data (e.g., the CD title or year of release) is called a data *field*. In addition to records and fields, the data file might contain additional information that is held in headers or footers. In this example the header contains a

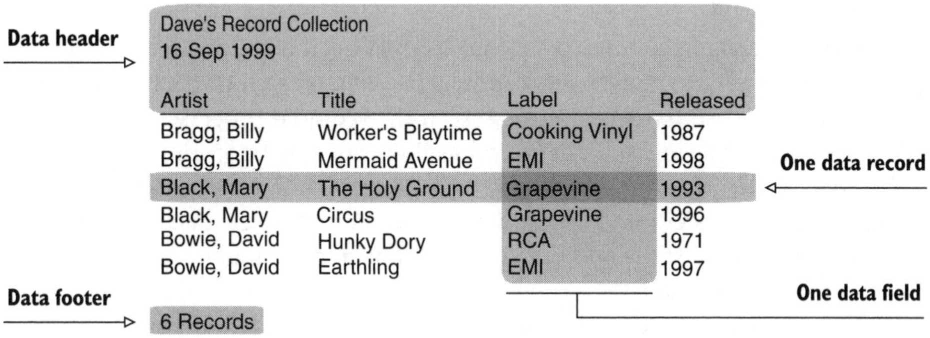

Figure 1.1 Sample data file

description of the data, followed by a header row which describes the meaning of each individual data field. The footer contains the number of records in the file. This can be useful to ensure that we have processed (or even received) the whole file.

We will return to this example throughout the book to demonstrate data munging techniques.

1.1.2 Data recognition

You won't be able to do very much with this data unless you can recognize what data you have. Data recognition is about examining your source data and working out which parts of the data are of interest to you. More specifically, it is about a computer program examining your source data and comparing what it finds against pre-defined patterns which allow it to determine which parts of the data represent the data items that are of interest.

In our CD example there is a lot of data and the format varies within different parts of the file. Depending on what we need to do with the data, the header and footer lines may be of no interest to us. On the other hand, if we just want to report that on Sept. 16, 1999 I owned six CDs, then all the data we are interested in is in the header and footer records and we don't need to examine the actual data records in any detail.

An important part of recognizing data is realizing what *context* the data is found in. For example, data items that are in header and footer records will have to be processed completely differently from data items which are in the body of the data.

It is therefore very important to understand what our input data looks like and what we need to do with it.

1.1.3 Data parsing

Having recognized your data you need to be able to do something with it. Data parsing is about taking your source data and storing it in data structures that make it easier for you to carry out the rest of the required processes.

If we are parsing our CD file, we will presumably be storing details of each CD in a data structure. Each CD may well be an element in a list structure and perhaps the header and footer information will be in other variables. Parsing will be the process that takes the text file and puts the useful data into variables that are accessible from within our program.

As with data recognition, it is far easier to parse data if you know what you are going to do with it, as this will affect the kinds of data structures that you use.

In practice, many data munging programs are written so that the data recognition and data parsing phases are combined.

1.1.4 Data filtering

It is quite possible that your source data contains too much information. You will therefore have to reduce the amount of data in the data set. This can be achieved in a number of ways.

- *You can reduce the number of records returned.* For example, you could list only CDs by David Bowie or only CDs that were released in the 1990s.
- *You can reduce the number of fields returned.* For example, you could list only the artist, title, and year of release of all of the CDs.
- *You can summarize the data in a variety of ways.* For example, you could list only the total number of CDs for each artist or list the number of CDs released in a certain year.
- *You can perform a combination of these processes.* For example, you could list the number of CDs by Billy Bragg.

1.1.5 Data transformation

Having recognized, parsed, and filtered our data, it is very likely that we need to transform it before we have finished with it. This transformation can take a variety of forms.

- *Changing the value of a data field*—For example, a customer number needs to be converted to a different identifier in order for the data to be used in a different system.

- *Changing the format of the data record*—For example, in the input record, the fields were separated by commas, but in the output record they need to be separated by tab characters.

- *Combining data fields*—In our CD file example, perhaps we want to make the name of the artist more accessible by taking the "surname, forename" format that we have and converting it to "forename surname."

1.2   Why is data munging important?

As I mentioned previously, data munging is at the heart of what most computer systems do. Just about any computer task can be seen as a number of data munging tasks. Twenty years ago, before everyone had a PC on a desk, the computing department of a company would have been known as the Data Processing department as that was their role—they processed data. Now, of course, we all deal with an Information Systems or Information Technology department and the job has more to do with keeping our PCs working than actually doing any data processing. All that has happened, however, is that the data processing is now being carried out by everyone, rather than a small group of computer programmers and operators.

1.2.1   Accessing corporate data repositories

Large computer systems still exist. Not many larger companies run their payroll system on a PC and most companies will have at least one database system which contains details of clients, products, suppliers, and employees. A common task for many office workers is to input data into these corporate data repositories or to extract data from them. Often the data to be loaded onto the system comes in the form of a spreadsheet or a comma-separated text file. Often the data extracted will go into another spreadsheet where it will be turned into tables of data or graphs.

1.2.2   Transferring data between multiple systems

It is obviously convenient for any organization if its data is held in one format in one place. Every time you duplicate a data item, you increase the likelihood that the two copies can get out of step with each other. As part of any database design project, the designers will go through a process known as normalization which ensures that data is held in the most efficient way possible.

It is equally obvious that if data is held in only one format, then it will not be in the most appropriate format for all of the systems that need to access that data. While this format may not be particularly convenient for any individual system, it should be chosen to allow maximum flexibility and ease of processing to simplify conversion into other formats. In order to be useful to all of the people who want to make use of the data, it will need to be transformed in various ways as it moves from one system to the next.

This is where data munging comes in. It lives in the interstices between computer systems, ensuring that data produced by one system can be used by another.

1.2.3   *Real-world data munging examples*

Let's look at a couple of simple examples where data munging can be used. These are simplified accounts of tasks that I carried out for large investment banks in the city of London.

Loading multiple data formats into a single database

In the first of these examples, a bank was looking to purchase some company accounting data to drive its equities research department. In any large bank the equity research department is full of people who build complex financial models of company performance in order to try to predict future performance, and hence share price. They can then recommend shares to their clients who buy them and (hopefully) get a lot richer in the process.

This particular bank needed more data to use in its existing database of company accounting data. There are many companies that supply this data electronically and a short list of three suppliers had been drawn up and a sample data set had been received from each. My task was to load these three data sets, in turn, onto the existing database.

The three sets of data came in different formats. I therefore decided to design a canonical file format and write a Perl script that would load that format onto the database. I then wrote three other Perl scripts (one for each input file) which read the different input files and wrote a file in my standard format. In this case I was reading from a number of sources and writing to one place.

Sharing data using a standard data format

In the second example I was working on a trading system which needed to send details of trades to various other systems. Once more, the data was stored in a relational database. In this case the bank had made all interaction between systems much easier by designing an XML file format[1] for data interchange. Therefore, all we needed to do was to extract our data, create the necessary XML file, and send it on to the systems that required it. By defining a standard data format, the bank

---

[1] The definition of an XML file format is known as a Document Type Definition (DTD), but we'll get to that in chapter 10.

ensured that all of its systems would only need to read or write one type of file, thereby saving a large amount of development time.

1.3   *Where does data come from? Where does it go?*

As we saw in the previous section, the point of data munging is to take data in one format, carry out various transformations on it, and write it out in another format. Let's take a closer look at where the data might come from and where it might go.

First a bit of terminology. The place that you receive data from is known as your *data source*. The place where you send data to is known as your *data sink*.

Sources and sinks can take a number of different forms. Some of the most common ones that you will come across are:

- Data files
- Databases
- Data pipes

Let's look at these data sources and sinks in more detail.

1.3.1   *Data files*

Probably the most common way to transfer data between systems is in a file. One application writes a file. This file is then transferred to a place where your data munging process can pick it up. Your process opens the file, reads in the data, and writes a new file containing the transformed data. This new file is then used as the input to another application elsewhere.

Data files are used because they represent the lowest common denominator between computer systems. Just about every computer system has the concept of a disk file. The exact format of the file will vary from system to system (even a plain ASCII text file has slightly different representations under UNIX and Windows) but handling that is, after all, part of the job of the data munger.

File transfer methods

Transferring files between different systems is also something that is usually very easy to achieve. Many computer systems implement a version of the *File Transfer Protocol* (FTP) which can be used to copy files between two systems that are connected by a network. A more sophisticated system is the *Network File System* (NFS) protocol, in which file systems from one computer can be viewed as apparently local files systems on another computer. Other common methods of transferring files are by using removable media (CD-ROMs, floppy disks, or tapes) or even as a MIME attachment to an email message.

Ensuring that file transfers are complete

One difficulty to overcome with file transfer is the problem of knowing if a file is complete. You may have a process that sits on one system, monitoring a file system where your source file will be written by another process. Under most operating systems the file will appear as soon as the source process begins to write it. Your process shouldn't start to read the file until it has all been transferred. In some cases, people write complex systems which monitor the size of the file and trigger the reading process only once the file has stopped growing. Another common solution is for the writing process to write another small flag file once the main file is complete and for the reading process to check for the existence of this flag file. In most cases a much simpler solution is also the best—simply write the file under a different name and only rename it to the expected name once it is complete.

Data files are most useful when there are discrete sets of data that you want to process in one chunk. This might be a summary of banking transactions sent to an accounting system at the end of the day. In a situation where a constant flow of data is required, one of the other methods discussed below might be more appropriate.

1.3.2 Databases

Databases are becoming almost as ubiquitous as data files. Of course, the term "database" means vastly differing things to different people. Some people who are used to a Windows environment might think of dBase or some similar nonrelational database system. UNIX users might think of a set of DBM files. Hopefully, most people will think of a relational database management system (RDBMS), whether it is a single-user product like Microsoft Access or Sybase Adaptive Server Anywhere, or a full multi-user product such as Oracle or Sybase Adaptive Server Enterprise.

Imposing structure on data

Databases have advantages over data files in that they impose structure on your data. A database designer will have defined a *database schema*, which defines the shape and type of all of your data objects. It will define, for example, exactly which data items are stored for each customer in the database, which ones are optional and which ones are mandatory. Many database systems also allow you to define relationships between data objects (for example, "each order must contain a customer identifier which must relate to an existing customer"). Modern databases also contain executable code which can define some of your business logic (for example, "when the status of an order is changed to 'delivered,' automatically create an invoice object relating to that order").

Of course, all of these benefits come at a price. Manipulating data within a database is potentially slower than equivalent operations on data files. You may also need to invest in new hardware as some larger database systems like to have their own CPU (or CPUs) to run on. Nevertheless, most organizations are prepared to pay this price for the extra flexibility that they get from a database.

Communicating with databases

Most modern databases use a dialect of Structured Query Language (SQL) for all of their data manipulation. It is therefore very likely that if your data source or sink is an RDBMS that you will be communicating with it using SQL. Each vendor's RDBMS has its own proprietary interface to get SQL queries into the database and data back into your program, but Perl now has a vendor-independent database interface (called DBI) which makes it much easier to switch processing between different databases.[2]

1.3.3 Data pipes

If you need to constantly monitor data that is being produced by a system and transform it so it can be used by another system (perhaps a system that is monitoring a real-time stock prices feed), then you should look at using a data pipe. In this system an application writes directly to the standard input of your program. Your program needs to read data from its input, deal with it (by munging it and writing it somewhere), and then go back to read more input. You can also create a data pipe (or continue an existing one) by writing your munged data to your standard output, hoping that the next link in the pipe will pick it up from there.

We will look at this concept in more detail when discussing the UNIX "filter" model in chapter 2.

1.3.4 Other sources/sinks

There are a number of other types of sources and sinks. Here, briefly, are a few more that you might come across. In each of these examples we talk about receiving data from a source, but the concepts apply equally well to sending data to a sink.

- *Named Pipe*—This is a feature of many UNIX-like operating systems. One process prepares to write data to a named pipe which, to other processes, looks like a file. The writing process waits until another process tries to read from the file. At that point it writes a chunk of data to the named pipe, which the reading process sees as the contents of the file. This is useful if the reading process has been written to expect a file, but you want to write constantly changing data.

---

[2] As long as you don't make any use of vendor-specific features.

- *TCP/IP Socket*—This is a good way to send a stream of data between two computers that are on the same network.[3] The two systems define a TCP/IP port number through which they will communicate. The data munging process then sets itself up as a TCP/IP server and listens for connections on the right port. When the source has data to send, it instigates a connection on the port. Some kind of (application-defined) handshaking then takes place, followed by the source sending the data across to the waiting server.

- *HTTP*[4]—This method is becoming more common. If both programs have access to the Internet, they can be on opposite sides of the world and can still talk to each other. The source simply writes the data to a file somewhere on the publicly accessible Internet. The data munging program uses HTTP to send a request for the file to the source's web server and, in response, the web server sends the file. The file could be an HTML file, but it could just as easily be in any other format. HTTP also has some basic authentication facilities built into it, so it is feasible to protect files to which you don't want the public to have access.

1.4   *What forms does data take?*

Data comes in many different formats. We will be examining many formats in more detail later in the book, but for now we'll take a brief survey of the most popular ones.

1.4.1   *Unstructured data*

While there is a great deal of unstructured data in the world, it is unlikely that you will come across very much of it, because the job of data munging is to convert data from one structure to another. It is very difficult for a computer program to impose structure on data that isn't already structured in some way. Of course, one common data munging task is to take data with no apparent structure and bring out the structure that was hiding deep within it.

The best example of unstructured data is plain text. Other than separating text into individual lines and words and producing statistics, it is difficult to do much useful work with this kind of data.

---

[3] Using the term "network" in a very wide sense. Most Internet protocols are based on TCP/IP so that while your modem is dialed into your Internet Service Provider, your PC is on the same network as the web server that you are downloading MP3s from.

[4] Strictly speaking, HTTP is just another protocol running on top of TCP/IP, but it is important enough to justify discussing it separately.

Nonetheless, we will examine unstructured data in chapter 5. This is largely because it will give us the chance to discuss some general mechanisms, such as reading and writing files, before moving on to better structured data.

1.4.2 *Record-oriented data*

Most of the simple data that you will come across will be record-oriented. That is, the data source will consist of a number of records, each of which can be processed separately from its siblings. Records can be separated from each other in a number of ways. The most common way is for each line in a text file to represent one record,[5] but it is also possible that a blank line or a well-defined series of characters separates records.

Within each record, there will probably be fields, which represent the various data items of the record. These will also be denoted in several different ways. There may well be a particular character between different fields (often a comma or a tab), but it is also possible that a record will be padded with spaces or zeroes to ensure that it is always a given number of characters in width.

We will look at record-oriented data in chapter 6.

1.4.3 *Hierarchical data*

This is an area that will be growing in importance in the coming years. The best example of hierarchical data is the *Standardized General Mark-up Language* (SGML), and its two better known offspring, the *Hypertext Mark-up Language* (HTML) and the *Extensible Mark-up Language* (XML). In these systems, each data item is surrounded by tags which denote its position in the hierarchy of the data. A data item is contained by its parent and contains its own children.[6] At this point, the record-at-a-time processing methods that we will have been using on simpler data types no longer work and we will be forced to find more powerful tools.

We will look at hierarchical data (specifically HTML and XML) in chapters 9 and 10.

1.4.4 *Binary data*

Finally, there is binary data. This is data that you cannot successfully use without software which has been specially designed to handle it. Without having access to an explanation of the structure of a binary data file, it is very difficult to make any sense

---

[5] There is, of course, potential for confusion over exactly what constitutes a line, but we'll discuss that in more detail later.

[6] This family metaphor can, of course, be taken further. Two nodes which have the same parent are known as *sibling* nodes, although I've never yet heard two nodes with the same grandparents described as *cousins*.

of it. We will take a look at some publicly available binary file formats and see how to get some meaningful data out of them.

We will look at binary data in chapter 7.

1.5   *What is Perl?*

Perl is a computer programming language that has been in use since 1987. It was initially developed for use on the UNIX operating system, but it has since been ported to more operating systems than just about any other programming language (with the possible exception of C).

Perl was written by Larry Wall to solve a particular problem, but instead of writing something that would just solve the question at hand, Wall wrote a general tool that he could use to solve other problems later.

What he came up with was just about the most useful data processing tool that anyone has created.

What makes Perl different from many other computer languages is that Wall has a background in linguistics and brought a lot of this knowledge to bear in the design of Perl's syntax. This means that a lot of the time you can say things in a more natural way in Perl and the code will mean what you expect it to mean.

For example, most programming languages have an `if` statement which you can use to write something like this:

```
if (condition) {
  do_something();
}
```

but what happens if you want to do some special processing only if the condition is false? Of course you can often write something like:

```
if (not condition) {
  do_something()
}
```

but it's already starting to look a bit unwieldy. In Perl you can write:

```
unless (condition) {
  do_something()
}
```

which reads far more like English. In fact you can even write:

```
do_something() unless condition;
```

which is about as close to English as a programming language ever gets.

A Perl programmer once explained to me the moment when he realized that Perl and he were made for each other was when he wrote some pseudocode which described a possible solution to a problem and accidentally ran it through the Perl interpreter. It ran correctly the first time.

As another example of how Perl makes it easier to write code that is easier to read, consider opening a file. This is something that just about any kind of program has to do at some point. This is a point in a program where error checking is very important, and in many languages you will see large amounts of code surrounding a file open statement. Code to open a file in C looks like this:

```
if ((f = fopen("file.txt", "r")) == NULL) {
  perror("file.txt");
  exit(0);
}
```

whereas in Perl you can write it like this:

```
open(FILE, 'file.txt') or die "Can't open file.txt: $!";
```

This opens a file and assigns it to the file handle FILE which you can later use to read data from the file. It also checks for errors and, if anything goes wrong, it kills the program with an error message explaining exactly what went wrong. And, as a bonus, once more it almost reads like English.

Perl is not for everyone. Some people enjoy the verbosity of some other languages or the rigid syntax of others. Those who do make an effort to understand Perl typically become much more effective programmers.

Perl is not for every task. Many speed-critical routines are better written in C or assembly language. In Perl, however, it is possible to split these sections into separate modules so that the majority of the program can still be written in Perl if desired.

1.5.1 Getting Perl

One of the advantages of Perl is that it is free.[7] The source code for Perl is available for download from a number of web sites. The definitive site to get the Perl source code (and, indeed, for all of your other Perl needs) is www.perl.com, but the Perl source is mirrored at sites all over the world. You can find the nearest one to you listed on the main site. Once you have the source code, it comes with simple instructions on how to build and install it. You'll need a C compiler and a make utility.[8]

---

[7] Free as in both the "free speech" and "free beer" meanings of the word. For a longer discussion of the advantages of these, please visit the Free Software Foundation at www.fsf.org.

[8] If you don't have these, then you can get copies of the excellent gcc and GNU make from the Free Software Foundation.

Downloading source code and compiling your own tools is a common procedure on UNIX systems. Many Windows developers, however, are more used to installing prepackaged software. This is not a problem, as they can get a prebuilt binary called ActivePerl from ActiveState at www.activestate.com. As with other versions of Perl, this distribution is free.

1.6 *Why is Perl good for data munging?*

Perl has a number of advantages that make it particularly useful as a data munging language. Let's take a look at a few of them.

- *Perl is interpreted*—Actually Perl isn't really interpreted, but it looks as though it is to the programmer. There is no separate compilation phase that the programmer needs to run before executing a Perl program. This makes the development of a Perl program very quick as it frees the programmer from the edit-compile-test-debug cycle, which is typical of program development in languages like C and C++.

- *Perl is compiled*—What actually happens is that a Perl program is compiled automatically each time it is run. This gives a slight performance hit when the program first starts up, but means that once the program is running you don't get any of the performance problems that you would from a purely interpreted language.

- *Perl has powerful data recognition and transformation features*—A lot of data munging consists of recognizing particular parts of the input data and then transforming them. In Perl this is often achieved by using regular expressions. We will look at regular expressions in some detail later in the book, but at this point it suffices to point out that Perl's regular expression support is second to none.

- *Perl supports arbitrarily complex data structures*—When munging data, you will usually want to build up internal data structures to store the data in interim forms before writing it to the output file. Some programming languages impose limits on the complexity of internal data structures. Since the introduction of Perl 5, Perl has had no such constraints.

- *Perl encourages code reuse*—You will often be munging similar sorts of data in similar ways. It makes sense to build a library of reusable code to make writing new programs easier. Perl has a very powerful system for creating modules of code that can be slotted into other scripts very easily. In fact, there is a global repository of reusable Perl modules available across the Internet at www.cpan.org. CPAN stands for the Comprehensive Perl Archive Network. If someone else has previously solved your particular problem then you will find a solution there. If you are the first person to address a particular problem, once you've solved it, why not submit the solution to the CPAN. That way everyone benefits.

- *Perl is fun*—I know this is a very subjective opinion, but the fact remains that I have seen jaded C programmers become fired up with enthusiasm for their jobs once they've been introduced to Perl. I'm not going to try to explain it, I'm just going to suggest that you give it a try.

1.7 *Further information*

The best place to get up-to-date information about Perl is the Perl home page at www.perl.com.

Appendix B contains a brief overview of the Perl language, but if you want to learn Perl you should look at one of the many Perl tutorial books. If you are a non-programmer then *Elements of Programming with Perl* by Andrew Johnson (Manning) would be a good choice. Programmers looking to learn a new language should look at *Learning Perl (2nd edition)* by Randal Schwartz and Tom Christiansen (O'Reilly) or *Perl: The Programmer's Companion* by Nigel Chapman (Wiley).

The definitive Perl reference book is *Programming Perl (3rd edition)* by Larry Wall, Tom Christiansen and Jon Orwant (O'Reilly).

Perl itself comes with a huge amount of documentation. Once you have installed Perl, you can type `perldoc perl` at your command line to get a list of the available documents.

1.8 *Summary*

- Data munging is the process of taking data from one system (a data source) and converting it so that it is suitable for use by a different system (a data sink).
- Data munging consists of four stages—data recognition, parsing, filtering, and transformation.
- Data can come from (and be written to) a large number of different types of sources and sinks.
- Data itself can take a large number of forms, text or binary, unstructured or structured, record oriented or hierarchical.
- Perl is a language which is very well suited for the whole range of data munging jobs.

General munging
practices

When munging data there are a number of general principles which will be useful across a large number of different tasks. In this chapter we will take a look at some of these techniques.

2.1   *Decouple input, munging, and output processes*

When written in pseudocode, most data munging tasks will look very similar. At the highest level, the pseudocode will look something like this:

```
Read input data
Munge data
Write output data
```

Obviously, each of these three subtasks will need to be broken down into greater detail before any real code can be written; however, looking at the problem from this high level can demonstrate some useful general principles about data munging.

Suppose that we are combining data from several systems into one database. In this case our different data sources may well provide us with data in very different formats, but they all need to be converted into the same format to be passed on to our data sink. Our lives will be made much easier if we can write one output routine that handles writing the output from all of our data inputs. In order for this to be possible, the data structures in which we store our data just before we call the combined output routines will need to be in the same format. This means that the data munging routines need to leave the data in the same format, no matter which of the data sinks we are dealing with. One easy way to ensure this is to use the same data munging routines for each of our data sources. In order for this to be possible, the data structures that are output from the various data input routines must be in the same format. It may be tempting to try to take this a step further and reuse our input routines, but as our data sources can be in completely different formats, this is not likely to be possible. As figures 2.1 and 2.2 show, instead of writing three

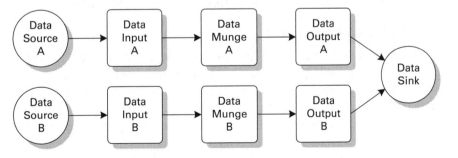

Figure 2.1   Separate munging and output processes

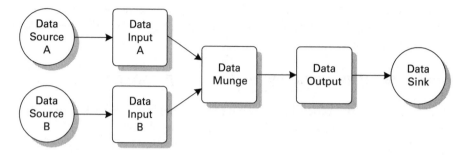

Figure 2.2   Combined munging and output processes

routines for each data source, we now need only write an input routine for each source with common munging and output routines.

A very similar argument can be made if we are taking data from one source and writing it to a number of different data sinks. In this case, only the data output routines need to vary from sink to sink and the input and munging routines can be shared.

There is another advantage to this decoupling of the various stages of the task. If we later need to read data from the same data source, or write data to the same data sink for another task, we already have code that will do the reading or writing for us. Later in this chapter we will look at some ways that Perl helps us to encapsulate these routines in reusable code libraries.

2.2   Design data structures carefully

Probably the most important way that you can make your data munging code (or, indeed, any code) more efficient is to design the intermediate data structures carefully. As always in software design, there are compromises to be made, but in this section we will look at some of the factors that you should consider.

2.2.1   Example: the CD file revisited

As an example, let's return to the list of compact disks that we discussed in chapter 1. We'll assume that we have a tab-separated text file where the columns are artist, title, record label, and year of release. Before considering what internal data structures we will use, we need to know what sort of output data we will be creating. Suppose that we needed to create a list of years, together with the number of CDs released in that year.

Solution 1: simple hash

The immediately obvious solution is to use a hash in which the keys are years and the values are the numbers of CDs. In this case, there will be no need for a separate data munging process, as all of the required munging will be carried out in the input routine. We might create a first draft script something like this:

```
my %years;
while (<STDIN>) {
  chomp;
  my $year = (split /\t/)[3];

  $years{$year}++;
}

foreach (sort keys %years) {
  print "In $_, $years{$_} CDs were released.\n";
}
```

1971	1
1987	1
1993	1
1996	1
1997	1
1998	1

Figure 2.3 Initial data structure design

This provides a solution to our problem in a reasonably efficient manner. The data structure that we build is very simple and is shown in figure 2.3.

Solution 2: adding flexibility

But how often are requirements as fixed as these?[1] Suppose later someone decides that, instead of having a list of the number of CDs released, they also need a list of the actual CDs. In this case, we will need to go back and rewrite our script completely to something like this:

```
my %years;
while (<STDIN>) {
  chomp;
  my ($artist, $title, $label, $year) = split /\t/;

  my $rec = {artist => $artist,
             title  => $title,
             label  => $label};
  push @ {$years{$year}}, $rec;
}

foreach my $year (sort keys %years) {
  my $count = scalar @{$years{$year}};
  print "In $year, $count CDs were released.\n";
  print "They were:\n";
  print map { "$_->{title} by $_->{artist}\n" } @{$years{$year}};
}
```

---

[1] There are, of course, many times when the requirements won't change—because this is a one-off data load process or you are proving a concept or building a prototype.

As you can see, this change has entailed an almost complete rewrite of the script. In the new version, we still have a hash where the keys are the years, but each value is now a reference to an array. Each element of this array is a reference to a hash which contains the artist, title, and label of the CD. The output section has also grown more complex as it needs to extract more information from the hash.

Notice that the hash stores the CD's label even though we don't use it in the output from the script. Although the label isn't required in our current version, it is quite possible that it will become necessary to add it to the output at some point in the future. If this happens we will no longer need to make any changes to the input section of our script as we already have the data available in our hash. This is, in itself, an important data munging principle—if you're reading in a data item, you may as well store it in your data structure. This can be described more succinctly as "Don't throw anything away." This improved data structure is shown in figure 2.4.

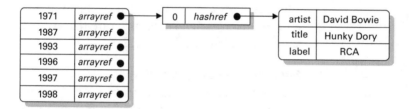

Figure 2.4   Improved data structure design

Solution 3: separating parsing from munging

What happens, however, if the requirements change completely so that we now need to display counts by artist for a different report? Our current script is of no use at all. There is no part of it that is reusable to help us achieve our new goals. Perhaps we need to rethink our strategy from the start.

In all of the scripts above we were not following the advice of the previous section. We were trying to do too much in the input section and left ourselves nothing to do in the data munging section. Perhaps if we went back to a more decoupled approach, we would have more success.

This leaves us contemplating our original question again—what structure would offer the best way to represent our data inside the program? Let's take another look at the data. What we have is a list of records, each of which has a well-defined set of attributes. We could use either a hash or an array to model our list of records and we have the same choices to model each individual record. In this case we will use an array of hashes[2] to model our data. A good argument could be made for just about any other combination of arrays and hashes, but the representation that I have chosen seems more natural to me. Our input routine will therefore look like this:

```
my @CDs;
sub input {
  my @attrs = qw(artist title label year);
  while (<STDIN>) {
    chomp;
    my %rec;
    @rec{@attrs} = split /\t/;
    push @CDs, \%rec;
  }
}
```

This third and final data structure is shown in figure 2.5.

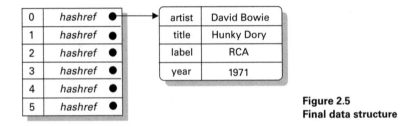

Figure 2.5
Final data structure

More examples: using our flexible data structure

Based on this data structure, we can then write any number of data munging routines to produce specific output reports. For example, to produce our original list of the CDs released in a year we would write a routine like this:

```
sub count_cds_by_year {
  my %years;

  foreach (@CDs) {
    $years{$_->{year}}++;
  }

  return \%years;
}
```

This routine returns a reference to a hash which is identical in structure to our original hash and can therefore be printed out using code identical to the output section of our original script.

---

[2] Or, more accurately, an array of references to hashes.

To produce a list of the number of CDs released by each artist we can write a similar routine like this:

```
sub count_cds_by_artist {
  my %artists;

  foreach (@CDs) {
    $artists{$_->{artist}}++;
  }

  return \%artists;
}
```

In fact these two routines are so similar, that it is possible to write a generic version which handles both of these cases (along with the cases where you want to count CDs by label or even by title).

```
sub count_cds_by_attr {
  my $attr = shift;

  my %counts;

  foreach (@CDs) {
    $counts{$_->{$attr}}++;
  }

  return \%counts;
}
```

A complete program to produce counts of CDs by any attribute which is passed in on the command line would look like this:

```
#!/usr/bin/perl -w

use strict;

my @CDs;

sub input {
  my @attrs = qw(artist title label year);
  while (<STDIN>) {
    chomp;
    my %rec;
    @rec{@attrs} = split /\t/;
    push @CDs, \%rec;
  }
}

sub count_cds_by_attr {
  my $attr = shift;

  my %counts;

  foreach (@CDs) {
    $counts{$_->{$attr}}++;
```

```
    }
    return \%counts;
}
sub output {
  my $counts = shift;
  foreach (sort keys %{$counts}) {
    print "$_: $counts->{$_}\n";
  }
}

my $attr = shift;

input();
my $counts = count_cds_by_attr($attr);
output($counts);
```

And, assuming that the program file is called count_cds.pl and you have the CD list in a file called cd.txt, it would be called like this:

```
count_cds.pl year < cds.txt > cds_by_year.txt
count_cds.pl label < cds.txt > cds_by_label.txt
count_cds.pl artist < cds.txt > cds_by_artist.txt
count_cds.pl title < cds.txt > cds_by_title.txt
```

In most cases you will have to make similar decisions when designing data structures. A data structure that is designed for one job will, in general, be simpler than one that is designed to be more flexible. It is up to you to decide whether it is worth taking the extra effort to make the design more flexible. (A hint—it usually is!)

2.3   *Encapsulate business rules*

Much of the logic in your data munging programs will be modeling what might be described as "business rules." These are the rules about what particular data items mean, what their valid sets of values are, and how they relate to other values in the same or other records.[3] Examples of these three types of business rules are:

- Customer number is a unique identifier for a customer.
- Customer number is always in the format CUS-XXXXX, where XXXXX is a unique integer.
- Each customer record must be linked to a valid salesperson record.

---

[3] I've described these constraints as "business rules," as I think that's easier to remember than something like "domain specific constraints." Of course, what you're encoding might well have nothing to do with "business."

In any system where these data items are used, the business rules must always hold true. No matter what your program does to a customer record, the customer number must remain unique and in the given format, and the customer must be linked to a valid salesperson record. Nothing that you do to a customer record is allowed to leave the data in a state that breaks any of these rules.

2.3.1 Reasons to encapsulate business rules

In a real-world system, there will probably be many other programs that are accessing the same data items for their own purposes. Each of these other programs will have to abide by exactly the same set of business rules for each customer record that it accesses. Therefore each of these programs will have logic within it that encodes these rules. This can lead to a couple of problems:

- It is possible that not every programmer who writes these programs has exactly the same understanding of the rules. Therefore, each program may have subtly different interpretations of the rules.

- At some point in the future these rules may be changed. When this happens, the same changes in logic will need to be made to each of the programs that use the existing business rules. This may be a large job, and the more times the changes have to be made, the higher the chance that errors will creep in.

2.3.2 Ways to encapsulate business rules

The most common solution to both of these problems is to write code that models the business rules in one place and to reuse that code in each program that needs to use the rules. Most programming languages have a facility that allows code to be reused across many programs, and Perl has a particularly powerful implementation of this functionality.

In Perl you would create a module that contains the business rules for a particular type of business record (say, a customer) and include this module in any other Perl programs that needed to understand the business rules that control the use of customer records. In fact, Perl gives you a couple of ways to implement this functionality. If your rules are relatively simple you can write a module that contains functions called things like `get_next_custno` or `save_cust_record` which get called at relevant points in your programs. For a more robust solution, you should consider writing a Perl object to implement your customer record. Let's look at examples of both of these approaches.

2.3.3 *Simple module*

Assume that we want to model the three business rules mentioned at the start of this section. We will write a module called `Customer_Rules.pm` that will contain the two functions `get_next_cust_no` and `save_cust_record` which we suggested above. The following example omits some of the lower level functions.

```
package Customer_Rules;

use strict;
use Carp;
use vars qw(@EXPORT @ISA);

@EXPORT = qw(get_next_cust_no save_cust_record);
@ISA = qw(Exporter);

require Exporter;

sub get_next_cust_no {
  my $prev_cust = get_max_cust_no()
    || croak "Can't allocate new customer reference.\n";

  my ($prev_no) = $prev_cust =~ /(\d+)/;
  $prev_no++;

  return "CUS-$prev_no";
}
sub save_cust_record {
  my $cust = shift;

  $cust->{cust_no} ||= get_next_cust_no();

  is_valid_sales_ref($cust->{salesperson})
    || croak "Invalid salesperson ref: $cust->{salesperson}.";

  write_sales_record($cust);
}
```

How Customer_Rules.pm works

In this example we have encapsulated our business rules in functions which, in turn, make use of other lower level functions. These lower level functions haven't been shown, as they would contain implementation-specific details which would only cloud the picture.

In the `get_next_cust_no` function we begin by getting the customer number of the most recently created customer record. This might be stored in a database table or in a text file or in some other format. In all of these cases there will need to be some kind of transaction-level locking to ensure that no other process gets the same value for the previous customer number. This would potentially lead to nonunique customer numbers in the system, which would break one of our business rules.

Having retrieved the previous customer number we simply extract the integer portion, increment it, and return it with the string CUS- prepended to it.

In the `save_cust_record` function, we assume that the customer record is stored internally in some complex data structure and that we are passed a reference to that structure. The first thing that we do is to ensure that we have a customer number in the record. We then check that the `$cust->{salesperson}` value represents a valid salesperson in our system. Again, the list of valid salespeople could be stored in a number of different forms. It may be possible that more data is required in order to validate the salesperson code. For example, a salesperson may only deal with customers in a certain region. In this case the region in which the customer is based will also need to be passed into the `is_valid_sales_ref` function.

Eventually, we get a true or false value back from `is_valid_sales_ref` and can proceed appropriately. If the salesperson is valid, we can write the customer record to whatever storage medium we are using; otherwise, we alert the user to the error. In a real-world system many other similar checks would probably need to be carried out.

Using Customer_Rules.pm

Having produced this module, we can make it available to all programmers who are writing applications by putting it into a project-wide library directory. To make use of these functions, a programmer only needs to include the line:

```
use Customer_Rules;
```

in a program. The program will now have access to the `get_next_cust_no` and `save_cust_record` functions. Therefore, we can ensure that every program has the same interpretation of the business rules and, perhaps more importantly, if the business rules change, we only need to change this module in order to change them in each program.

2.3.4 *Object class*

While the module of the previous section is useful, it still has a number of problems; not the least of which is the fact that the structure of the customer record is defined elsewhere in the application. If the module is reused in a number of applications, then each application will define its own customer record and it is possible that the definitions will become out of step with each other. The solution to this problem is to create an object class.

An object defines both the structure of a data record and all of the methods used to operate on the record. It makes the code far easier to reuse and maintain. A full discussion of the advantages of object-oriented programming (OOP) is beyond the scope of this book, but two very good places to get the full story are the *perltoot* manual page and Damian Conway's *Object Oriented Perl* (Manning).

Let's examine a cut-down customer object which is implemented in a module called `Customer.pm`.

```perl
package Customer;

use strict;

sub new {
  my $thing = shift;
  my $self = {};

  bless $self, ref($thing) || $thing;

  $self->init(@_);
  return $self;
}

sub init {
  my $self = shift;

  # Extract various interesting things from
  # @_ and use them to create a data structure
  # that represents a customer.
}

sub validate {
  my $self = shift;

  # Call a number of methods, each of which validates
  # one data item in the customer record.
  return $self->is_valid_sales_ref
         && $self->is_valid_other_attr
         && $self->is_valid_another_attr;
}

sub save {
  my $self = shift;

  if ($self->validate) {
    $self->{cust_no} ||= $self->get_next_cust_no;
    return $self->write;
  } else {
    return;
  }
}

# Various other object methods are omitted here, for example
# code to retrieve a customer object from the database or
# write a customer object to the database.

1; # Because all modules should return a true value.
```

The advantage that this method has over the previous example is that in addition to modeling the business rules that apply to a customer record, it defines a standard data structure to store customer data and a well defined set of actions that can be performed on a customer record. The slight downside is that incorporating this module into a program will take a little more work than simply using the functions defined in our previous module.

Example: using Customer.pm

As an example of using this module, let's look at a simple script for creating a customer record. We'll prompt the user for the information that we require.

```
use Customer;

my $cust = Customer->new;

print 'Enter new customer name: ';
my $name = <STDIN>;
$cust->name($name);

print 'Enter customer address: ';
my $addr = <STDIN>;
$cust->address($addr);

print 'Enter salesperson code: ';
my $sp_code = <STDIN>;
$cust->salesperson($sp_code);

# Write code similar to that above to get any other
# required data from the user.

if ($cust->save) {
  print "New customer saved successfully.\n";
  print "New customer code is ", $cust->code, "\n";
} else {
  print "Error saving new customer.\n";
}
```

In this case we create an empty customer object by calling the `Customer->new` method without any parameters. We then fill in the various data items in our customer object with data input by the user. Notice that we assume that each customer attribute has an access method which can be used to set or get the attribute value.[4]

---

[4] This is a common practice. For example, the `name` method counts the number of parameters that have been sent. If it has received a new value then it sets the customer's name to that value; if not, it just returns the previous value.

   An alternative practice is to have two separate methods called `get_name` and `set_name`. Which approach you use is a matter of personal preference. In either case, it is generally accepted that using access methods is better than accessing the attributes directly.

Having filled in all of the required data, we called `$cust->save` to save our new record. If the save is successful, the code attribute will have been filled in and we can display the new customer's code to the user by way of the `$cust->code` attribute access method.

If, on the other hand, we wanted to access an existing customer record, we would pass the customer to the `Customer->new` method (e.g., `Customer->new(id =>` `'CUS-00123')`) and the `init` method would populate our object with the customer's data. We could then either use this data in some way or alternatively alter it and use the `save` method to write the changed record back to the database.

2.4 Use UNIX "filter" model

UNIX filter programs give us a very good example to follow when it comes to building a number of small, reusable utilities each of which is designed to carry out one task.

2.4.1 Overview of the filter model

Many operating systems, principally UNIX and its variants, support a feature called I/O redirection. This feature is also supported in Microsoft Windows, although as it is a command line feature, it is not used as much as it is in UNIX. I/O redirection gives the user great flexibility over where a program gets its input and sends its output. This is achieved by treating all program input and output as file input and output. The operating system opens two special file handles called STDIN and STDOUT, which, by default, are attached to the user's keyboard and monitor.[5] This means that anything typed by the user on the keyboard appears to the program to be read from STDIN and anything that the program writes to STDOUT appears on the user's monitor.

For example, if a user runs the UNIX command

```
ls
```

then a list of files in the current directory will be written to STDOUT and will appear on the user's monitor.

There are, however a number of special character strings that can be used to redirect these special files. For example, if our user runs the command

```
ls > files.txt
```

then anything that would have been written to STDOUT is, instead, written to the file files.txt. Similarly, STDIN can be redirected using the < character. For example,

---

[5] In practice there is also a third file handle called STDERR which is a special output file to which error messages are written, but this file can be safely ignored for the purposes of this discussion.

```
sort < files.txt
```

would sort our previously created file in lexical order (since we haven't redirected the output, it will go to the user's monitor).

Another, more powerful, concept is I/O pipes. This is where the output of one process is connected directly to the input of another. This is achieved using the | character. For example, if our user runs the command

```
ls | sort
```

then anything written to the STDOUT of the ls command (i.e., the list of files in the current directory) is written directly to the STDIN of the sort command. The sort command processes the data that appears on its STDIN, sorts that data, and writes the sorted data to its STDOUT. The STDOUT for the sort command has not been redirected and therefore the sorted list of files appears on the user's monitor.

A summary of the character strings used in basic I/O redirection is given in table 2.1. More complex features are available in some operating systems, but the characters listed are available in all versions of UNIX and Windows.

Table 2.1 Common I/O redirection

String	Usage	Description
>	cmd > file	Runs cmd and writes the output to file, overwriting whatever was in file.
>>	cmd >> file	Runs cmd and appends the output to the end of file.
<	cmd < file	Runs cmd, taking input from file.
|	cmd1 | cmd2	Runs cmd1 and passes any output as input to cmd2

2.4.2 Advantages of the filter model

The filter model is a very useful concept and is fundamental to the way that UNIX works. It means that UNIX can supply a large number of small, simple utilities, each of which do one task and do it well. Many complex tasks can be carried out by plugging a number of these utilities together. For example, if we needed to list all of the files in a directory with a name containing the string "proj01" and wanted them sorted in alphabetical order, we could use a combination of ls, sort, and grep[6] like this:

```
ls -1 | grep proj01 | sort
```

---

[6] Which takes a text string as an argument and writes to STDOUT only input lines that contain that text.

Most UNIX utilities are written to support this mode of usage. They are known as *filters* as they read their input from STDIN, filter the data in a particular way, and write what is left to STDOUT.

This is a concept that we can make good use of in our data munging programs. If we write our programs so that they make no assumptions about the files that they are reading and writing (or, indeed, whether they are even reading from and writing to files) then we will have written a useful generic tool, which can be used in a number of different circumstances.

Example: I/O independence

Suppose, for example, that we had written a program called data_munger which munged data from one system into data suitable for use in another. Originally, we might take data from a file and write our output to another. It might be tempting to write a program that is called with two arguments which are the names of the input and output files. The program would then be called like this:

```
data_munger input.dat output.dat
```

Within the script we would open the files and read from the input, munge the data, and then write to the output file. In Perl, the program might look something like:

```perl
#!/usr/bin/perl -w

use strict;

my ($input, $output) = @ARGV;
open(IN, $input) || die "Can't open $input for reading: $!";
open(OUT, ">$output") || die "Can't open $output for writing: $!";

while (<IN>) {
  print OUT munge_data($_);
}
close(IN) || die "Can't close $input: $!";
close(OUT) || die "Can't close $output: $!";
```

This will certainly work well for as long as we receive our input data in a file and are expected to write our output data to another file. Perhaps at some point in the future, the programmers responsible for our data source will announce that they have written a new program called data_writer, which we should now use to extract data from their system. This program will write the extracted data to its STDOUT. At the same time the programmers responsible for our data sink announce a new program called data_reader, which we should use to load data into their system and which reads the data to be loaded from STDIN.

In order to use our program unchanged we will need to write some extra pieces of code in the script which drives our program. Our program will need to be called with code like this:

```
data_writer > input.dat
data_munger input.dat output.dat
data_reader < output.dat
```

This is already looking a little kludgy, but imagine if we had to make these changes across a large number of systems. Perhaps there is a better way to write the original program.

If we had assumed that the program reads from STDIN and writes to STDOUT, the program actually gets simpler and more flexible. The rewritten program looks like this:

```
#!/usr/bin/perl -w
while (<STDIN>) {
  print munge_data($_);
}
```

Note that we no longer have to open the input and output files explicitly, as Perl arranges for STDIN and STDOUT to be opened for us. Also, the default file handle to which the print function writes is STDOUT; therefore, we no longer need to pass a file handle to print. This script is therefore much simpler than our original one.

When we're dealing with input and output data files, our program is called like this:

```
data_munger < input.dat > output.dat
```

and once the other systems want us to use their data_writer and data_reader programs, we can call our program like this:

```
data_writer | data_munger | data_reader
```

and everything will work exactly the same without any changes to our program. As a bonus, if we have to cope with the introduction of data_writer before data_reader or vice versa, we can easily call our program like this:

```
data_writer | data_munger > output.dat
```

or this:

```
data_munger < input.dat | data_reader
```

and everything will still work as expected.

Rather than using the STDIN file handle, Perl allows you to make your program even more flexible with no more work, by reading input from the null file handle like this:

```
#!/usr/bin/perl -w
while (<>) {
  print munged_data($_);
}
```

In this case, Perl will give your program each line of every file that is listed on your command line. If there are no files on the command line, it reads from STDIN. This is exactly how most UNIX filter programs work. If we rewrote our data_munger program using this method we could call it in the following ways:

```
data_munger input.dat > output.dat
data_munger input.dat | data reader
```

in addition to the methods listed previously.

Example: I/O chaining

Another advantage of the filter model is that it makes it easier to add new functionality into your processing chain without having to change existing code. Suppose that a system is sending you product data. You are loading this data into the database that drives your company's web site. You receive the data in a file called products.dat and have written a script called load_products. This script reads the data from STDIN, performs various data munging processes, and finally loads the data into the database. The command that you run to load the file looks like this:

```
load_products < products.dat
```

What happens when the department that produces products.dat announces that because of a reorganization of their database they will be changing the format of your input file? For example, perhaps they will no longer identify each product with a unique integer, but with an alphanumeric code. Your first option would be to rewrite load_products to handle the new data format, but do you really want to destabilize a script that has worked very well for a long time? Using the UNIX filter model, you don't have to. You can write a new script called translate_products which reads the new file format, translates the new product code to the product identifiers that you are expecting, and writes the records in the original format to STDOUT. Your existing load_products script can then read records in the format that it accepts from STDIN and can process them in exactly the same way that it always has. The command line would look like this:

```
translate_products < products.dat | load_products
```

This method of working is known as *chain extension* and can be very useful in a number of areas.

In general, the UNIX filter model is very powerful and often actually simplifies the program that you are writing, as well as making your programs more flexible. You should therefore consider using it as often as possible.

2.5 *Write audit trails*

When transforming data it is often useful to keep a detailed audit trail of what you have done. This is particularly true when the end users of the transformed data question the results of your transformation. It is very helpful to be able to trace through the audit log and work out exactly where each data item has come from. Generally, problems in the output data can have only one of two sources, either errors in the input data or errors in the transformation program. It will make your life much easier if you can quickly work out where the problem has arisen.

2.5.1 *What to write to an audit trail*

At different points in the life of a program, different levels of auditing will be appropriate. While the program is being developed and tested it is common practice to have a much more detailed audit trail than when it is being used day to day in a production environment. For this reason, it is often useful to write auditing code that allows you to generate different levels of output depending on the value of a variable that defines the audit level. This variable might be read from an environment variable like this:

```
my $audit_level = $ENV{AUDIT_LEVEL} || 0;
```

In this example we set the value of $audit_level from the environment variable AUDIT_LEVEL. If this level is not set then we default to 0, the minimum level. Later in the script we can write code like:

```
print LOG 'Starting processing at ', scalar localtime, "\n"
  if $audit_level > 0;
```

to print audit information to the previously opened file handle, LOG.

Standards for audit trails will typically vary from company to company, but some things that you might consider auditing are:

- start and end times of the process
- source and sink parameters (filenames, database connection parameters, etc.)
- ID of every record processed
- results of each data translation
- final count of records processed

2.5.2 *Sample audit trail*

A useful audit trail for a data munging process that takes data from a file and either creates or updates database records might look like this:

```
Process: daily_upd started at 00:30:00 25 Mar 2000
Data source: /data/input/daily.dat
Data sink: database customer on server DATA_SERVER (using id 'maint')
Input record: D:CUS-00123
Action: Delete
Translation: CUS-00123 = database id 2364
Record 2364 deleted successfully
Input record: U:CUS-00124:Jones & Co| [etc ...]
Action: Update
Translation: CUS-00124 = database id 2365
Record 2365 updated successfully
Input record: I:CUS-01000:Magnum Solutions Ltd| [etc ...]
Action: Insert
Integrity Check: CUS-01000 does not exist on database
Record 3159 inserted successfully

[many lines omitted]

End of file on data source
1037 records processed (60 ins, 964 upd, 13 del)
Process: daily_upd complete at 00:43:14 25 Mar 2000
```

2.5.3 *Using the UNIX system logs*

Sometimes you will want to log your audit trail to the UNIX system log. This is a centralized process in which the administrator of a UNIX system can control where the log information for various processes is written. To access the system log from Perl, use the Sys::Syslog module. This module contains four functions called openlog, closelog, setlogmask, and syslog which closely mirror the functionality of the UNIX functions with the same names. For more details on these functions, see the Sys::Syslog module's documentation and your UNIX manual. Here is an example of their use:

```
use Sys::Syslog;

openlog('data_munger.pl', 'cons', 'user');

# then later in the program
syslog('info', 'Process started');

# then later again

closelog();
```

Notice that as the system logger automatically timestamps all messages, we don't need to print the start time in our log message.

2.6 *Further information*

For more information on writing objects in Perl see *Object Oriented Perl* by Damian Conway (Manning).

For more information about the UNIX filter model and other UNIX programming tricks see *The UNIX Programming Environment* by Brian Kernigan and Rob Pike (Prentice Hall) or *UNIX Power Tools* by Jerry Peek, Tim O'Reilly, and Mike Loukides (O'Reilly).

For more general programming advice see *The Practice of Programming* by Brian Kernigan and Rob Pike (Addison-Wesley) and *Programming Pearls* by Jon Bentley (Addison-Wesley).

2.7 *Summary*

- Decoupling the various stages of your program can cut down on the code that you have to write by making code more reusable.
- Designing data structures carefully will make your programs more flexible.
- Write modules or objects to encapsulate your business rules.
- The UNIX filter model can make your programs I/O independent.
- Always write audit logs.

Useful Perl idioms

3

There are a number of Perl idioms that will be useful in many data munging programs. Rather than introduce them in the text when they are first met, we will discuss them all here.

3.1 Sorting

Sorting is one of the most common tasks that you will carry out when data munging. As you would expect, Perl makes sorting very easy for you, but there are a few niceties that we'll come to later in this section.

3.1.1 Simple sorts

Perl has a built-in `sort` function which will handle simple sorts very easily. The syntax for the `sort` function is as follows:

```
@out = sort @in;
```

This takes the elements of the list `@in`, sorts them lexically, and returns them in array `@out`. This is the simplest scenario. Normally you will want something more complex, so `sort` takes another argument which allows you to define the sort that you want to perform. This argument is either the name of a subroutine or a block of Perl code (enclosed in braces). For example, to sort data numerically[1] you would write code like this:

```
@out = sort numerically @in;
```

and a subroutine called `numerically` which would look like this:

```
sub numerically {
  return $a <=> $b;
}
```

There are a couple of things to notice in this subroutine. First, there are two special variables, `$a` and `$b`, which are used in the subroutine. Each time Perl calls the subroutine, these variables are set to two of the values in the source array. Your subroutine should compare these two values and return a value that indicates which of the elements should come first in the sorted list. You should return –1 if `$a` comes before `$b`, 1 if `$b` comes before `$a`, and 0 if they are the same. The other thing to notice is the `<=>` operator which takes two values and returns –1, 0, or 1, depending on which value is numerically larger. This function, therefore, compares the two values and returns the values required by `sort`. If you wanted to sort the list in

---

[1] Rather than lexically, where 100 comes before 2.

descending numerical order, you would simply have to reverse the order of the comparison of $a and $b like so:

```
sub desc_numerically {
  return $b <=> $a;
}
```

Another way of handling this is to sort the data in ascending order and reverse the list using Perl's built-in `reverse` function like this:

```
@out = reverse sort numerically @in;
```

There is also another operator, `cmp`, which returns the same values but orders the elements lexically. The original default sort is therefore equivalent to:

```
@out = sort lexically @in;

sub lexically {
  return $a cmp $b;
}
```

3.1.2 *Complex sorts*

Sorts as simple as the ones we've discussed so far are generally not written using the subroutine syntax that we have used above. In these cases, the block syntax is used. In the block syntax, Perl code is placed between the `sort` function and the input list. This code must still work on $a and $b and must obey the same rules about what it returns. The sorts that we have discussed above can therefore be rewritten like this:

```
@out = sort { $a <=> $b } @in;
@out = sort { $b <=> $a } @in; # or @out = reverse sort { $a <=> $b } @in
@out = sort { $a cmp $b } @in;
```

The subroutine syntax can, however, be used to produce quite complex sort criteria. Imagine that you have an array of hashes where each hash has two keys, forename and surname, and you want to sort the list like a telephone book (i.e., surname first and then forename). You could write code like this:

```
my @out = sort namesort @in;

sub namesort {
  return $a->{surname} cmp $b->{surname}
    || $a->{forename} cmp $b->{forename};
}
```

Note that we make good use of the "short circuit" functionality of the Perl || operator. Only if the surnames are the same and the first comparison returns 0 is the second comparison evaluated.

We can, of course, mix numeric comparisons with lexical comparisons and even reverse the order on some comparisons. If our hash also contains a key for age, the following code will resolve two identical names by putting the older person first.

```
my @out = sort namesort @in;

sub namesort {
  return $a->{surname} cmp $b->{surname}
    || $a->{forename} cmp $b->{forename}
    || $b->{age} <=> $a->{age};
}
```

This default sort mechanism is implemented using a Quicksort algorithm. In this type of sort, each element of the list is compared with at least one other element in order to determine the correct sequence. This is an efficient method if each comparison is relatively cheap; however, there are circumstances where you are sorting on a value which is calculated from the element. In these situations, recalculating the value each time can have a detrimental effect on performance. There are a number of methods available to minimize this effect and we will now discuss some of the best ones.

3.1.3 *The Orcish Manoeuvre*

One simple way to minimize the effect of calculating the sort value multiple times is to cache the results of each calculation so that we only have to carry out each calculation once. This is the basis of the *Orcish Manoeuvre* (a pun on "or cache") devised by Joseph Hall. In this method, the results of previous calculations are stored in a hash. The basic code would look like this:

```
my %key_cache;

my @out = sort orcish @in;

sub orcish {
  return ($key_cache{$a} ||= get_sort_key($a))
    <=> ($key_cache{$b} ||= get_sort_key($b));
}

sub get_sort_key {
  # Code that takes the list element and returns
  # the part that you want to sort on
}
```

There is a lot going on here so it's worth looking at it in some detail.

The hash %key_cache is used to store the precalculated sort keys.

The function orcish carries out the sort, but for each element, before calculating the sort key, it checks to see if the key has already been calculated, in which case it will be stored in `%key_cache`. It makes use of Perl's `||=` operator to make the code more streamlined. The code

```
$key_cache{$a} ||= get_sort_key($a)
```

can be expanded to

```
$key_cache{$a} = $key_cache{$a} || get_sort_key($a)
```

The net effect of this code is that if `$key_cache{$a}` doesn't already exist then `get_sort_key` is called to calculate it and the result is stored in `$key_cache{$a}`. The same procedure is carried out for `$b` and the two results are then compared using `<=>` (this could just as easily be `cmp` if you need a lexical comparison).

Depending on how expensive your `get_sort_key` function is, this method can greatly increase your performance in sorting large lists.

3.1.4 *Schwartzian transform*

Another way of avoiding recalculating the sort keys a number of times is to use the Schwartzian transform. This was named after Randal L. Schwartz, a well-known member of the Perl community and author of a number of Perl books, who was the first person to post a message using this technique to the comp.lang.perl.misc newsgroup.

In the Schwartzian transform we precalculate all of the sort keys before we begin the actual sort.

As an example, let's go back to our list of CDs. If you remember, we finally decided that we would read the data file into an array of hashes, where each hash contained the details of each CD. Figure 3.1 is a slightly simplified diagram of the @CDs array (each hash has only two fields).

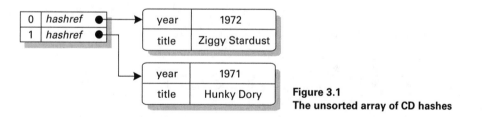

Figure 3.1
The unsorted array of CD hashes

Suppose that now we want to produce a list of CDs arranged in order of release date. The naïve way to write this using `sort` would be like this:

```
my @CDs_sorted_by_year = sort { $a->{year} <=> $b->{year} } @CDs;
```

We could then iterate across the sorted array and print out whatever fields of the hash were of interest to us.

As you can see, to get to the sort key (the release date) we have to go through a hash reference to get to that hash itself. Hash lookup is a reasonably expensive operation in Perl and we'd be better off if we could avoid having to look up each element a number of times.

Let's introduce an intermediate array. Each element of the array will be a reference to a two-element array. The first element will be the year and the second element will be a reference to the original hash. We can create this list very easily using map.

```
my @CD_and_year = map { [$_->{year}, $_] } @CDs;
```

Figure 3.2 shows what this new array would look like.

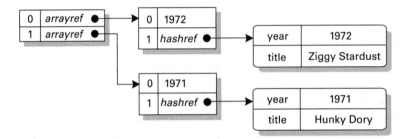

Figure 3.2 `@CD_and_year` **contains references to a two element array**

The year field in each hash has been extracted only once, which will save us a lot of time. We can now sort our new array on the first element of the array. Array lookup is much faster than hash lookup. The code to carry out this sort looks like this:

```
my @sorted_CD_and_year = sort { $a->[0] <=> $b->[0] } @CD_and_year;
```

Figure 3.3 shows this new array.

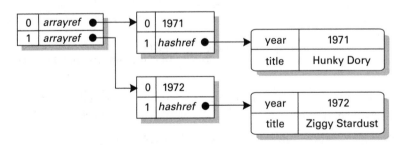

Figure 3.3 `@sorted_CD_and_year` **is** `@CD_and_year` **sorted by the first element of the array**

Now in `@sorted_CD_and_year` we have an array of references to arrays. The important thing, however, is that the array is ordered by year. In fact, we only need the second element of each of these arrays, because that is a reference to our original hash. Using `map` it is simple to strip out the parts that we need.

```
my @CDs_sorted_by_year = map { $_->[1] } @sorted_CD_and_year;
```

Figure 3.4 shows what this array would look like.

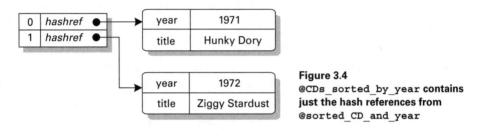

Figure 3.4
`@CDs_sorted_by_year` contains
just the hash references from
`@sorted_CD_and_year`

Let's put those three stages together.

```
my @CD_and_year = map { [$_, $_->{year}] } @CDs;
my @sorted_CD_and_year = sort { $a->[1] <=> $b->[1] } @CD_and_year;
my @CDs_sorted_by_year = map { $_->[0] } @sorted_CD_and_year;
```

That, in a nutshell, is the Schwartzian transform—a sort surrounded by two maps. There is one more piece of tidying up that we can do. As each of the maps and the sort take an array as input and return an array we can chain all of these transformations together in one statement and lose both of the intermediate arrays.

```
my @CDs_sorted_by_year = map { $_->[0] }
                 sort { $a->[1] <=> $b->[1] }
                 map { [$_, $_->{year}] } @CDs;
```

If this doesn't look quite like what we had before, try tracing it through in reverse. Our original array (`@CDs`) is passed in at the bottom. It goes through the `map` that dereferences the hash, then the `sort`, and finally the last `map`.

The chaining together of multiple list processing functions, where the output of the first map becomes the input to the sort and so on, is very similar to the I/O pipes that we saw when looking at the UNIX filter model earlier.

The Schwartzian transform can be used anywhere that you want to sort a list of data structures by one of the data values contained within it, but that's not all it can do. Here's a three-line script that prints out our CD file (read in through `STDIN`), sorted by the recording label.

```
print map { $_->[0] }
      sort { $a->[1] cmp $b->[1] }
      map { [$_, (split /\t/) [2]] } <STDIN>;
```

3.1.5 *The Guttman-Rosler transform*

At the 1999 Perl Conference, Uri Guttman and Larry Rosler presented a paper on sorting with Perl. It covered all of the techniques discussed so far and went a step further, by introducing the concept of the *packed-default* sort. They started from two premises:

1 Eliminating any hash or array dereferencing would speed up the sort.

2 The default lexical sort (without any sort subroutine or block) is the fastest.

The resulting method is an interesting variation on the Schwartzian transform. Instead of transforming each element of the list into a two element list (the sort key and the original data) and sorting on the first element of this list, Guttman and Rosler suggest converting each element of the original list into a string with the sort key at the beginning and the original element at the end. A list containing these strings can then be sorted lexically and the original data is extracted from the sorted list.

The example that they use in their paper is that of sorting IP addresses. First they convert each element to a string in which each part of the IP address is converted (using pack) to the character represented by that value in ASCII. This four-character string has the original data appended to the end:

```
my @strings = map { pack('C4', /(\d+)\.(\d+)\.(\d+)\.(\d+)/) . $_ } @IPs;
```

then the strings are lexically sorted using the default sort mechanism

```
my @sorted_strings = sort @strings;
```

and finally the original data is extracted.

```
my @sorted_IPs = map { substr($_, 4) } @sorted_strings;
```

Rewriting this to make it look more like the Schwartzian transform, we get this:

```
my @sorted_IPs = map { substr($_, 4) }
                 sort
                 map { pack('C4', /(\d+)\.(\d+)\.(\d+)\.(\d+)/) . $_ } @IPs;
```

This type of sort needs a bit more thought than the other methods that we have considered in order to create a suitable string for sorting; however, it can pay great dividends in the amount of performance improvement that you can see.

3.1.6 *Choosing a sort technique*

If you are having performance problems with a program that contains a complex sort, then it is quite possible that using one of the techniques from this section will speed up the script. It is, however, possible that your script could get slower. Each of the techniques will improve the actual sort time, but they all have an overhead which means that your sort will need to be quite large before you see any improvement.

When selecting a sort technique to use, it is important that you use the benchmarking methods, discussed in section 3.4, to work out which technique is most appropriate. Of course, if your script is only going to run once, then spending half a day benchmarking sorts for the purpose of shaving five seconds off the runtime isn't much of a gain.

This section has only really started to discuss the subject of sorting in Perl. If you'd like to know more, Guttman and Rosler's paper is a very good place to start. You can find it online at http://www.sysarch.com/perl/sort_paper.html.

3.2   *Database Interface (DBI)*

As discussed in chapter 1, a common source or sink for data is a database. For many years Perl has had mechanisms that enable it to talk to various database systems. For example, if you wanted to exchange data with an Oracle database you would use `oraperl` and if you had to communicate with a Sybase database you would use `sybperl`. Modules were also available to talk to many other popular database systems.

Most of these database access modules were a thin Perl wrapper around the programming APIs that were already provided by the database vendors. The mechanisms for talking to the various databases were all doing largely the same thing, but they were doing it in completely incompatible ways.

This has all changed in recent years with the introduction of the generic Perl Database Interface (DBI) module. This module was designed and written by Tim Bunce (the author and maintainer of `oraperl`). It allows a program to connect to any of the supported database systems and read and write data using exactly the same syntax. The only change required to connect to a different database system is to change one string that is passed to the DBI connect function. It does this by using different database driver (DBD) modules. These are all named `DBD::<db_name>`. You will need to obtain the DBD module for whichever database you are using separately from the main DBI module.

3.2.1   *Sample DBI program*

A sample DBI program to read data from a database would look like this:

```
1: #!/usr/local/bin/perl -w
2:
3: use strict;
4: use DBI;
5:
```

```
 6: my $user = 'dave';
 7: my $pass = 'secret';
 8: my $dbh = DBI->connect('dbi:mysql:testdb', $user, $pass,
 9:                         {RaiseError => 1})
10:    || die "Connect failed: $DBI::errstr";
11:
12: my $sth = $dbh->prepare('select col1, col2, col3 from my_table')
13:
14: $sth->execute;
15:
16: my @row;
17: while (@row = $sth->fetchrow_array) {
18:   print join("\t", @row), "\n";
19: }
20:
21: $sth->finish;
22: $dbh->disconnect;
```

While this is a very simple DBI program, it demonstrates a number of important DBI concepts and it is worth examining line by line.

Line 1 points to the Perl interpreter. Notice the use of the -w flag.

Line 3 switches on the strict pragma.

Line 4 brings in the DBI.pm module. This allows us to use the DBI functions.

Lines 6 and 7 define a username and password that we will use to connect to the database. Obviously, in a real program you probably wouldn't want to have a password written in a script in plain text.

Line 8 connects us to the database. In this case we are connecting to a database running MySQL. This free database program is very popular for web systems. This is the only line that would need to change if we were connecting to a different database system. The connect function takes a number of parameters which can vary depending on the database to which you are connecting. The first parameter is a connection string. This changes its precise meaning for different databases, but it is always a colon-separated string. The first part is the string dbi and the second part is always the name of the database system[2] that we are connecting to. In this case the string mysql tells DBI that we will be talking to a MySQL database, and it should therefore load the DBD::mysql module. The third section of the connection string in this case is the particular database that we want to connect to. Many database systems (including MySQL) can store many different databases on the same database server. In this case we want to connect to a database called testdb. The second and third parameters are valid usernames and passwords for connecting to this database.

---

[2] Or, more accurately, the name of the DBD module that we are using to connect to the database.

The fourth parameter to `DBI->connect` is a reference to a hash containing various configuration options. In this example we switch on the `RaiseError` option, which will automatically generate a fatal run-time error if a database error occurs.

The `DBI->connect` function returns a database handle, which can then be used to access other DBI functions. If there is an error, the function returns `undef`. In the sample program we check for this and, if there is a problem, the program dies after printing the value of the variable `$DBI::errstr` which contains the most recent database error message.

Line 12 prepares an SQL statement for execution against the database. It does this by calling the DBI function `prepare`. This function returns a statement handle which can be used to access another set of DBI functions—those that deal with executing queries on the database and reading and writing data. This handle is undefined if there is an error preparing the statement.

Line 14 executes the statement and dies if there is an error.

Line 16 defines an array variable which will hold each row of data returned from the database in turn.

Lines 17 to 19 define a loop which receives each row from the database query and prints it out. On line 17 we call `fetchrow_array` which returns a list containing one element for each of the columns in the next row of the result set. When the result set has all been returned, the next call to `fetchrow_array` will return the value `undef`.

Line 18 prints out the current row with a tab character between each element.

Lines 21 and 22 call functions that reclaim the memory used for the database and statement handles. This memory will be reclaimed automatically when the variables go out of scope, but it is tidier to clean up yourself.

This has been a very quick overview of using the DBI. There are a number of other functions and the most useful ones are listed in appendix A. More detailed documentation comes with the DBI module and your chosen DBD modules.

3.3 Data::Dumper

As your data structures get more and more complex it will become more and more useful to have an easy way to see what they look like. A very convenient way to do this is by using the `Data::Dumper` module which comes as a standard part of the Perl distribution. `Data::Dumper` takes one or more variables and produces a "stringified" version of the data contained in the variables.

We'll see many examples of `Data::Dumper` throughout the book but, as an example, let's use it to get a dump of the CD data structure that we built in the previous chapter. The data structure was built up using code like this:

```
my @CDs;
my @attrs = qw(artist title label year);
  while (<STDIN>) {
    chomp;
    my %rec;
    @rec{@attrs} = split /\t/;
    push @CDs, \%rec;
  }
```

In order to use Data::Dumper we just need to add a use Data::Dumper statement and a call to the Dumper function like this:

```
use Data::Dumper;
my @CDs;

my @attrs = qw(artist title label year);
while (<STDIN>) {
  chomp;
  my %rec;
  @rec{@attrs} = split /\t/;
  push @CDs, \%rec;
}

print Dumper(\@CDs);
```

Running this program using our CD files as input produces the following output:

```
$VAR1 = [
          {
            'artist' => 'Bragg, Billy',
            'title' => 'Workers\' Playtime',
            'year' => '1987',
            'label' => 'Cooking Vinyl'
          },
          {
            'artist' => 'Bragg, Billy',
            'title' => 'Mermaid Avenue',
            'year' => '1998',
            'label' => 'EMI'
          },
          {
            'artist' => 'Black, Mary',
            'title' => 'The Holy Ground',
            'year' => '1993',
            'label' => 'Grapevine'
          },
          {
            'artist' => 'Black, Mary',
            'title' => 'Circus',
            'year' => '1996',
            'label' => 'Grapevine'
          },
```

```
    {
      'artist' => 'Bowie, David',
      'title' => 'Hunky Dory',
      'year' => '1971',
      'label' => 'RCA'
    },
    {
      'artist' => 'Bowie, David',
      'title' => 'Earthling',
      'year' => '1998',
      'label' => 'EMI'
    }
  ];
```

This is a very understandable representation of our data structure.

Notice that we passed a reference to our array rather than the array itself. This is because Dumper expects a list of variables as arguments so, if we had passed an array, it would have processed each element of the array individually and produced output for each of them. By passing a reference we forced it to treat our array as a single object.

3.4   *Benchmarking*

When choosing between various ways to implement a task in Perl, it will often be useful to know which option is the quickest. Perl provides a module called Benchmark that makes it easy to get this data. This module contains a number of functions (see the documentation for details) but the most useful for comparing the performance of different pieces of code is called timethese. This function takes a number of pieces of code, runs them each a number of times, and returns the time that each piece of code took to run. You should, therefore, break your options down into separate functions which all do the same thing in different ways and pass these functions to timethese. For example, there are four ways to put the value of a variable into the middle of a fixed string. You can interpolate the variable directly within the string

```
$str = "The value is $x (or thereabouts)";
```

or join a list of values

```
$str = join '', 'The value is ', $x, ' (or thereabouts)';
```

or concatenate the values

```
$s = 'The value is ' . $x . ' (or thereabouts)';
```

or, finally, use sprintf.

```
$str = sprintf 'The value is %s (or thereabouts)', $x;
```

In order to calculate which of these methods is the fastest, you would write a script like this:

```perl
#!/usr/bin/perl -w
use strict;
use Benchmark qw(timethese);

my $x = 'x' x 100;

sub using_concat {
  my $str = 'x is ' . $x . ' (or thereabouts)';
}

sub using_join {
  my $str = join '', 'x is ', $x, ' (or thereabouts)';
}

sub using_interp {
  my $str = "x is $x (or thereabouts)";
}

sub using_sprintf {
  my $str = sprintf("x is %s (or thereabouts)", $x);
}

timethese (1E6, {
  'concat'  => \&using_concat,
  'join'    => \&using_join,
  'interp'  => \&using_interp,
  'sprintf' => \&using_sprintf,
});
```

On my current computer,[3] running this script gives the following output:

```
Benchmark: timing 1000000 iterations of concat, interp, join, sprintf …
    concat: 8 wallclock secs ( 7.36 usr +  0.00 sys =  7.36 CPU) @ 135869.57/s (n=1000000)
    interp: 8 wallclock secs ( 6.92 usr + -0.00 sys =  6.92 CPU) @ 144508.67/s (n=1000000)
      join: 9 wallclock secs ( 8.38 usr +  0.03 sys =  8.41 CPU) @ 118906.06/s (n=1000000)
    sprintf: 12 wallclock secs (11.14 usr +  0.02 sys = 11.16 CPU) @ 89605.73/s
    (n=1000000)
```

What does this mean? Looking at the script, we can see that we call the function timethese, passing it an integer followed by a reference to a hash. The integer is the number of times that you want the tests to be run. The hash contains details of the code that you want tested. The keys to the hash are unique names for each of the subroutines and the values are references to the functions themselves. timethese will run each of your functions the given number of times and will print out the

---

[3] A rather old 200 MHz P6 with 64 MB of RAM, running Microsoft Windows 98 and ActivePerl build 521.

results. As you can see from the results we get above, our functions fall into three sets. Both concat and interp took about 8 seconds of CPU time to run 1,000,000 times; join was a little longer at 9 seconds; and sprintf came in at 12 seconds of CPU time.

You can then use these figures to help you decide which version of the code to use in your application.

3.5 *Command line scripts*

Often data munging scripts are written to carry out one-off tasks. Perhaps you have been given a data file which you need to clean up before loading it into a database. While you can, of course, write a complete Perl script to carry out this munging, Perl supplies a set of command line options which make it easy to carry out this kind of task from the command line. This approach can often be more efficient.

The basic option for command line processing is -e. The text following this option is treated as Perl code and is passed through to the Perl interpreter. You can therefore write scripts like:

```
perl -e 'print "Hello world\n"'
```

You can pass as many -e options as you want to Perl and they will be run in the order that they appear on the command line. You can also combine many statements in one -e string by separating them with a semicolon.

If the code that you want to run needs a module that you would usually include with a use statement, you can use the -M option to load the module. For example, this makes it easy to find the version of any module that is installed on your system[4] using code like this:

```
perl -MCGI -e 'print $CGI::VERSION'
```

These single-line scripts can sometimes be useful, but there is a whole set of more powerful options to write file processing scripts. The first of these is -n, which adds a loop around your code which looks like this:

```
LINE:
while (<>) {
  # Your -e code goes here
}
```

This can be used, for example, to write a simple grep-like script such as:

```
perl -ne 'print if /search text/' file.txt
```

---

[4] Providing that the module uses the standard practice of defining a $VERSION variable.

which will print any lines in `file.txt` that contain the string "search text". Notice the presence of the `LINE` label which allows you to write code using `next LINE`.

If you are transforming data in the file and want to print a result for every line, then you should use the -p option which prints the contents of `$_` at the end of each iteration of the `while` loop. The code it generates looks like this:

```
LINE:
while (<>) {
  # Your -e code goes here
} continue {
  print
}
```

As an example of using this option, imagine that you wanted to collapse multiple zeroes in a record to just one. You could write code like this:

```
perl -pe 's/0+/0/g' input.txt > output.txt
```

With the examples we've seen so far, the output from the script is written to STDOUT (that is why we redirected STDOUT to another file in the last example). There is another option, -i, which allows us to process a file in place and optionally create a backup containing the previous version of the file. The -i takes a text string which will be the extension added to the backup of the file, so we can rewrite our previous example as:

```
perl -i.bak -pe 's/0+/0/g' input.txt
```

This option will leave the changed data in `input.txt` and the original data in `input.txt.bak`. If you don't give -i an extension then no backup is made (so you'd better be pretty confident that you know what you're doing!).

There are a number of other options that can make your life even easier. Using -a turns on autosplit, which in turn splits each input row into `@F`. By default, autosplit splits the string on any white space, but you can change the split character using -F. Therefore, in order to print out the set of user names from /etc/passwd you can use code like this:

```
perl -a -F':' -ne 'print "$F[0]\n"' < /etc/passwd
```

The –1 option switches on line-end processing. This automatically does a `chomp` on each line when used with -n or -p. You can also give it an optional octal number which will change the value of the output record separator ($\).[5] This value is

---

[5] Special variables like $\ are covered in more detail in chapter 6.

appended to the end of each output line. Without the octal number, $\backslash$ is set to the same value as the input record separator ($/). The default value for this is a newline. You can change the value of $/ using the -0 (that's dash-zero, not dash-oh) option.

What this means is that in order to have newlines automatically removed from your input lines and automatically added back to your output line, just use -l. For instance, the previous /etc/passwd example could be rewritten as:

```
perl -a -F':' -nle 'print $F[0]' < /etc/passwd
```

For more information about these command line options see the perlrun manual page which is installed when you install Perl.

3.6 *Further information*

More discussion of the Schwartzian transform, the Orcish Manoeuvre, and other Perl tricks can be found in *Effective Perl Programming* by Joseph Hall with Randal Schwartz (Addison-Wesley) and *The Perl Cookbook* by Tom Christiansen and Nathan Torkington (O'Reilly).

The more academic side of sorting in Perl is discussed in *Mastering Algorithms with Perl* by Jon Orwant, Jarkko Hietaniemi, and John Macdonald (O'Reilly).

More information about benchmarking can be found in the documentation for the Benchmark.pm module.

Further information about the DBI and DBD modules can be found in *Programming the Perl DBI* by Tim Bunce and Alligator Descartes (O'Reilly) and in the documentation that is installed along with the modules. When you have installed the DBI module you can read the documentation by typing

```
perldoc DBI
```

at your command line. Similarly you can read the documentation for any installed DBD module by typing

```
perldoc DBD::<name>
```

at your command line. You should replace <name> with the name of the DBD module that you have installed, for example "Sybase" or "mysql".

3.7 Summary

- Sorting can be very simple in Perl, but for more complex sorts there are a number of methods which can make the sort more efficient.
- Database access in Perl is very easy using the DBI.
- `Data::Dumper` is very useful for seeing what your internal data structures look like.
- Benchmarking is very important, but can be quite tricky to do correctly.
- Command line scripts can be surprisingly powerful.

Pattern matching

A lot of data munging involves the use of pattern matching. In fact, it's probably fair to say that the vast majority of data munging uses pattern matching in one way or another. Most pattern matching in Perl is carried out using regular expressions.[1] It is therefore very important that you understand how to use them. In this chapter we take an overview of regular expressions in Perl and how they can be used in data munging, but we start with a brief look at a couple of methods for pattern matching that don't involve regular expressions.

4.1   String handling functions

Perl has a number of functions for handling strings and these are often far simpler to use and more efficient than the regular expression-based methods that we will discuss later. When considering how to solve a particular problem, it is always worth seeing if you can use a simpler method before going straight for a solution using regular expressions.

4.1.1   Substrings

If you want to extract a particular portion of a string then you can use the substr function. This function takes two mandatory parameters: a string to work on and the offset to start at, and two optional parameters: the length of the required substring and another string to replace it with. If the third parameter is omitted, then the substring will include all characters in the source string from the given offset to the end. The offset of the first character in the source string is 0.[2] If the offset is negative then it counts from the end of the string. Here are a few simple examples:

```
my $string = 'Alas poor Yorick. I knew him Horatio.';
my $sub1 = substr($string, 0, 4);     # $sub1 contains 'Alas'
my $sub2 = substr($string, 10, 6);    # $sub2 contains 'Yorick'
my $sub3 = substr($string, 29);       # $sub3 contains 'Horatio.'
my $sub4 = substr($string, -12, 3);   # $sub4 contains 'him'
```

Many programming languages have a function that produces substrings in a similar manner, but the clever thing about Perl's substr function is that the result of the operation can act as an lvalue. That is, you can assign values to it, like this:

```
my $string = 'Alas poor Yorick. I knew him Horatio.';

substr($string, 10, 6) = 'Robert';
substr($string, 29) = 'as Bob';

print $string;
```

---

[1] In fact, it's often suggested that regular expressions in Perl are overused.

[2] Or, more accurately, it is the value of the special $[variable, but as that is initially set to zero and there is really no good reason to change it, your strings should always start from position zero.

which will produce the output:

```
Alas poor Robert. I knew him as Bob
```

Notice the second assignment in this example which demonstrates that the substring and the text that you are replacing it with do not have to be the same length. Perl will take care of any necessary manipulation of the strings. You can even do something like this:

```
my $short = 'Short string';
my $long  = 'Very, very, very, very long';

substr($short, 0, 5) = $long;
```

which will leave `$short` containing the text "Very, very, very, very long string".

4.1.2 *Finding strings within strings (index and rindex)*

Two more functions that are useful for this kind of text manipulation are index and rindex. These functions do very similar things—index finds the first occurrence of a string in another string and rindex finds the last occurrence. Both functions return an integer indicating the position[3] in the source string where the given substring begins, and both take an optional third parameter which is the position where the search should start. Here are some simple examples:

```
my $string = 'To be or not to be.';

my $pos1 = index($string, 'be');      # $pos1 is 3
my $pos2 = rindex($string, 'be');     # $pos2 is 16
my $pos3 = index($string, 'be', 5);   # $pos3 is 16
my $pos4 = index($string, 'not');     # $pos4 is 9
my $pos5 = rindex($string, 'not');    # $pos5 is 9
```

It's worth noting that $pos3 is 16 because we don't start looking until position 5; and $pos4 and $pos5 are equal because there is only one instance of the string 'not' in our source string.

It is, of course, possible to use these three functions in combination to carry out more complex tasks. For example, if you had a string and wanted to extract the middle portion that was contained between square brackets ([and]), you could do something like this:

```
my $string = 'Text with an [important bit] in brackets';

my $start = index($string, '[');
my $end = rindex($string, ']');

my $keep = substr($string, $start+1, $end-$start-1);
```

---

[3] Again, the positions start from 0—or the value of $[.

although in this case, the regular expression solution would probably be more easily understood.

4.1.3 Case transformations

Another common requirement is to alter the case of a text string, either to change the string to all upper case, all lower case, or some combination. Perl has functions to handle all of these eventualities. The functions are uc (to convert a whole string to upper case), ucfirst (to convert the first character of a string to upper case), lc (to convert a whole string to lower case), and lcfirst (to convert the first character of a string to lower case).

There are a couple of traps that seem to catch unwary programmers who use these functions. The first of these is with the ucfirst and lcfirst functions. It is important to note that they do exactly what they say and affect only the first character in the given string. I have seen code like this:

```
$string = ucfirst 'UPPER';    # This doesn't work
```

where the programmer expects to end up with the string 'Upper'. The correct code to achieve this is:

```
$string = ucfirst lc 'UPPER';
```

The second trap for the unwary is that these functions will respect your local language character set, but to make use of that, you need to switch on Perl's locale support by including the line use locale in your program.

4.2   Regular expressions

In this section we take a closer look at regular expressions. This is one of Perl's most powerful tools for data munging, but it is also a feature that many people have difficulty understanding.

4.2.1 What are regular expressions?

"Regular expression" is a very formal computer science sounding term for something that would probably scare people a great deal less if we simply called it "pattern matching," because that is basically what we are talking about.

If you have some data and you want to know whether or not certain strings are present within the data set, then you need to construct a regular expression that describes the data that you are looking for and see whether it matches your data. Exactly how you construct the regular expression and match it against your data will be covered later in the chapter. First we will look at the kinds of things that you can match with regular expressions.

Many text-processing tools support regular expressions. UNIX tools like vi, sed, grep, and awk all support them to varying degrees. Even some Windows-based tools like Microsoft Word allow you to search text using basic kinds of regular expressions. Of all of these tools, Perl has the most powerful regular expression support.

Among others, Perl regular expressions can match the following:

- A text phrase
- Phrases containing optional sections
- Phrases containing repeated sections
- Alternate phrases (i.e., either *this* or *that*)
- Phrases that must appear at the start or end of a word
- Phrases that must appear at the start or end of a line
- Phrases that must appear at the start or end of the data
- Any character from a group of characters
- Any character not from a group of characters

Recent versions of Perl have added a number of extensions to the standard regular expression set, some of which are still experimental at the time of this writing. For the definitive, up-to-date regular expression documentation for your version of Perl see the perlre documentation page.

4.2.2 Regular expression syntax

In Perl you can turn a string of characters into a regular expression by enclosing it in slash characters (/). So, for example

```
/regular expression/
```

is a regular expression which matches the string "regular expression".

Regular expression metacharacters

Within a regular expression most characters will match themselves[4] unless their meaning is modified by the presence of various metacharacters. The list of metacharacters that can be used in Perl regular expressions is

```
\ | ( ) [ { ^ $ * + ? .
```

---

[4] That is, a letter "a" in a regular expression will match the character "a" in the target string.

Any of these metacharacters can be used to match itself in a regular expression by preceding it with a backslash character (\). You'll see that the backslash is itself a metacharacter, so to match a literal backslash you'll need to have two backslashes in your regular expression /foo\\bar/ matches "foo\bar".

The dot character (.) matches any character.

The normal escape sequences that are familiar from many programming languages are also available. A tab character is matched by \t, a newline by \n, a carriage return by \r, and a form feed by \f.

Character classes

You can match any character in a group of characters (known in Perl as a *character class*) by enclosing the list of characters within square brackets ([and]). If a group of characters are consecutive in your character set, then you can use a dash character (-) to denote a range of characters. Therefore the regular expression

```
/[aeiouAEIOU]/
```

will match any vowel and

```
/[a-z]/
```

will match any lower case letter.

To match any character that is not in a character class, put a caret (^) at the start of the group, so

```
/[^aeiouAEIOU]/
```

matches any nonvowel (note that this does not just match consonants; it will also match punctuation characters, spaces, control characters—and even extended ASCII characters like ñ, «, and é).

Escape sequences

There are a number of predefined character classes that can be denoted using escape sequences. Any digit is matched by \d. Any word character (i.e., digits, upper and lower case letters, and the underscore character) is matched by \w and any white space character (space, tab, carriage return, line feed, or form feed) is matched by \s. The inverses of these classes are also defined. Any nondigit is matched by \D, any nonword character is matched by \W, and any nonspace character is matched by \S.

Matching alternatives

The vertical bar character (|) is used to denote alternate matches. A regular expression, such as:

```
/regular expression|regex/
```

will match either the string "regular expression" or the string "regex". Parentheses ((and)) can be used to group strings, so while

`/regexes are cool|rubbish/`

will match the strings "regexes are cool" or "rubbish",

`/regexes are (cool|rubbish)/`

will match "regexes are cool" or "regexes are rubbish".

Capturing parts of matches

A side effect of grouping characters using parentheses is that if a string matches a regular expression, then the parts of the string which match the sections in parentheses will be stored in special variables called $1, $2, $3, etc. For example, after matching a string against the previous regular expression, then $1 will contain the string "cool" or "rubbish." We will see more examples of this later in the chapter.

Quantifying matches

You can also quantify the number of times that a string should appear using the +, *, or ? characters. Putting + after a character (or string of characters in a parentheses or a character class) allows that item to appear one or more times, * allows the item to appear zero or more times, and ? allows the item to appear zero or one time (i.e., it becomes optional). For example:

`/so+n/`

will match "son", "soon", or "sooon", etc., whereas

`/so*n/`

will match "sn", "son", "soon", and "sooon", etc., and

`/so?n/`

will only match "sn", and "son".

   Similarly for groups of characters,

`/(so)+n/`

will match "son", "soson", or "sososon", etc., whereas

`/(so)*n/`

will match "n", "son", "soson", and "sososon", etc., and

`/(so)?n/`

will match only "n" and "son".

You can have more control over the number of times that a term appears using the {n,m} syntax. In this syntax the term to be repeated is followed by braces containing up to two numbers separated by a comma. The numbers indicate the minimum and maximum times that the term can appear. For example, in the regular expression

`/so{1,2}n/`

the "o" will match if it appears once or twice, so "son" or "soon" will match, but "sooon" will not. If the first number is omitted, then it is assumed to be zero and if the second number is omitted then there is assumed to be no limit to the number of occurrences that will match. You should notice that the +, *, and ? forms that we used earlier are not strictly necessary as they could be indicated using {1,}, {0,}, and {0,1}. If only one number appears without a comma then the expression will match if the term appears exactly that number of times.

Anchoring matches

It is also possible to anchor parts of your regular expression at various points of the data. If you want to match a regular expression only at the start of your data you can use a caret (^). Similarly, a dollar sign ($) matches at the end of the data. To match an email header line which consists of a string such as "From", "To", or "Subject" followed by a colon, an optional space and some more text, you could use a regular expression like this:[5]

`/^[^:]+: ?.+$/`

which matches the start of the line followed by at least one noncolon character, followed by a colon, an optional space, and at least one other character before the end of the line.

Other special terms can be used to match at word boundaries. The term \b matches only at the start or end of a word (i.e., between a \w character and a \W character) and its inverse \B only matches within a word (i.e., between two \w characters). For instance, if we wanted to match "son", but didn't want to match it at the end of names like "Johnson" and "Robertson" we could use a regular expression like:

`/\bson\b/`

and if we were only interested in occurrences of "son" at the end of other words, we could use:

`/\Bson\b/`

---

[5] You could also write this as /^.+?: ?.+$/, but we don't cover the syntax for nongreedy matching until later in the chapter.

More complex regular expressions

Recent versions of Perl have added more complexity to regular expressions allowing you to define more complex rules against which you match your strings. The full explanation of these enhancements is in your Perl documentation, but the most important additions are:

- (?: ...)—These parentheses group in the same way that normal brackets do, but when they match, their contents don't get assigned to $1, $2, etc.
- (?= ...)—This is known as positive lookahead. It enables you to check that whatever is between the parentheses exists there in the string, but it doesn't actually consume the next part of the string that is being matched.
- (?! ...)—This is negative lookahead, which is the opposite of positive lookahead. You will only get a match if whatever is in the parentheses does *not* match the string there.

4.2.3 Using regular expressions

Most regular expressions are used in Perl programs in one of two ways. The simpler way is to check if a data string matches the regular expression, and the slightly more complex way is to replace parts of data strings with other strings.

String matching

To match a string against a regular expression in Perl we use the match operator—which is normally called m//, although it is quite possible that it looks nothing like that when you use it.

By default, the match operator works on the $_ variable. This works very well when you are looping through an array of values. Imagine, for example, that you have a text file containing email messages and you want to print out all of the lines containing "From" headers. You could do something like this:

```
open MAIL, 'mail.txt' or die "Can't open mail.txt: $!";

while (<MAIL>) {
  print if m/^From:/;
}
```

The while loop reads in another line from the file each time around and stores the line in $_. The match operator checks for lines beginning with the string "From:" (note the ^ character that matches the start of the line) and returns true for lines that match. These lines are then printed to STDOUT.

One nice touch with the match operator is that in many cases the m is optional so we can write the match statement in our scripts as

```
print if /^From:/;
```

and that is how you will see it in most scripts that you encounter. It is also possible
to use delimiters other than the / character, but in this case the m becomes mandatory. To see why you might want to do this, look at this example:

```
open FILES 'files.txt' or die "Can't open files.txt: $!";

while (<FILES>) {
  print if /\/davec\//;
}
```

In this script we are doing a very similar thing to the previous example, but in this
case we are scanning a list of files and printing the ones that are under a directory
called davec. The directory separator character is also a slash, so we need to escape
it within the regular expression with back-slashes and the whole thing ends up looking a little inelegant (this is sometimes known as leaning toothpick syndrome). To
get around this, Perl allows us to choose our own regular expression delimiter. This
can be any punctuation character, but if we choose one of the paired delimiter characters ((, {, [or <) to open our regular expression we must use the opposite character (), },] or >) to close it, otherwise we just use the same character. We can
therefore rewrite our match line as

```
print if m(/davec/);
```

or

```
print if m|/davec/|;
```

or even

```
print if m=/davec/=;
```

any of which may well be easier to read than the original. Note that in all of these
cases we have to use the m at the start of the expression.

More capturing
Once a match has been successful, Perl sets a number of special variables. For each
bracketed group in your regular expression, Perl sets a variable. The first bracket
group goes into $1, the second into $2, and so on. Bracketed groups can be nested,
so the order of assignment to these variables depends upon the order of the opening bracket of the group. Going back to our earlier email header example, if we had
an email in a text file and wanted to print out all of the headers, we could do something like this:[6]

---

[6] This simplified example conveniently ignores the fact that email headers can continue onto more than one
line and that an email body can contain the character ":".

```
open MAIL, 'mail.txt' or die "Can't open mail.txt: $!";

while (<MAIL>) {
   if (/^([^:]+): ?(.+)$/) {
      print "Header $1 has the value $2\n";
}
```

We have added two sets of brackets to the original regular expression which will capture the header name and value into $1 and $2 so that we can print them out in the next line. If a match operation is evaluated in an array context, it returns the values of $1, $2, and so forth in a list. We could, therefore, rewrite the previous example as:

```
open MAIL, 'mail.txt' or die "Can't open mail.txt: $!";

my ($header, $value);
while (<MAIL>) {
   if (($header, $value) = /^([^:]+): ?(.+)$/) {
     print "Header $header has the value $value\n";
   }
}
```

There are other variables that Perl sets on a successful match. These include $& which is set to the part of the string that matched the whole regular expression, $` which is set to the part of the string before the part that matched the regular expression, and $' which is set to the part of the string after the part that matched the regular expressions. Therefore after executing the following code:

```
$_ = 'Matching regular expressions';
m/regular expression/;
```

$& will contain the string "regular expression", $` will contain "Matching ", and $' will contain "s". Obviously these variables are far more useful if your regular expression is not a fixed string.

There is one small downside to using these variables. Perl has to do a lot more work to keep them up to date. If you don't use them it doesn't set them. However, if you use them in just one match in your program, Perl will then keep them updated for every match. Using them can therefore have an effect on performance.

Matching against other variables

Obviously not every string that you are going to want to match is going to be in $_, so Perl provides a binding operator which binds the match to another variable. The operator looks like this:

```
$string =~ m/regular expression/
```

This statement searches for a match for the string "regular expression" within the text in the variable `$string`.

Match modifiers

There are a number of optional modifiers that can be applied to the match operator to change the way that it works. These modifiers are all placed after the closing delimiter. The most commonly used modifier is `i` which forces the match to be case-insensitive, so that

```
m/hello/i
```

will match "hello", "HELLO", "Hello", or any other combination of cases. Earlier we saw a regular expression for matching vowels that looked like this

```
/[aeiouAEIOU]/
```

Now that we have the `i` modifier, we can rewrite this as

```
/[aeiou]/i
```

The next two modifiers are `s` and `m` which force the match to treat the data string as either single or multiple lines. In single line mode, "." will match a newline character (which would not happen by default). In multiple line mode, `^` and `$` will match at the start and end of any line. To match the start and end of the entire string you can use the anchors `\A` and `\Z`.

The final modifier is `x`. This allows you to put white space and comments within your regular expressions. The regular expressions that we have looked at so far have been very simple, but regular expressions are largely what give Perl its reputation of being written in line noise. If we look again at the regular expression we used to match email headers, is it easier to follow like this:

```
m/^[^:]+\s?.+$/
```

or like this

```
m/^      # start of line
  [^:]+ # at least one non-colon
  :     # a colon
  \s?   # an optional white space character
  .+    # at least one other character
  $/x   # end of line
```

And that's just a simple example!

String replacement

The string replacement operation looks strikingly similar to the string-matching operator, and works in a quite similar fashion. The operator is usually called s/// although, like the string-matching operator, it can actually take many forms.

The simplest way of using the string replacement operator is to replace occurrences of one string with another string. For example to replace "Dave" with "David" you would use this code:

```
s/Dave/David/;
```

The first expression (Dave) is evaluated as a regular expression. The second expression is a string that will replace whatever matched the regular expression in the original data string. This replacement string can contain any of the variables that get set on a successful match. It is therefore possible to rewrite the previous example as:

```
s/(Dav)e/${1}id/
```

As with the match operator, the operation defaults to affecting whatever is in the variable $_, but you can bind the operation to a different variable using the =~ operator.

Substitution modifiers

All of the match operator modifiers (i, s, m, and x) work in the same way on the substitution operator but there are a few extra modifiers. By default, the substitution only takes place on the first string matched in the data string. For example:

```
my $data = "This is Dave's data. It is the data belonging to Dave";

$data =~ s/Dave/David/;
```

will result in $data containing the string "This is David's data. It is the data belonging to Dave". The second occurrence of Dave was untouched. In order to affect all occurrences of the string we can use the g modifier.

```
my $data = "This is Dave's data. It is the data belonging to Dave";

$data =~ s/Dave/David/g;
```

This works as expected and leaves $data containing the string "This is David's data. It is the data belonging to David".

The other two new modifiers only affect the substitution if either the search string or the replacement string contains variables or executable code. Consider the following code:

```
my ($new, $old) = @ARGV;

while (<STDIN>) {
s/$old/$new/g;
```

```
    print;
}
```

which is a very simple text substitution filter. It takes two strings as arguments. The first is a string to search for and the second is a string to replace it with. It then reads whatever is passed to it on STDIN and replaces one string with the other. This certainly works, but it is not very efficient. Each time around, the loop Perl doesn't know that the contents of $old haven't changed so it is forced to recompile the regular expression each time. We, however, know that $old has a fixed value. We can therefore let Perl know this, by adding the o modifier to the substitution operator. This tells Perl that it is safe to compile the regular expression once and to reuse the same version each time around the loop. We should change the substitution line to read

```
s/$old/$new/go;
```

There is one more modifier to explain and that is the e modifier. When this modifier is used, the replacement string is treated as executable code and is passed to eval. The return value from the evaluation is then used as the replacement string.[7] As an example, here is a fairly strange way to print out a table of squares:

```
foreach (1 .. 12) {
  s/(\d+)/print "$1 squared is ", $1*$1, "\n"/e;
}
```

which produces the following output:

```
1 squared is 1
2 squared is 4
3 squared is 9
4 squared is 16
5 squared is 25
6 squared is 36
7 squared is 49
8 squared is 64
9 squared is 81
10 squared is 100
11 squared is 121
12 squared is 144
```

4.2.4 *Example: translating from English to American*

To finish this overview of regular expressions, let's write a script that translates from English to American. To make it easier for ourselves we'll make a few assumptions.

---

[7] Actually it isn't quite that simple, as you can have multiple instances of the e modifier and the replacement string is evaluated for each one.

We'll assume that each English word has just one American translation.[8] We'll also store our translations in a text file so it is easy to add to them. The program will look something like this:

```
 1: #!/usr/bin/perl -w
 2: use strict;
 3:
 4: while (<STDIN>) {
 5:
 6:    s/(\w+)/translate($1)/ge;
 7:    print;
 8: }
 9:
10: my %trans;
11: sub translate {
12:    my $word = shift;
13:
14:    $trans{lc $word} ||= get_trans(lc $word);
15: }
16:
17: sub get_trans {
18:    my $word = shift;
19:
20:    my $file = 'american.txt';
21:    open(TRANS, $file) || die "Can't open $file: $!";
22:
23:    my ($line, $english, $american);
24:    while (defined($line = <TRANS>)) {
25:      chomp $line;
26:      ($english, $american) = split(/\t/, $line);
27:      do {$word = $american; last; } if $english eq $word;
28:    }
29:    close TRANS;
30:    return $word;
31: }
```

How the translation program works

Lines 1 and 2 are the standard way to start a Perl script.

The loop starting on line 4 reads from STDIN and puts each line in turn in the $_ variable.

Line 6 does most of the work. It looks for groups of word characters. Each time it finds one it stores the word in $1. The replacement string is the result of executing the code translate($1). Notice the two modifiers: g which means that every

---

[8] We'll also conveniently ignore situations where an English phrase should be replaced by a different phrase in American, such as "car park" and "parking lot."

word in the line will be converted, and e which forces Perl to execute the replacement string before putting it back into the original string.

Line 7 prints the value of $_, which is now the translated line. Note that when given no arguments, print defaults to printing the contents of the $_ variable—which in this case is exactly what we want.

Line 10 defines a caching hash which the translate function uses to store words which it already knows how to translate.

The translate function which starts on line 11 uses a caching algorithm similar to the Orcish Manoeuvre. If the current word doesn't exist in the %trans hash, it calls get_trans to get a translation of the word. Notice that we always work with lower case versions of the word.

Line 17 starts the get_trans function, which will read any necessary words from the file containing a list of translatable words.

Line 20 defines the name of the translations file and line 21 attempts to open it. If the file can't be opened, then the program dies with an error message.

Line 24 loops though the translations file a line at a time, putting each line of text into $line and line 25 removes the newline character from the line.

Line 26 splits the line on the tab character which separates the English and American words.

Line 27 sets $word to the American word if the English word matches the word we are seeking.

Line 29 closes the file.

Line 30 returns either the translation or the original word if a translation is not found while looping through the file. This ensures that the function always returns a valid word and therefore that the %trans hash will contain an entry for every word that we've come across. If we didn't do this, then for each word that didn't need to be translated, we would have no entry in the hash and would have to search the entire translations file each time. This way we only search the translations file once for each unique word.

Using the translation program

As an example of the use of this script, create a file called american.txt which contains a line for each word that you want to translate. Each line should have the English word followed by a tab character and the equivalent American word. For example:

```
hello<TAB>hiya
pavement<TAB>sidewalk
```

Create another file containing the text that you want to translate. In my test, I used

```
Hello.
Please stay on the pavement.
```

and running the program using the command line

```
translate.pl < in.txt
```

produced the output

```
hiya.
Please stay on the sidewalk.
```

If you wanted to keep the translated text in another text file then you could run the program using the command line

```
translate.pl < in.txt > out.txt
```

Once again we make use of the power of the UNIX filter model as discussed in chapter 2.

This isn't a particularly useful script. It doesn't, for example, handle capitalization of the words that it translates. In the next section we'll look at something a little more powerful.

4.2.5 *More examples: /etc/passwd*

Let's look at a few more examples of real-world data munging tasks for which you would use regular expressions. In these examples we will use a well-known standard UNIX data file as our input data. The file we will use is the `/etc/passwd` file which stores a list of users on a UNIX system. The file is a colon-separated, record-based file. This means that each line in the file represents one user, and the various pieces of information about each user are separated with a colon. A typical line in one of these files looks like this:

```
dave:Rg6kuZvwIDF.A:501:100:Dave Cross:/home/dave:/bin/bash
```

The seven sections of this line have the following meanings:

1. The username
2. The user's password (in an encrypted form)[9]
3. The unique ID of the user on this system
4. The ID of the user's default group
5. The user's full name[10]
6. The path to the user's home directory
7. The user's command shell

---

[9] On a system using shadow passwords, the encrypted password won't be in this field.

[10] Strictly, this field can contain any text that the system administrator chooses—but this is my system and I've chosen to store full names here.

The precise meaning of some of these fields may not be clear to non-UNIX users, but it should be clear enough to understand the following examples.

Example: reading /etc/passwd

Let's start by writing a routine to read the data into internal data structures. This routine can then be used by any of the following examples. As always, for flexibility, we'll assume that the data is coming in via STDIN.

```
sub read_passwd {

  my %users;

  my @fields = qw/name pword uid gid fullname home shell/;

  while (<STDIN>) {
    chomp;
    my %rec;

    @rec{@fields} = split(/:/);

    $users{$rec{name}} = \%rec;
  }

  return \%users;
}
```

In a similar manner to other input routines we have written, this routine reads the data into a data structure and returns a reference to that data structure. In this case we have chosen a hash as the main data structure, as the users on the system have no implicit ordering and it seems quite likely that we will want to get the information on a specific user. A hash allows us to do this very easily. This raises one other issue: what is the best choice for the key of the hash? The answer depends on just what we are planning to do with the data, but in this case I have chosen the username. In other cases the user ID might be a useful choice. All of the other columns would be bad choices, as they aren't guaranteed to be unique across all users.[11]

So, we have decided on a hash where the keys are the usernames. What will the values of our hash be? In this case I have chosen to use another level of hash where the keys are the names of the various data values (as defined in the array @fields) and the values are the actual values.

Our input routine therefore reads each line from STDIN and splits it on colons and puts the values directly into a hash called %rec. A reference to %rec is then stored in the main %users hash. Notice that because %rec is a lexical variable that is scoped to within the while loop, each time around the loop we get a new variable

---

[11] It seems unlikely that the home directory of a user would be nonunique, but it is (just) possible to imagine scenarios where it makes sense for two or more users to share a home directory.

and therefore a new reference. If %rec were declared outside the loop it would always be the same variable and every time around the loop we would be overwriting the same location in memory.

   Having created a hash for each line in the input file and assigned it to the correct record in %users, our routine finally returns a reference to %users. We are now ready to start doing some real work.

Example: listing users

To start with, let's produce a list of all of the real names of all of the users on the system. As that would be a little too simple we'll introduce a couple of refinements. First, included in the list of users in /etc/passwd are a number of special accounts that aren't for real users. These will include root (the superuser), lp (a user ID which is often used to carry out printer administration tasks) and a number of other task-oriented users. Assuming that we can detect these uses by the fact that their full names will be empty, we'll exclude them from the output. Secondly, in the original file, the full names are in the format <forename> <surname>. We'll print them out as <surname>, <forename>, and sort them in surname order. Here's the script:

```
 1: use strict;
 2:
 3: my $users = read_passwd();
 4:
 5: my @names;
 6: foreach (keys %{$users}) {
 7:   next unless $users->{$_}{fullname};
 8:
 9:   my ($forename, $surname) = split(/\s+/, $users->{$_}{fullname}, 2);
10:
11:   push @names, "$surname, $forename";
12: }
13:
14: print map { "$_\n" } sort @names;
```

Most of this script is self-explanatory. The key lines are:

   Line 6 gets each key in the %users hash in turn.

   Line 7 skips any record that doesn't have a full name, thereby ignoring the special users.

   Line 9 splits the full name on white space. Note that we pass a third argument to split.[12] This limits the number of elements in the returned list.

---

[12] Notice, however, that we are making assumptions here about the format of the name. This algorithm assumes that the first word in the name is the forename and everything else is the surname. If the name is not in this format then things will go wrong. For example, think about what would happen if the name were "Dame Elizabeth Taylor" or "Randal L. Schwartz." As always, it is very important to know your data.

Line 11 builds the reversed name and pushes it onto another array.

Line 14 prints the array of names in sorted order.

Example: listing particular users

Now suppose we want to get a report on the users that use the Bourne shell (/bin/sh). Maybe we want to email them to suggest that they use bash instead. We might write something like this:

```
1: use strict;
2:
3: my $users = read_passwd();
4:
6: foreach (keys %{$users}) {
7:   print "$_\n" if $users->{$_}{shell} eq '/bin/sh';
8: }
```

Again we have a very simple script. Most of the real work is being done on line 7. This line checks the value in `$users->{$_}{shell}` against the string "/bin/sh", and if it matches it prints out the current key (which is the username). Notice that we could also have chosen to match against a regular expression using the code

```
print "$_\n" if $users->{$_}{shell} =~ m|^/bin/sh$|
```

If performance is important to you, then you could benchmark the two solutions and choose the faster one. Otherwise the solution you choose is a matter of personal preference.

4.2.6 Taking it to extremes

Of course, using regular expressions for transforming data is a very powerful technique and, like all powerful techniques, it is open to abuse. As an example of what you can do with this technique, let's take a brief look at the `Text::Bastardize` module which is available from the CPAN at http://search.cpan.org/search?dist=Text-Bastardize.

This module will take an innocent piece of text and will abuse it in various increasingly bizarre ways. The complete set of transformations available in the current version (0.06 as of the time of writing) is as follows:

- *rdct*—Converts the text to hyperreductionist English. This removes vowels within words, changes "you" to "u" and "are" to "r" and carries out a number of other conversions.

- *pig*—Converts the text to Pig Latin. Pig Latin is a bizarre corruption of English in which the first syllable of a word is moved to the end of the word and the sound "ay" is appended.

- *k3wlt0k*—Converts the text to "cool-talk" as used by certain denizens of the Internet (the d00dz who deal in k3wl war3z).

- *rot13*—Applies rot13 "encryption" to the text. In this very basic type of encryption, each letter is replaced with one that is thirteen letters past it in the alphabet. This method is often used in newsgroup posts to disguise potential plot spoilers or material which might give offense to casual readers.
- *rev*—Reverses the order of the letters in the text.
- *censor*—Censors text which might be thought inappropriate. It does this by replacing some of the vowels with asterisks.
- *n20e*—Performs numerical abbreviations on the text. Words over six letters in length have all but their first and last letters removed and replaced with a number indicating the number of letters removed.

It is, of course, unlikely that this module is ever used as anything other than an example of a text transformation tool, but it is a very good example of one and it can be very instructive to look at the code of the module.

As an example of the use of the module, here is a script that performs all of the transformations in turn on a piece of text that is read from STDIN. Notice that the piece of text that is to be transformed is set using the charge function.

```perl
#!/usr/perl/bin/perl -w

use strict;
use Text::Bastardize;

my $text = Text::Bastardize->new;

print 'Say something: ';
while (<STDIN>) {
  chomp;
  $text->charge($_);
  foreach my $xfm (qw/rdct pig k3wlt0k rot13 rev censor n20e/) {
    print "$xfm: ";
    print eval "\$text->$xfm";
    print "\n";
  }
}
```

4.3 *Further information*

The best place to obtain definitive information about regular expressions is from the perlre manual page that comes with every installation of Perl. You can access this by typing

```
perldoc perlre
```

on your command line.

You can get more information than you will ever need from *Mastering Regular Expressions*, by Jeffrey Friedl (O'Reilly).

4.4 Summary

- Perl has very powerful text matching and processing facilities.
- Often you can achieve what you want using basic text-processing functions such as `substr`, `index`, and `uc`.
- Regular expressions are a more powerful method of describing text that you want to match.
- Regular expressions are most often used in the text matching (`m//`) and text substitution (`s///`) operators.

Part II

Data munging

In which our heroes first come into contact with the data munging beast. Three times they battle it, and each time the beast takes on a different form.

At first the beast appears without structure and our heroes fight valiantly to impose structure upon it. They learn new techniques for finding hidden structure and emerge triumphant.

The second time the beast appears structured into records. Our heroes find many ways to split the records apart and recombine them in other useful ways.

The third time the beast appears in even more strongly structured forms. Once again our heroes discover enough new techniques to see through all of their enemies' disguises.

Our heroes end this section of the tale believing that they can handle the beast in all of its guises, but disappointment is soon to follow.

Unstructured data 5

The simplest kind of data that can require munging is unstructured data. This is data that has no internal structure imposed on it in any way. In some ways this is the most difficult data to deal with as there is often very little that you can do with it.

A good example of unstructured data is a plain ASCII file that contains text. In this chapter we will look at some of the things that we can do with a file like this.

5.1   ASCII text files

An ASCII text file contains data that is readable by a person. It can be created in a text editor like vi or emacs in UNIX, Notepad in Windows, or edit in DOS. You should note that the files created by most word processors are not ASCII text, but some proprietary text format.[1] It is also possible that the file could be created by some other computer system.

An ASCII text file, like all data files, is nothing but a series of bytes of binary data. It is only the software that you use to view the file (an editor perhaps) that interprets the different bytes of data as ASCII characters.

5.1.1   Reading the file

One of the simplest things that we can do with an ASCII file is to read it into a data structure for later manipulation. The most suitable format for the data structure depends, of course, on the exact nature of the data in the file and what you are planning to do with it, but for readable text an array of lines will probably be the most appropriate structure. If you are interested in the individual words in each line then it will probably make sense to split each line into an array of words. Notice that because order is important when reading text we use Perl arrays (which are also ordered) to store the data, rather than hashes (which are unordered).

Example: Reading text into an array of arrays

Let's write an input routine that will read an unstructured text file into an array of arrays. As always we will assume that the file is coming to us via STDIN.

```
1: sub read_text {
2:
3:    my @file;
4:
5:    push @file, [split] while <STDIN>;
6:
7:    return \@file;
8: }
```

---

[1] Most word processors do have a facility to save the document in ASCII text format; however, this will destroy most of the formatting of the document.

Let's look at this line by line.

Line 3 defines a variable that will contain the array of lines. Each element of this array will be a reference to another array. Each element of these second-level arrays will contain one of the words from the line.

Line 5 does most of the work. It might be easier to follow if you read it in reverse. It is actually a contraction of code that, when expanded, looks something like this:

```
while (<STDIN>) {
  my @line = split(/\s+/, $_);
  push @file, [@line];
}
```

which may be a little easier to follow. For each line in the file, we split the line wherever we see one or more white space characters. We then create an anonymous array which is a copy of the array returned by split and push the reference returned by the anonymous array constructor onto an `@file`.

Also implicit in this line is our definition of a word. In this case we are using Perl's built-in `\s` character class to define our word separators as white space characters (recall that `split` uses `\s+` as the delimiter by default). Your application may require something a little more complicated.

Line 7 returns a reference to the array.

Our new function can be called like this:

```
my $file = read_text;
```

and we can then access any line of the file using

```
my $line = $file->[$x];
```

where `$x` contains the number of the line that we are interested in. After this call, `$line` will contain a reference to the line array. We can, therefore, access any given word using

```
my $word = $line->[$y];
```

or, from the original `$file` reference:

```
my $word = $file->[$x][$y];
```

Of course, all of this is only a very good idea if your text file is of a reasonable size, as attempting to store the entire text of "War and Peace" in memory may cause your computer to start swapping memory to disk, which will slow down your program.[2]

---

[2] Then again, if you have enough memory that you can store the entire text of *War and Peace* in it without swapping to disk, that would be the most efficient way to process it.

Finer control of input

If you are, however, planning to store all of the text in memory then there are a couple of tricks that might be of use to you. If you want to read the file into an array of lines without splitting the lines into individual words, then you can do it in one line like this:

```
my @file = <FILE>;
```

If, on the other hand, you want the whole text to be stored in one scalar variable then you should look at the $/ variable. This variable is the input record separator and its default value is a newline character. This means that, by default, data read from a <> operator will be read until a newline is encountered. Setting this variable to undef will read the whole input stream in one go.[3] You can, therefore, read in a whole file by doing this

```
local $/ = undef;
my $file = <FILE>;
```

You can set $/ to any value that your program will find useful. Another value that is often used is an empty string. This puts Perl into paragraph mode where a blank line is used as the input delimiter.

If your file is too large to fit efficiently into memory then you are going to have to process a row at a time (or a record at a time if you have changed $/). We will look at line-based and record-based data in the next chapter, but for the rest of this chapter we will assume that we can get the whole file in memory at one time.

5.1.2 Text transformations

Having read the file into our data structures, the simplest thing to do is to transform part of the data using the simple regular expression techniques that we discussed in the last chapter. In this case the lines or individual words of the data are largely irrelevant to us, and our lives become much easier if we read the whole file into a scalar variable.

Example: simple text replacement

For example, if we have a text file where we want to convert all instances of "Windows" to "Linux", we can write a short script like this:

```
my $file;

{
  local $/ = undef;
```

---

[3] Note that $/ (like most Perl internal variables) is, by default, global, so altering it in one place will affect your whole program. For that reason, it is usually a good idea to use local and enclosing braces to ensure that any changes have a strictly limited scope.

```
    $file = <STDIN>;
}

$file =~ s/Windows/Linux/g;

print $file;
```

Notice how the section that reads the data has been wrapped in a bare block in order to provide a limited scope for the local copy of the $/ variable. Also, we have used the g modifier on the substitution command in order to change all occurrences of Windows.

All of the power of regular expression substitutions is available to us. It would be simple to rewrite our translation program from the previous chapter to translate the whole input file in one operation.

5.1.3 *Text statistics*

One of the useful things that we can do is to produce statistics on the text file. It is simple to produce information on the number of lines or words in a file. It is only a little harder to find the longest word or to produce a table that counts the occurrences of each word. In the following examples we will assume that a file is read in using the read_text function that we defined earlier in the chapter. This function returns a reference to an array of arrays. We will produce a script that counts the lines and words in a file and then reports on the lengths of words and the most-used words in the text.

Example: producing text statistics

```
 1: # Variables to keep track of where we are in the file
 2: my ($line, $word);
 3:
 4: # Variables to store stats
 5: my ($num_lines, $num_words);
 6: my (%words, %lengths);
 7:
 8: my $text = read_text();
 9:
10: $num_lines = scalar @{$text};
11:
12: foreach $line (@{$text}) {
13:   $num_words += scalar @{$line};
14:
15:   foreach $word (@{$line}) {
16:     $words{$word}++;
17:     $lengths{length $word}++;
18:   }
19: }
20:
```

```
21: my @sorted_words = sort { $words{$b} <=> $words{$a} } keys %words;
22: my @sorted_lengths = sort { $lengths{$b} <=> $lengths{$a} } keys %lengths;
23:
24: print "Your file contains $num_lines lines ";
25: print "and $num_words words\n\n";
26:
27: print "The 5 most popular words were:\n";
28: print map { "$_ ($words{$_} times)\n" } @sorted_words[0 .. 4];
29:
30: print "\nThe 5 most popular word lengths were:\n";
31: print map { "$_ ($lengths{$_} words)\n" } @sorted_lengths[0 .. 4];
```

Line 2 declares two variables that we will use to keep track of where we are in the file.

Lines 5 and 6 declare four variables that we will use to produce the statistics. $num_lines and $num_words are the numbers of lines and words in the file. %words is a hash that will keep a count of the number of times each word has occurred in the file. Its key will be the word and its value will be the number of times the word has been seen. %lengths is a hash that keeps count of the frequency of word lengths in a similar fashion.

Line 8 calls our read_text function to get the contents of the file.

Line 10 calculates the number of lines in the file. This is simply the number of elements in the $text array.

Line 12 starts to loop around each line in the array.

Line 13 increases the $num_words variable with the number of elements in the $line array. This is equal to the number of words in the line.

Line 15 starts to loop around the words on the line.

Lines 16 and 17 increment the relevant entries in the two hashes.

Lines 21 and 22 create two arrays which contain the keys of the %words and %lengths hashes, sorted in the order of decreasing hash values.

Lines 24 and 25 print out the total number of words and lines in the file.

Lines 27 and 28 print out the five most popular words in the file by taking the first five elements in the @sorted_words array and printing the value associated with that key in the %words hash. Lines 30 and 31 do the same thing for the @sorted_lengths array.

Example: calculating average word length

As a final example of producing text file statistics, let's calculate the average word length in the files. Once again we will use the existing read_text function to read in our text.

```
my ($total_length, $num_words);
my $text = read_text();
```

```
my ($word, $line);
foreach $line (@{$text}) {
  $num_words += scalar @{$line};

  foreach $word (@{$line}) {
    $total_length += length $word;
  }
}

printf "The average word length is %.2f\n", $total_length / $num_words;
```

5.2   *Data conversions*

One of the most useful things that you might want to do to unstructured data is to perform simple data format conversions on it. In this section we'll take a look at three typical types of conversions that you might need to do.

5.2.1   *Converting the character set*

Most textual data that you will come across will be in ASCII, but there may well be occasions when you have to deal with other character sets. If you are exchanging data with IBM mainframe systems then you will often have to convert data to and from EBCDIC. You may also come across multibyte characters if you are dealing with data from a country where these characters are commonplace (like China or Japan).

Unicode
For multibyte characters, Perl version 5.6 includes some support for Unicode via the new utf8 module. This was introduced in order to make it easier to work with XML using Perl (XML uses Unicode in UTF-8 format to define all of its character data). If you have an older version of Perl you may find the Unicode::Map8 and Unicode::String modules to be interesting.

Converting between ASCII and EBCDIC
For converting between ASCII and EBCDIC you can use the Convert::EBCDIC module from the CPAN. This module can be used either as an object or as a traditional module. As a traditional module, it exports two functions called ascii2ebcdic and ebcdic2ascii. Note that these functions need to be explicitly imported into your namespace. As an object, it has two methods called toascii and toebcdic. The following example uses the traditional method to convert the ASCII data arriving on STDIN into EBCDIC.

```
use strict;
use Convert::EBCDIC qw/ascii2ebcdic/;

my $data;
```

```
{
  local $/ = undef;
  $data = <STDIN>;
}
```

```
print ascii2ebcdic($data);
```

The second example uses the object interface to convert EBCDIC data to ASCII.

```
use strict;
use Convert::EBCDIC;

my $data;
my $conv = Convert::EBCDIC->new;

my $data;

{
  local $/ = undef;
  $data = <STDIN>;
}

print $conv->toascii($data);
```

The `Convert::EBCDIC` constructor takes one optional parameter which is a 256 character string which defines a translation table.

5.2.2 *Converting line endings*

As I mentioned above, an ASCII text file is no more than a stream of binary data. It is only the software that we use to process it that interprets the data in such a way that it produces lines of text. One important character (or sequence of characters) in a text file is the character which separates different lines of text. When, for example, a text editor reaches this character in a file, it will know that the following characters must be displayed starting at the first column of the following line of the user's display.

Different line end characters

Over the years, two characters in particular have come to be the most commonly used line end characters. They are the characters with the ASCII codes 10 (line feed) and 13 (carriage return). The line feed is used by UNIX (and Linux) systems. Apple Macintoshes use the carriage return. DOS and Windows use a combination of both characters, the carriage return followed by the line feed.

This difference in line endings causes no problems when data files are used on the same system on which they were created, but when you start to transfer data files between different systems it can lead to some confusion. You may have edited a file that was created under Windows in a UNIX text editor. If so you will have seen an extra ^M character at the end of each line of text.[4] This is the printable equivalent of the carriage return character that Windows inserts before each line feed. Similarly, a UNIX text file opened in Windows Notepad will have no carriage returns before the line feed and, therefore, Notepad will not recognize the end of line character sequence. All the lines will subsequently be run together, separated only by a black rectangle, which is Windows' way of representing the unprintable line feed character.

There are ways to avoid this problem. Transferring files between systems using FTP in ASCII mode, for example, will automatically convert the line endings into the appropriate form. It is almost guaranteed, however, that at some point you will find yourself dealing with a data file that has incorrect line endings for your system. Perl is, of course, the perfect language for correcting this problem.

Example: a simple line end conversion filter

The following program can be used as a filter to clean up problem files. It takes two parameters, which are the line endings on the source and target systems. These are the strings CR, LF, or CRLF.

In the program, instead of using \n and \r we use the ASCII control character sequences \cM and \cJ (Ctrl-M and Ctrl-J). This is because Perl is cleverer than we might like it to be in this case. Whenever Perl sees a \n sequence in a program it actually converts it to the correct end-of-line character sequence for the current system. This is very useful most of the time (it means, for example, that you don't need to use print "some text\r\n"; to output text when using Perl on a Windows system). But in this situation it masks the very problem that we're trying to solve—so we have to go to a lower level representation of the characters.

```
#!/usr/local/bin/perl -w

use strict;

(@ARGV == 2) or die "Error: source and target formats not given.";

my ($src, $tgt) = @ARGV;

my %conv = (CR =>    "\cM",
            LF =>    "\cJ",
            CRLF => "\cM\cJ");

$src = $conv{$src};
$tgt = $conv{$tgt};

$/ = $src;
while (<STDIN>) {
```

---

[4] This is becoming less common as many editors will now display the lines without the ^M, and indicate the newline style in the status line.

```
s/$src/$tgt/go;
  print;
}
```

Notice that we use the `o` modifier on the substitution as we know that the source will not change during the execution of the `while` loop.

5.2.3 Converting number formats

Sometimes the unstructured data that you receive will contain numerical data and the only changes that you will want to make are to reformat the numbers into a standardized format. This breaks down into two processes. First you have to recognize the numbers you are interested in, then you need to reformat them.

Recognizing numbers

How do you recognize a number? The answer depends on what sort of numbers you are dealing with. Are they integers or floating points? Can they be negative? Do you accept exponential notation (such as 1E6 for 1×10^6)? When you answer these questions, you can build a regular expression that matches the particular type of number that you need to process.

To match natural numbers (i.e., positive integers) you can use a simple regular expression such as:

```
/\d+/
```

To match integers (with optional +/- signs) use

```
/[-+]?\d+/
```

To match a floating point number use

```
/[-+]?(\d+(\.\d*)?|\.\d+)/
```

To match a number that can optionally be in exponential notation, use

```
/[-+]?(?=\d|\.\d)\d*(\.\d*)?([eE]([-+]?\d+))?/
```

As these become rather complex, it might be a suitable time to consider using Perl's precompiled regular expression feature and creating your number-matching regular expressions in advance. You can do something like this:

```
my $num_re = qr/[-+]?(?=\d|\.\d)\d*(\.\d*)?([eE]([-+]?\d+))?/;

my @nums;
while ($data =~ /($num_re)/g) {
  push @nums, $1;
}
```

to print out a list of all of the numbers in `$data`.

If you have a function, `reformat`, that will change the numbers into your preferred format then you can use code like this:

```
$data =~ s/$num_re/reformat($1)/ge;
```

which makes use, once more, of the `e` modifier to execute the replacement string before using it.

Reformatting numbers with sprintf

The simplest way to reformat a number is to pass it through `sprintf`. This will enable you to do things like fix the number of decimal places, pad the start of the number with spaces or zeroes, and right or left align the number within its field. Here is an example of the sort of things that you can do:

```
my $number = 123.456789;

my @fmts = ('0.2f', '.2f', '10.4f', '-10.4f');

foreach (@fmts) {
  my $fmt = sprintf "%$_", $number;
  print "$_: [$fmt]\n";
}
```

which gives the following output:

```
0.2f: [123.46]
.2f: [123.46]
10.4f: [  123.4568]
-10.4f: [123.4568  ]
```

(The brackets are there to show the exact start and end of each output field.)

Reformatting numbers with CPAN modules

There are, however, a couple of modules available on the CPAN which allow you to do far more sophisticated formatting of numbers. They are `Convert::SciEng` and `Number::Format`.

Convert::SciEng

`Convert::SciEng` is a module for converting numbers to and from a format in which they have a postfix letter indicating the magnitude of the number. This conversion is called *fixing* and *unfixing* the number. The module recognizes two different schemes of fixes, the SI scheme and the SPICE scheme. The module interface is via an object interface. A new object is created by calling the class `new` method and passing it a string indicating which fix scheme you want to use (SI or SPICE).

```
my $conv = Convert::SciEng->new('SI');
```

You can then start fixing and unfixing numbers. The following:

```
print $conv->unfix('2.34u');
```

will print the value 2.34e-06. The "u" is taken to mean the SI symbol for microunits. You can also pass an array to unfix, as in

```
print map { "$_\n" } $conv->unfix(qw/1P 1T 1G 1M 1K 1 1m 1u 1p 1f 1a/);
```

which will produce the output

```
1e+015
1000000000000
1000000000
1000000
1000
1
0.001
1e-006
1e-012
1e-015
1e-018
```

(and also demonstrates the complete range of postfixes understood by the SI scheme).

You can also adjust the format in which the results are returned in by using the `format` method and passing it a new format string. The format string is simply a string that will be passed to `sprintf` whenever a value is required. The default format is `%5.5g`.

There is, of course, also a `fix` method that takes a number and returns a value with the correct postfix letter appended:

```
print $conv->fix(100_000)
```

prints "100K" and

```
print $conv->fix(1_000_000)
```

prints "1M".

Number::Format

The `Number::Format` module is a more general-purpose module for formatting numbers in interesting ways. Like `Convert::SciEng`, it is accessed through an object-oriented interface. Calling the `new` method creates a new formatter object. This method takes as its argument a hash which contains various formatting options. These options are detailed in appendix A along with the other object methods contained within `Number::Format`.

Here are some examples of using this module:

```
my $fmt = Number::Format->new; # use all defaults
my $number = 1234567.890;
```

```
print $fmt->round($number), "\n";
print $fmt->format_number($number), "\n";
print $fmt->format_negative($number), "\n";
print $fmt->format_picture($number, '###########'), "\n";
print $fmt->format_price($number), "\n";
print $fmt->format_bytes($number), "\n";
print $fmt->unformat_number('1,000,000.00'), "\n";
```

This results in:

```
1234567.89
1,234,567.89
-1234567.89
     1234568
USD 1,234,567.89
1.18M
1000000
```

Changing the formatting options slightly:

```
my $fmt = Number::Format->new(INTL_CURRENCY_SYMBOL => 'GBP',
                              DECIMAL_DIGITS => 1);

my $number = 1234567.890;

print $fmt->round($number), "\n";
print $fmt->format_number($number), "\n";
print $fmt->format_negative($number), "\n";
print $fmt->format_picture($number, '###########'), "\n";
print $fmt->format_bytes($number), "\n";
print $fmt->unformat_number('1,000,000.00'), "\n";
```

results in:

```
1234567.9
1,234,567.9
-1234567.89
     1234568
GBP 1,234,567.89
1.18M
1000000
```

If we were formatting numbers for a German system, we might try something like this:

```
my $de = Number::Format->new(INT_CURR_SYMBOL => 'DEM ',
                             THOUSANDS_SEP => '.',
                             DECIMAL_POINT => ',');

my $number = 1234567.890;

print $de->format_number($number), "\n";
print $de->format_negative($number), "\n";
print $de->format_price($number), "\n";
```

which would result in:

```
1.234.567,89
-1234567.89
DEM 1.234.567,89
```

And finally, if we were accountants, we might want to do something like this:

```
my $fmt = Number::Format->new(NEG_FORMAT=> '(x)');

my $debt = -12345678.90;

print $fmt->format_negative($debt);
```

which would give us:

```
(12345678.90)
```

It is, of course, possible to combine `Number::Format` with some of the other techniques that we were using earlier. If we had a text document that contained numbers in different formats and we wanted to ensure that they were all in our standard format we could do it like this:

```
use Number::Format;

my $data;

{
  local $/ = undef;
  $data = <STDIN>;
}

my $fmt = Number::Format->new;

my $num_re = qr/[-+]?(?=\d|\.\d)\d*(\.\d*)?([eE]([-+]?\d+))?/;

$data =~ s/$num_re/$fmt->format_number($1)/ge;

print $data;
```

5.3   *Further information*

For more information about input control variables such as `$/`, see the `perldoc perlvar` manual pages.

For more information about the Unicode support in Perl, see the `perldoc perlunicode` and `perldoc utf8` manual pages.

For more information about `sprintf`, see the `perldoc -f sprintf` manual page.

Both `Convert::SciEng` and `Number::Format` can be found on the CPAN. Once you have installed them, their documentation will be available using the `perldoc` command.

5.4 Summary

- Most unstructured data is found in ASCII text files.
- Perl can be used to extract statistics from text files very easily.
- Many useful data format conversions can be carried out either using the standard Perl distribution or with the addition of modules from the CPAN.

Record-oriented data

What this chapter covers:

- Reading, writing, and processing simple
  record-oriented data
- Caching data
- Currency conversion
- The comma separated value format
- Creating complex data records
- Problems with date fields

A very large proportion of the data that you will come across in data munging tasks will be record oriented. In this chapter we will take a look at some common ways to deal with this kind of data.

6.1 Simple record-oriented data

We have already seen examples of simple record-oriented data. The CD data file that we examined in previous chapters had one line of data for each CD in my collection. Each of these lines of data is a record. As we will see later, a record can be larger or smaller than one line, but we will begin by looking in more detail at files where each line is one record.

6.1.1 Reading simple record-oriented data

Perl makes it very easy to deal with record-oriented data, particularly simple records of the type we are discussing here. We have seen before the idiom where you can read a file a line at a time using a construct like

```
while (<FILE>) {
  chomp; # remove newline
  # each line in turn is assigned to $_
}
```

Let's take a closer look and see what Perl is doing here to make life easier.

The most important part of the construct is the use of <FILE> to read data from the file handle FILE which has presumably been assigned to a file earlier in the program by a call to the open function. This file input operator can return two different results, depending on whether it is used in scalar context or array context.

When called in a scalar context, the file input operator returns the next record from the file handle. This begs the obvious question of what constitutes a record. The answer is that input records are separated by a sequence of characters called (logically enough) the input record separator. This value is stored in the variable $/. The default value is a newline \n (which is translated to the appropriate actual characters for the specific operating system), but this can be altered to any other string of characters. We will look at this usage in more detail later, but for now the default value will suffice.

When called in an array context, the file input operator returns a list in which each element is a record from the input file.

You can, therefore, call the file input operator in one of these two ways:

```
my $next_line = <FILE>;
my @whole_file = <FILE>;
```

In both of these examples it is important to realize that each record—whether it is the record stored in $next_line or one of the records in @whole_file—will still contain the value of $/ at the end.[1] Often you will want to get rid of this and the easiest way to do it is by using the chomp function. chomp is passed either a scalar or an array and removes the value of $/ from the end of the scalar or each element of the array. If no argument is passed to chomp then it works on $_.[2]

Reading data a record at a time (from first principles)

Now that we understand a little more about the file input operator and chomp, let's see if we can build our standard data munging input construct from first principles.

A first attempt at processing each line in a file might look something like this:

```
my $line;
while ($line = <FILE>) {
  chomp $line;
  ...
}
```

This is a good start, but it has a subtle bug in it. The conditional expression in the while loop is checking for the truth of the scalar variable $line. This variable is set from the next line taken from FILE. Generally this is fine, but there are certain conditions when a valid line in a file can evaluate to false. The most obvious of these is when the final line in a file contains the value 0 (zero) and has no end of line characters after it.[3] In this case, the variable $line will contain the value 0 which will evaluate as false and the final line of the file will not be processed.

Although this bug is a little obscure, it is still worthwhile finding a solution that doesn't exhibit this problem. This is simple enough to do by checking that the line is defined instead of evaluating to true. The contents of a variable are said to be defined if they are not the special Perl value undef. Any variable that contains a value that evaluates to false will still be defined. Whether or not a value is defined can be tested using the defined function. The file input operator returns undef when the end of the file is reached. We can therefore rewrite our first attempt into something like this:

---

[1]   Except, possibly, the last line in the file.

[2]   In versions of Perl before Perl 5, the chomp function did not exist. Instead we had to use a function called chop, which simply removed the last character from a string without checking what it was. As this is still an occasionally useful thing to do to a string, chop is still available in Perl, but most of the time chomp is more appropriate.

[3]   It would have to the be last line, because for any other line, the existence of the end of line characters following the data will ensure that there is enough data in the string for it to evaluate as true.

```
my $line;
while (defined($line = <FILE>)) {
  chomp $line;
  ...
}
```

and this will exhibit all of the behavior that we need. There are still a couple of improvements that we can make, but these are more about making the code Perlish than about fixing bugs.

The first of the changes is to make use of the Perl default variable $_. A lot of Perl code can be made more streamlined by using $_. In this case it makes a small amount of difference. We no longer need to define $line and we can make use of the fact that chomp works on $_ by default. Our code will now look like this:

```
while (defined($_ = <FILE>)) {
  chomp;
  ...
}
```

The last piece of optimization is one that you wouldn't be able to guess at, as it uses a piece of syntactic sugar that was put in by the authors of Perl when they realized what a common task this would be. If the file input operator is the only thing that is in the conditional expression of a while loop, then the result of the operator is magically assigned to the $_ variable and the resulting value is checked to see that it is defined (rather than checking that it is true.) This means that you can write:

```
while (<FILE>)) {
  chomp;
  ...
}
```

at which point we are back with our original code (but, hopefully, with a deeper understanding of the complexities beneath the surface of such simple looking code).

Notice that this final optimization is dependent on two things being true:

1   The file input operator must be the only thing in the conditional expression, so you can't write things like

```
while (<FILE> and $_ ne 'END') { # THIS DOESN'T WORK!
  ...
}
```

2   The conditional expression must be part of a while loop, so you can't write things like

```
if (<FILE>) { # THIS DOESN'T WORK EITHER!
  print;
} else {
  print "No data\n";
}
```

Counting the current record number

While looping through a file like this it is often useful to know which line you are currently processing. This useful information is stored in the $.$ variable.[4] The value is reset when the file handle is closed, which means that this works:

```
open FILE, 'input.txt' or die "Can't open input file: $!\n";
while (<FILE>) {
  # do stuff
}

print "$. records processed.\n";
close FILE;
```

but the following code is wrong as it will always print zero.

```
# THIS CODE DOESN'T WORK
open FILE, "input.txt" or die "Can't open input file: $!\n";
while (<FILE>) {
  # do stuff
}

close FILE;
print "$. records processed.\n";
```

In many of these examples, I have moved away from using STDIN, simply to indicate that these methods will work on any file handle. To finish this section, here is a very short example using STDIN that will add line numbers to any file passed to it.

```
#!/usr/local/bin/perl -w
use strict;

print "$.: $_" while <STDIN>;
```

6.1.2 Processing simple record-oriented data

So now that we know how to get our records from the input stream (either one at a time or all together in an array) what do we do with them? Of course, the answer to that question depends to a great extent on what your end result should be, but here are a few ideas.

Extracting data fields

Chances are that within your record there will be individual data items (otherwise known as fields) and you will need to break up the record to access these fields. Fields can be denoted in a record in a number of ways, but most methods fall into

---

[4] Actually, $.$ contains the current line number in the file handle that you read most recently. This allows you to still use $.$ if you have more than one file open. It's also worth mentioning that the definition of a line is determined by the contents of the input separator variable ($/$), which we'll cover in more detail later.

one of two camps. In one method the start and end of a particular field is denoted by a sequence of characters that won't appear in the fields themselves. This is known as delimited or separated data.[5] In the other method each field is defined to take up a certain number of characters and is space—or zero—padded if it is less than the defined size. This is known as fixed-width data. We will cover fixed-width data in more detail in the next chapter and for now will limit ourselves to separated and delimited data.

We have seen separated data before. The CD example that we have looked at in previous chapters is an example of a tab-separated data file. In the file each line represents one CD, and within a line the various fields are separated by the tab character. An obvious way to deal with this data is the one that we used before, i.e., using `split` to separate the record into individual fields like this:

```
my $record = <STDIN>;
chomp $record;
my @fields = split(/\t/, $record);
```

The fields will then be in the elements of `@fields`. Often, a more natural way to model a data record is by using a hash. For example, to build a `%cd` hash from a record in our CD file, we could do something like this:

```
my $record = <STDIN>;
chomp $record;
my %cd;
($cd{artist}, $cd{title}, $cd{label}, $cd{year}) = split (/\t/, $record);
```

We can then access the individual fields within the record using:

```
my $label = $cd{label};
my $title = $cd{title};
```

and so on.

Within the actual CD file input code from chapter 3 we simplified this code slightly by writing it like this:

```
my @fields = qw/artist title label year/;
my $record = <FILE>;
chomp $record;
my %cd;
@cd{@fields} = split(/\t/, $record);
```

---

[5] Strictly speaking, there is a difference between separated and delimited data. *Separated data* has a character sequence between each field and *delimited data* has a character sequence at the start and end of each field. In practical terms, however, the methods for dealing with them are very similar and many people tend to use the terms as if they are interchangeable.

In this example we make use of a hash slice to make assigning values to the hash much easier. Another side effect is that it makes maintenance a little easier as well. If a new field is added to the input file, then the only change required to the input routine is to add another element to the @fields array.

We now have a simple and efficient way to read in simple record-oriented data and split each record into its individual fields.

6.1.3 *Writing simple record-oriented data*

Of course, having read in your data and carried out suitable data munging, you will next need to output your data in some way. The obvious choice is to use print, but there are other options and even print has a few subtleties that will make your life easier.

Controlling output—separating output records

In the same way that Perl defines a variable ($/) that contains the input record separator, it defines another variable ($\) which contains the output record separator. Normally this variable is set to undef which leaves you free to control exactly where you output the record separator. If you set it to another value, then that value will be appended to the end of the output from each print statement. If you know that in your output file each record must be separated by a newline character, then instead of writing code like this:

```
foreach (@output_records) {
  print "$_\n";
}
```

you can do something like this:

```
{
  local $\ = "\n";
  foreach (@output_records) {
    print;
  }
}
```

(Notice how we've localized the change to $\ so that we don't inadvertently break any print statements elsewhere in the program.)

Generally people don't use this variable because it isn't really any more efficient.

Controlling output—printing lists of items

Other variables that are much more useful are the output field separator ($,) and the output list separator ($"). The output field separator is printed between the elements of the list passed to a print statement and the output list separator is printed between the elements of a list that is interpolated in a double quoted string. These concepts are dangerously similar so let's see if we can make it a little clearer.

In Perl the `print` function works on a list. This list can be passed to the function in a number of different ways. Here are a couple of examples:

```
print 'This list has one element';
print 'This', 'list', 'has', 'five', 'elements';
```

In the first example the list passed to `print` has only one element. In the second example the list has five elements that are separated by commas. The output field separator (`$,`) controls what is printed between the individual elements. By default, this variable is set to the empty string (so the second example above prints `Thislisthasfiveelements`). If we were to change the value of `$,` to a space character before executing the `print` statement, then we would get something a little more readable. The following:

```
$, = ' ';
print 'This', 'list', 'has', 'five', 'elements';
```

produces the output

This list has five elements

This can be useful if your output data is stored in a number of variables. For example, if our CD data was in variables called `$band`, `$title`, `$label`, and `$year` and we wanted to create a tab separated file, we could do something like this:

```
$\ = "\n";
$, = "\t";
print $band, $title, $label, $year;
```

which would automatically put a tab character between each field and a newline character on the end of the record.

Another way that a list is often passed to `print` is in an array variable. You will sometimes see code like this:

```
my @list = qw/This is a list of items/;
print @list;
```

in which case the elements of `@list` are printed with nothing separating them (`Thisisalistofitems`). A common way to get round this is to use `join`:

```
my @list = qw/This is a list of items/;
print join(' ', @list);
```

which will put spaces between each of the elements being printed.

A more elegant way to handle this is to use the list separator variable (`$"`). This variable controls what is printed between the elements of an array when the array is in double quotes. The default value is a space. This means that if we change our original code to

```
my @list = qw/This is a list of items/;
print "@list";
```

then we will get spaces printed between the elements of our list. In order to print the data with tabs separating each record we simply have to set $" to a tab character (\t). In chapter 3 when we were reading in the CD data file we stored the data in an array of hashes. An easy way to print out this data would be to use code like this:

```
my @fields = qw/name title label year/;

local $" = "\t";
local $\ = "\n";

foreach (@CDs) {
  my %CD = %$_;
  print "@CD{@fields}";
}
```

Controlling output—printing to different file handles

Recall that the syntax of the `print` statement is one of the following:

```
print;
print LIST;
print FILEHANDLE LIST;
```

In the first version the contents of $_ are printed to the default output file handle (usually STDOUT). In the second version the contents of LIST are printed to the default output file handle. In the third version the contents of LIST are printed to FILEHANDLE.

Notice that I said that the default output file handle is *usually* STDOUT. If you are doing a lot of printing to a different file handle, then it is possible to change the default using the `select` function.[6] If you call `select` with no parameters, it will return the name of the currently selected output file handle, so

```
print select;
```

will normally print main::STDOUT. If you call `select` with the name of a file handle, it will replace the current default output file handle with the new one. It returns the previously selected file handle so that you can store it and reset it later. If you needed to write a lot of data to a particular file, you could use code like this:

```
open FILE, '>out.txt' or die "Can't open out.txt: $!";
my $old = select FILE;
```

---

[6] Or rather one of the `select` functions. Perl has two functions called `select` and knows which one you mean by the number of arguments you pass it. This one has either zero arguments or one argument. The other one (which we won't cover in this book as it is used in network programming) has four arguments.

```
foreach (@data) {
  print;
}
select $old;
```

Between the two calls to `select`, the default output file handle is changed to be `FILE` and all `print` statements without a specific file handle will be written to `FILE`. Notice that when we have finished we reset the default file handle to whatever it was before we started (we stored this value in `$old`). You shouldn't assume that the default file handle is `STDOUT` before you change it, as some other part of the program may have changed it already.

Another variable that is useful when writing data is `$|`. Setting this variable to a nonzero value will force the output buffer to be flushed immediately after every `print` (or `write`) statement. This has the effect of making the output stream look as if it were unbuffered. This variable acts on the currently selected output file handle. If you want to unbuffer any other file handle, you will need to select it, change the value of `$|`, and then reselect the previous file handle using code like this:

```
my $file = select FILE;
$| = 1;
select $file;
```

While this works, it isn't as compact as it could be, so in many Perl programs you will see this code instead:

```
select((select(FILE), $| = 1)[0]);
```

This is perhaps one of the strangest looking pieces of Perl that you'll come across but it's really quite simple if you look closely.

The central part of the code is building a list. The first element of the list is the return value from `select(FILE)`, which will be the previously selected file handle. As a side effect, this piece of code selects `FILE` as the new default file handle. The second element of the list is the result of evaluating `$| = 1`, which is always 1. As a side effect, this code will unbuffer the current default file handle (which is now `FILE`). The code now takes the first element of this list (which is the previously selected file handle) and passes that to `select`, thereby returning the default file handle to its previous state.

6.1.4 Caching data

One common data munging task is translating data from one format to another using a lookup table. Often a good way to handle this is to cache data as you use it, as the next example will demonstrate.

Example: currency conversion

A good example of data translation would be converting data from one currency to another. Suppose that you were given a data file with three columns, a monetary amount, the currency that it is in,[7] and the date that should be used for currency conversions. You need to be able to present this data in any of a hundred or so possible currencies. The daily currency rates are stored in a database. In pseudocode, a first attempt at this program might look something like this:

```
Get target currency
For each data row
  Split data into amount, currency, and date
  Get conversion rate between source and target currencies on given date
  Multiply amount by conversion rate
  Output converted amount
Next
```

This would, of course, do the job but is it the most efficient way of doing it? What if the source data was all in the same currency and for the same date? We would end up retrieving the same exchange rate from the database each time.

Maybe we should read all of the possible exchange rates in at the start and store them in memory. We would then have very fast access to any exchange rate without having to go back to the database. This option would work if we had a reasonably small number of currencies and a small range of dates (perhaps we are only concerned with U.S. dollars, Sterling, and Deutschmarks over the last week). For any large number of currencies or date range, the overhead of reading them all into memory would be prohibitive. And, once again, if the source data all had the same currency and date then we would be wasting a lot of our time.

The solution to our problem is to cache the exchange rates that we have already read from the database. Look at this script:

```perl
#!/usr/bin/perl -w
my $target_curr = shift;
my %rates;
while (<STDIN>) {
chomp;
  my ($amount, $source_curr, $date) = split(/\t/);
  $rates{"$source_curr|$target_curr|$date"} ||= get_rate($source_curr,
                                                         $target_curr,
                                                         $date);
  $amount *= $rates{"$source_curr|$target_curr|$date"};
  print "$amount\t$target_curr\t$date\n";
}
```

---

[7] The International Standards Organization (ISO) defines a list of three letter codes for each internationally recognized currency (USD for U.S. Dollar, GBP for the pound sterling, and a hundred or so others).

In this script we assume that the `get_rate` function goes to the database and returns the exchange rate between the source and target currencies on the given date. We have introduced a hash which caches the return values from this function. Remember that in Perl

```
$a ||= $b;
```

means the same thing as

```
$a = $a || $b;
```

and also that the Perl `||` operator is short-circuiting, which means that the expression after the operator is only evaluated if the expression before the operator is false.

Bearing this in mind, take another look at this line of the above script:

```
$rates{"$source_curr|$target_curr|$date"} ||= get_rate($source_curr,
                                                        $target_curr,
                                                        $date);
```

The first time that this line is reached, the `%rates` hash is empty. The `get_rate` function is therefore called and the exchange rate that is returned is written into the hash with a key made up from the three parameters.

The next time that this line is reached with the same combination of parameters, a value is found in the hash and the `get_rate` function does not get called.[8]

Taking caching further—Memoize.pm

This trick is very similar to the Orcish Manoeuvre which we saw when we were discussing sorting techniques in chapter 3. It is, however, possible to take things one step further. On the CPAN there is a module called `Memoize.pm` which was written by Mark-Jason Dominus. This module includes a function called `memoize` which will automatically wrap caching functionality around any function in your program. We would use it in our currency conversion script like this:

```
#!/usr/bin/perl -w
use Memoize;
memoize 'get_rate';
   my $target_curr = shift;
     while (<STDIN>) {
     chomp;
```

---

[8] You might notice that we're checking the *value* in the hash rather than the *existence* of a value. This may cause a problem if the value can legitimately be zero (or any other value which is evaluated as false—the string "0", the empty string, or the value `undef`). In this case the existence of a zero exchange rate may cause a few more serious problems than a bug in a Perl script, so I think that we can safely ignore that possibility. You may need to code around this problem.

```
  my ($amount, $source_curr, $date) = split(/\t/);
    $amount *= get_rate($source_curr, $target_curr, $date);
  print "$amount\t$target_curr\t$date\n";
}
```

Notice how the introduction of Memoize actually simplifies the code. What Memoize does is it replaces any call to a memoized function (get_rate in our example) with a call to a new function. This new function checks an internal cache and calls the original function only if there is not an appropriate cached value already available. An article explaining these concepts in some detail appeared in issue 13 (Vol. 4, No. 1) Spring 1999 of *The Perl Journal*.

Not every function call is a suitable candidate for caching or memoization but, when you find one that is, you can see a remarkable increase in performance.

6.2 *Comma-separated files*

A very common form of record-oriented data is the comma-separated value (CSV) format. In this format each record is one line of the data file and within that record each field is separated with commas. This format is often used for extracting data from spreadsheets or databases.

6.2.1 *Anatomy of CSV data*

At first glance it might seem that there is nothing particularly difficult about dealing with comma-separated data. The structure is very similar to the tab or pipe separated files that we have looked at before. The difference is that while tab and pipe characters are relatively rare in many kinds of data, the comma can quite often appear in data records, especially if the data is textual. To get around these problems there are a couple of additions to the CSV definition. These are:

- A comma should not be classed as a separator if it is in a string that is enclosed in double quotes.
- Within a double quoted string, a double quote character is represented by two consecutive double quotes.

Suddenly things get a bit more complex. This means that the following is a valid CSV record:

```
"Cross, Dave",07/09/1962,M,"Field with ""embedded"" quotes"
```

We can't simply split this data on commas, as we would have done before because the extra comma in the first field will generate an extra field. Also, the double quotes around the first and last fields are not part of the data and need to be stripped off and the doubled double quotes in the last field need to be converted to single double quotes!

6.2.2 *Text::CSV_XS*

Fortunately, this problem has already been solved for you. On the CPAN there is a module called `Text::CSV_XS`[9] which will extract the data from CSV files and will also generate CSV records from your data. The best way to explain how it works is to leap right in with an example or two. Suppose that we had a CSV file which contained data like the previous example line. The code to extract and print the data fields would look like this:

```
use Text::CSV_XS;

my $csv = Text::CSV->new;

$csv->parse(<STDIN>);
my @fields = $csv->fields;

local $" = '|';
print "@fields\n";
```

Assuming the input line above, this will print:

```
Cross, Dave|07/09/1962|M|Field with "embedded" quotes
```

Notice the use of `$"` to print pipe characters between the fields.

`Text::CSV_XS` also works in reverse. It will create CSV records from your data. As an example, let's rebuild the same data line from the individual data fields.

```
my @new_cols = ('Cross, Dave', '07/09/1962', 'M',
        'Field with "embedded" quotes');
$csv->combine(@new_cols);

print $csv->string;
```

This code prints:

```
"Cross, Dave",07/09/1962,M,"Field with ""embedded"" quotes"
```

which is back to our original data.

The important functions in `Text:CSV` are therefore:

- *new*—Creates a CSV object through which all other functions can be called.
- *parse($csv_data)*—Parses a CSV data string that is passed to it. The extracted columns are stored internally within the CSV object and can be accessed using the fields method.
- *fields*—Returns an array containing the parsed CSV data fields.

---

[9] `Text::CSV_XS` is a newer and faster version of the older `Text::CSV` module. As the name implies, `Text::CSV_XS` is partially implemented in C, which makes it faster. The `Text::CSV` module is pure Perl.

- *combine (@fields)*—Takes a list of data fields and converts them into a CSV data record. The CSV record is stored internally within the CSV object and can be accessed using the string method.
- *string*—Returns a string which is the last created CSV data record.

With this in mind, it is simple to create generic CSV data reading and writing routines.

```
use Text::CSV;

sub read_csv {
  my $csv = Text::CSV->new;

  my @data;

  while (<STDIN>) {
    $csv->parse($_);
    push @data, [$csv->fields];
  }

  return \@data;
}

sub write_csv {
  my $data = shift;
  my $csv = Text::CSV->new;

  foreach (@$data) {
    $csv->combine(@$_);
    print $csv->string;
  }
}
```

These functions would be called from within a program like this:

```
my $data = read_csv;

foreach (@$data) {
  # Do something to each record.
  # Individual fields are accessed as
  #   $_->[0], $_->[1], etc …
}

write_csv($data);
```

6.3   *Complex records*

All of the data we have seen up to now has had one line per record, but as I hinted earlier it is quite possible for data records to span more than one line in a data file. Perl makes it almost as simple to deal with nearly any kind of data. The secret to handling more complex data records is to make good use of the Perl variables that we mentioned in previous sections.

6.3.1 *Example: a different CD file*

Imagine, for example, if our CD file was in a slightly different format, like this:

```
Name: Bragg, Billy
Title: Workers' Playtime
Label: Cooking Vinyl
Year: 1987
%%
Name: Bragg, Billy
Title: Mermaid Avenue
Label: EMI
Year: 1998
%%
Name: Black, Mary
Title: The Holy Ground
Label: Grapevine
Year: 1993
%%
Name: Black, Mary
Title: Circus
Label: Grapevine
Year: 1996
%%
Name: Bowie, David
Title: Hunky Dory
Label: RCA
Year: 1971
%%
Name: Bowie, David
Title: Earthling
Label: EMI
Year: 1997
```

In this case the data is exactly the same, but a record is now spread over a number of lines. Notice that the records are separated by a line containing the character sequence %%.[10] This will be our clue in working out the best way to read these records. Earlier we briefly mentioned the variable $/ which defines the input record separator. By setting this variable to an appropriate value we can get Perl to read the file one whole record at a time. In this case the appropriate value is \n%%\n. We can now read in records like this:

```
local $/ = "\n%%\n";
while (<STDIN>) {
  chomp;
  print "Record $. is\n$_";
}
```

---

[10] This is a surprisingly common record separator, due to its use as the record separator in the data files read by the UNIX fortune program.

Remember that when Perl reads to the next occurrence of the input record separator, it includes the separator character sequence in the string that it returns. We therefore use chomp to remove that sequence from the string before processing it.

So now we have the record in a variable. How do we go about extracting the individual fields from within the records? This is relatively easy as we can go back to using split to separate the fields. In this case the field separator is a newline character so that is what we need to split on.

```
local $/ = "\n%%\n";
while (<STDIN>) {
  chomp;
  print join('|', split(/\n/)), "\n";
}
```

This code will print each of the records on one line with the fields separated by a pipe character. We are very close to having all of the fields in a form that we can use, but there is one more step to take.

Making use of the extra data

One difference between this format and the original (one record per line) format for the CD file is that the individual fields are now labeled. We need to lose these labels, but we can first make good use of them. Eventually we want each of our records to end up in a hash. The values of the hash will be the values of the data fields, but what are the keys? In previous versions of the CD input routines we have always hard-coded the names of the data fields, but here we have been given them. Let's use them to create the keys of our hash. This will hopefully become clearer when you see this code:

```
 1: $/ = "%%\n";
 2:
 3: my @CDs;
 4:
 5: while (<STDIN>) {
 6:   chomp;
 7:   my (%CD, $field);
 8:
 9:   my @fields = split(/\n/);
10:   foreach $field (@fields) {
11:     my ($key, $val) = split (/:\s*/, $field, 2);
12:     $CD{lc $key} = $val;
13:   }
14:
15:   push @CDs, \%CD;
16: }
```

Let's examine this code line by line.

Line 1 sets the input record separator to be %%\n.

Line 3 defines an array variable that we will use to store the CDs.

Line 5 starts the while loop which reads each line from STDIN in to $_.

Line 6 calls chomp to remove the %%\n characters from the end of $_.

Line 7 defines two temporary variables. %CD will store the data for one CD and $field will be used as temporary storage when processing the fields.

Line 9 creates an array @fields which contains each of the fields in the record, split on the newline character. Notice that split throws away the separator character so that the fields in the array do not have newline characters at the end of them.

Line 10 starts a foreach loop which processes each field in the record in turn. The field being processed is stored in $field.

Line 11 splits the field into its key and its value, assigning the results to $key and $value. Note that the regular expression that we split on is /:\s*/. This matches a colon followed by zero or more white space characters. In our sample data, the separator is always a colon followed by exactly one space, but we have made our script a little more flexible. We also pass a limit to split so that the list returned always contains two or fewer elements.

Line 12 assigns the value to the key in the %CD hash. Notice that we actually use the lower-case version of $key. Again this just allows us to cope with a few more potential problems in the input data.

Line 13 completes the foreach loop. At this point the %CD hash should have four records in it.

Line 15 pushes a reference to the %CD onto the @CDs array.

Line 16 completes the while loop. At this point the @CDs array will contain a reference to one hash for each of the CDs in the collection.

6.3.2 *Special values for $/*

There are two other commonly used values for $/—undef and the empty string. Setting $/ to undef puts Perl into "slurp mode." In this mode there are no record separators and the whole input file will be read in one go. Setting $/ to the empty string puts Perl into "paragraph mode." In this mode, records are separated by one or more blank lines. Note that this is not the same as setting $/ to \n\n. If a file has two or more consecutive blank lines then setting $/ to \n\n will give you extra empty records, whereas setting it to the empty string will soak up any number of blank lines between records. There are, of course, times when either of these behaviors is what is required.

You can also set $/ to a reference to a scalar (which should contain an integer). In this case Perl will read that number of bytes from the input stream. For example:

```
local $/ = \1024;
my $data = <DATA>;
```

will read in the next kilobyte from the file handle DATA. This idiom is more useful when reading binary files.

One thing that you would sometimes like to do with $/ is set it to a regular expression so that you can read in records that are delimited by differing record markers. Unfortunately, you must set $/ to be a fixed string, so you can't do this. The best way to get around this is to read the whole file into a scalar variable (by setting $/ to undef) and then use split to break it up into an array of records. The first parameter to split is interpreted as a regular expression.

6.4 Special problems with date fields

It is very common for data records to contain dates.[11] Unfortunately, Perl's date handling seems to be one of the areas that confuses a large number of people, which is a shame, because it is really very simple. Let's start with an overview of how Perl handles dates.

6.4.1 Built-in Perl date functions

As far as Perl is concerned, all dates are measured as a number of seconds since the epoch. That sounds more complex than it is. The epoch is just a date and time from which all other dates are measured. This can vary from system to system, but on many modern computer systems (including all UNIX systems) the epoch is defined as 00:00:00 GMT on Thursday, Jan. 1, 1970. The date as I'm writing this is 943011797, which means that almost a billion seconds have passed since the beginning of 1970.

Getting the current date and time with time functions

You can attain the current date and time in this format using the time function. I generated the number in the last paragraph by running this at my command line:

```
perl -e "print time";
```

This can be useful for calculating the time that a process has taken to run. You can write something like this:

```
my $start = time;

# Do lots of clever stuff
```

---

[11] When I mention dates in this section, I generally mean dates and times.

```
my $end = time;

print "Process took ", $end - $start, " seconds to run.";
```

More readable dates and times with localtime

This format for dates isn't very user friendly, so Perl supplies the `localtime` function to convert these values into readable formats, adjusted for your current time zone.[12] `localtime` takes one optional argument, which is the number of seconds since the epoch. If you don't pass this argument it calls `time` to get the current time. `localtime` returns different things depending on whether it is called in scalar or array context. In a scalar context it returns the date in a standard format. You can see this by running

```
perl -e "print scalar localtime"
```

at your command line. Notice the use of `scalar` to force a scalar context on the function call, as `print` gives its arguments an array context. To find when exactly a billion seconds will have passed since the epoch you can run:

```
perl -e "print scalar localtime(1_000_000_000)"
```

(which prints "Sun Sep 9 01:46:40 2001" on my system) and to find out when the epoch is on your system use:

```
perl -e "print scalar localtime(0)"
```

In an array context, `localtime` returns an array containing the various parts of the date. The elements of the array are:

- the number of seconds $(0-60)$[13]
- the number of minutes $(0-59)$
- the hour of the day $(0-23)$
- the day of the month $(1-31)$
- the month of the year $(0-11)$
- the year, as the number of years since 1900.
- the day of the week (0 is Sunday and 6 is Saturday)
- the day of the year
- a Boolean flag indicating whether daylight savings time is in effect.

Some of these fields cause a lot of problems.

---

[12] There is another function, `gmtime`, which does the same as `localtime`, but doesn't make time zone adjustments and returns values for GMT.

[13] The 61st second is there to handle leap seconds.

The month and the day of the week are given as zero-based numbers. This is because you are very likely to convert these into strings using an array of month or day names.

The year is given as the number of years since 1900. This is well-documented and has always been the case, but the fact that until recently this has been a two-digit number has led many people to believe that it returns a two-digit year. This has led to a number of broken scripts gaining a great deal of currency and it is common to see scripts that do something like this:

```
my $year = (localtime)[5];
$year = "19$year"; # THIS IS WRONG!
```

or (worse)

```
$year = ($year < 50) ? "20$year" : "19$year"; # THIS IS WRONG!
```

The correct way to produce a date using `localtime` is to do something like this:

```
my @months = qw/January February March April May June July August
        September October November December/;
my @days   = qw/Sunday Monday Tuesday Wednesday Thursday Friday Saturday/;

my @now = localtime;

$now[5] += 1900;

my $date = sprintf '%s %02d %s %4d, %02d:%02d:%02d',
                    $days[$now[6]], $now[3], $months[$now[4]], $now[5],
                    $now[2], $now[1], $now[0];
```

As hinted in the code above, if you don't need all of the date information, it is simple enough to use an array slice to get only the parts of the array that you want. These are all valid constructions:

```
my $year = (localtime)[5];
my ($d, $m, $y) = (localtime)[3 .. 5];
my ($year, $day_no) = (localtime)[5, 7];
```

Getting the epoch seconds using timelocal

It is therefore easy enough to convert the return value from `time` to a readable date string. It would be reasonable to want to do the same in reverse. In Perl you can do that by using the `timelocal` function. This function is not a Perl built-in function, but is included in the standard Perl library in the module `Time::Local`.

To use `timelocal`, you pass it a list of time values in the same format as they are returned by `localtime`. The arguments are seconds, minutes, hours, day of month, month (January is 0 and December is 11), and year (in number of years since 1900; e.g., 2000 would be passed in as 100). For example to find out how many seconds will have passed at the start of the third millennium (i.e., Jan. 1, 2001) you can use code like this:

```
use Time::Local;

my $secs = timelocal(0, 0, 0, 1, 0, 101);
```

Examples: date and time manipulation using Perl built-in functions

With `localtime` and `timelocal` it is possible to do just about any kind of data manipulation that you want. Here are a few simple examples.

Finding the date in x days time

This is, in principle, simple but there is one small complexity. The method that we use is to find the current time (in seconds) using `localtime` and add 86,400 (24 x 60 x 60) for each day that we want to add. The complication arises when you try to calculate the date near the time when daylight saving time either starts or finishes. At that time you could have days of either 23 or 25 hours and this can affect your calculation. To counter this we move the time to noon before carrying out the calculation.

```
use Time::Local;

my @now = localtime;                # Get the current date and time

my @then = (0, 0, 12, @now[3 .. 5]); # Normalize time to 12 noon

my $then = timelocal(@then);        # Convert to number of seconds

$then += $x * 86_400;               # Where $x is the number of days to add

@then = localtime($then);           # Convert back to array of values

@then[0 .. 2] = @now[0 .. 2];       # Replace 12 noon with real time

$then = timelocal(@then);           # Convert back to number of seconds

print scalar localtime $then;       # Print result
```

Finding the date of the previous Saturday

Again, this is pretty simple, with just one slightly complex calculation, which is explained in the comments. We work out the current day of the week and, therefore, can work out the number of days that we need to go back to get to Saturday.

```
my @days = qw/Sunday Monday Tuesday Wednesday Thursday Friday
              Saturday/;
my @months = qw/January February March April May June July August
                September October November December/;

my $when = 6; # Saturday is day 6 in the week.
              # You can change this line to get other days of the week.

my $now = time;
my @now = localtime($now);

# This is the tricky bit.
# $diff will be the number of days since last Saturday.
# $when is the day of the week that we want.
```

```
# $now[6] is the current day of the week.
# We take the result modulus 7 to ensure that it stays in the
# range 0 - 6.
my $diff = ($now[6] - $when + 7) % 7;

my $then = $now - (24 * 60 * 60 * $diff);

my @then = localtime($then);

$then[5] += 1900;

print "$days[$then[6]] $then[3] $months[$then[4]] $then[5]";
```

Finding the date of the first Monday in a given year

This is very similar in concept to the last example. We calculate the day of the week that January 1 fell on in the given year, and from that we can calculate the number of days that we have to move forward to get to the first Monday.

```
use Time::Local;

# Get the year to work on
my $year = shift || (localtime)[5] + 1900;

# Get epoch time of Jan 1st in that year
my $jan_1 = timelocal(0, 0, 0, 1, 0, $year - 1900);

# Get day of week for Jan 1
my $day = (localtime($jan_1))[6];

# Monday is day 1 (Sunday is day 0)
my $monday = 1;

# Calculate the number of days to the first Monday
my $diff = (7 - $day + $monday) % 7;

# Add the correct number of days to $jan_1
print scalar localtime($jan_1 + (86_400 * $diff));
```

Better date and time formatting with POSIX::strftime

There is one other important date function that comes with the Perl standard library. This is the strftime function that is part of the POSIX module. POSIX is an attempt to standardize system calls across a number of computer vendors' systems (particularly among UNIX vendors) and the Perl POSIX module is an interface to these standard functions. The strftime function allows you to format dates and times in a very controllable manner. The function takes as arguments a format string and a list of date and time values in the same format as they are returned by localtime. The format string can contain any characters, but certain character sequences will be replaced by various parts of the date and time. The actual set of sequences supported will vary from system to system, but most systems should support the sequences shown in table 6.1.

Table 6.1 `POSIX::strftime` **character sequences**

%a	short day name (Sun to Sat)
%A	long day name (Sunday to Saturday)
%b	short month name (Jan to Dec)
%B	long month name (January to December)
%c	full date and time in the same format as `localtime` returns in scalar context
%d	day of the month (01 to 31)
%H	hour in 24-hour clock (00 to 23)
%I	hour in 12-hour clock (01 to 12)
%j	day of the year (001 to 366)
%m	month of the year (01 to 12)
%M	minutes after the hour (00 to 59)
%p	AM or PM
%S	seconds after the minute (00 to 59)
%w	day of the week (0 to 6)
%y	year of the century (00 to 99)
%Y	year (0000 to 9999)
%Z	time zone string (e.g., GMT)
%%	a percent character

Here is a simple script which uses `strftime`.

```
use POSIX qw(strftime);

foreach ('%c', '%A %d %B %Y', 'Day %j', '%I:%M:%S%p (%Z)') {
  print strftime($_, localtime), "\n";
}
```

which gives the following output:

```
22/05/00 14:38:38
Monday 22 May 2000
Day 143
02:38:38PM (GMT Daylight Time)
```

International issues with date formats

One of the most intractable problems with dates has nothing to do with computer software, but with culture. If I tell you that I am writing this on 8/9/2000, without knowing whether I am European or American you have no way of knowing if I mean the 8th of September or the 9th of August. For that reason I'd recommend that whenever possible you always use dates that are in the order year, month, and day as that is far less likely to be misunderstood. There is an ISO standard (number 8601) which recommends that dates and times are displayed in formats which can be reproduced using the POSIX::strftime templates %Y-%m-%dT%h:%M:%S (for date and time) or %Y-%m-%d (for just the date).

All of the functions that we have just discussed come with every distribution of Perl. You should therefore see that it is quite easy to carry out complex date manipulation with vanilla Perl. As you might suspect, however, on the CPAN there are a number of modules that will make your coding life even easier. We will look in some detail at two of them: Date::Calc and Date::Manip.

6.4.2 Date::Calc

Date::Calc contains a number of functions for carrying out calculations using dates.

One important thing to know about Date::Calc is that it represents dates differently from Perl's internal functions. In particular when dealing with months, the numbers will be in the range 1 to 12 (instead of 0 to 11), and when dealing with days of the week the numbers will be in the range 1 to 7 instead of 0 to 6.

Examples: date and time manipulation with Date::Calc

Let's look at using Date::Calc for solving the same three problems that we discussed in the section on built-in functions.

Finding the date in x days time

With Date::Calc, this becomes trivial as we simply call Today to get the current date and then call Add_Delta_Days to get the result. Of course we can also call Date_to_Text to get a more user friendly output. The code would look like this:

```
print Date_to_Text(Add_Delta_Days(Today(), $x)); # Where $x is the
                                                  # number of days to add
```

Finding the date of the previous Saturday

There are a number of different ways to solve this problem but here is a reasonably simple one. We find the week number of the current week and then calculate the date of Monday in this week. We then subtract two days to get to the previous Saturday.

```
my ($year, $month, $day) = Today;
my $week = Week_Number($year, $month, $day);

print Date_to_Text(Add_Delta_Days(Monday_of_Week($week, $year), -2));
```

Finding the date of the first Monday in a given year
This isn't as simple as it sounds. The obvious way would be to do this:

```
print Date_to_Text(Monday_of_Week(1, $year));
```

but if you try this for 2001 you'll get Mon 31-Dec 2000. The problem is in the definition of week one of a year. Week one of a year is defined to be the week that contains January 4. You can, therefore, see that if the first Monday of the year is January 5, then that day is defined as being in week two and the Monday of week one is, in fact, December 29 of the previous year. We will need to do something a little more sophisticated. If we calculate which week number contains January 7 and then find the Monday of that week, we will always get the first Monday in the year. The code looks like this:

```
my $week = Week_Number($year, 1, 7);
print Date_to_Text(Monday_of_Week($week, $year));
```

6.4.3   *Date::Manip*

`Date::Manip` is, if possible, even bigger and more complex than `Date::Calc`. Many of the same functions are available (although, obviously, they often have different names).

Examples: date and time manipulation with Date::Manip

Let's once more look at solving our three standard problems.

Finding the date in x days time
With `Date::Manip`, the code would look like this:

```
print UnixDate(DateCalc(ParseDateString('now'), "+${x}d"),
         "%d/%m/%Y %H:%M:%S");
# Where $x is the number of days to add
```

Finding the date of the previous Saturday
Again this is very simple with `Date::Manip`. We can use the `Date_GetPrev` function to get the date immediately. In the call to `Date_GetPrev`, 6 is for Saturday and 0 is the `$curr` flag so it won't return the current date if today is a Saturday.

```
my $today = ParseDateString('today');
my $sat = Date_GetPrev($today, 6, 0);

print UnixDate($sat, "%d/%m/%Y");
```

Finding the date of the first Monday in a given year
This is another problem that is much easier with `Date::Manip`. We can use `Date_GetNext` to get the date of the first Monday after January 1, passing it 1 in the `$curr` flag so it returns the current date if it is a Monday.

```
my $jan_1 = ParseDateString("1 Jan $year");
my $mon = Date_GetNext($jan_1, 1, 1);

print UnixDate($mon, "%d/%m/%Y");
```

6.4.4 Choosing between date modules

We have seen a number of different ways to handle problems involving dates. It might be difficult to see how to choose between these various methods. My advice: use built-in Perl functions unless you have a really good reason not to.

The major reason for this is performance. Date::Manip is a very large module which does a number of very complex things and they are all implemented in pure Perl code. Most things can be handled much more efficiently with custom written Perl code. I hope I've demonstrated that there are very few date manipulations which can't be achieved with the standard Perl functions and modules. It is a question of balancing the ease of writing the program against the speed at which it runs.

Benchmarking date modules

As an example, look at this benchmark program which compares the speed of the Data::Manip ParseDate function with that of a piece of custom Perl code which builds up the same string using localtime.

```
#!/usr/bin/perl -w

use strict;

use Date::Manip;
use Benchmark;

timethese(5000, {'localtime' => \&ltime, date_manip => \&dmanip});

sub ltime {
  my @now = localtime;

  sprintf("%4d%02d%02d%02d:%02d:%02d",
          $now[5] + 1900, ++$now[4], $now[3], $now[2], $now[1], $now[0]);
}
sub dmanip {
  ParseDate('now');
}
```

Running this script gives the following output:

```
Benchmark: timing 5000 iterations of date_manip, localtime …
date_manip: 29 wallclock secs (28.89 usr +  0.00 sys = 28.89 CPU)
 localtime:  2 wallclock secs ( 2.04 usr +  0.00 sys =  2.04 CPU)
```

As you can see, the standard Perl version is almost fifteen times faster.

Having seen this evidence, you might be wondering if it is ever a good idea to use Date::Manip. There is one very good reason for using Date::Manip, and it is the `ParseDate` function itself. If you are ever in a position where you are reading in a date and you are not completely sure which format it will be in, then `ParseDate` will most likely be able to read the date and convert it into a standard form. Here are some of the more extreme examples of that in action:

```
use Date::Manip;

my @times = ('tomorrow',
             'next wednesday',
             '5 weeks ago');

foreach (@times) {
  print UnixDate(ParseDate($_), '%d %b %Y'), "\n";
}
```

which displays:

```
08 Feb 2000
09 Feb 2000
03 Jan 2000
```

(or, rather, the equivalent dates for the date when it is run).

6.5 Extended example: web access logs

One of the most common sources of line-oriented data is a web server access log. It seems that everyone needs to wring as much information as possible from these files in order to see if their web site is attracting a large enough audience to justify the huge sums of money spent on it.

Most web servers write access logs in a standard format. Here is a sample of a real access log. This sample comes from a log written by an Apache web server. Apache is the Open Source web server which runs more web sites than any other server.

```
158.152.136.193 - - [31/Dec/1999:21:27:27 -0800] "GET /index.html HTTP/1.1" 200 2987
158.152.136.193 - - [31/Dec/1999:21:27:27 -0800] "GET /head.gif HTTP/1.1" 200 4389
158.152.136.193 - - [31/Dec/1999:21:27:28 -0800] "GET /menu.gif HTTP/1.1" 200 7317
```

Each of these lines represents one access request that the server has received. Let's look at the fields in one of these lines and see what each one represents.

The first field is the IP address from which the request came. It is possible in most web servers to have these addresses resolved to hostnames before they are logged, but on a heavily used site this can seriously impact performance, so most webmasters leave this option turned off.

The second and third fields (the two dash characters) denote which user made this request. These fields will contain interesting data only if the requested page is not public, so the user must go through some kind of authorization in order to see it.

The fourth field is the date and time of the access. It shows the local date and time together with the difference from UTC (so in this case the server is hosted in the Pacific time zone of the U.S.A.).

The fifth field shows the actual HTTP request that was made. It is in three parts: the request type (in this case, GET), the URL that was requested, and the protocol used (HTTP/1.1).

The final two fields contain the response code that was returned to the browser (200 means that the request was successful and the contents of the URL have been sent) and the number of bytes returned.

Armed with this knowledge we can look at the three lines and work out exactly what happened. At half past nine on New Year's Eve someone at IP address 158.152.136.193 made three requests to the web site. The person requested index.html, head.gif, and menu.gif. Each of these requests was successful and we returned a total of 14,000 bytes to them.

This kind of analysis is very useful and not very difficult, but a busy web site will have many thousands of hits every day. How are you supposed to get meaningful information from that amount of input data? Using Perl, of course.

It wouldn't be very difficult to write something to break apart a log line and analyze the data, but it's not completely simple—some fields are separated by spaces, others have embedded spaces. Luckily this is such a common task that someone has already written a module to process web access logs. It is called Logfile and you can find it on the CPAN.

Using Logfile is very simple. It consists of a number of submodules, each tuned to handle a particular type of web server log. They are all subclasses of the module Logfile::Base. As our access log was generated by Apache we will use Logfile::Apache.

Logfile is an object-oriented module, so all processing is carried out via a Logfile object. The first thing we need to do is create a Logfile object.

```
my $log = Logfile::Apache->new(File => 'access_log',
                               Group => [qw(Host Date File Bytes User)]);
```

The named parameters to this function make it very easy to follow what is going on. The File parameter is the name of the access log that you want to analyze. Group is a reference to a list of indexes that you will want to use to produce reports. The five indexes listed in the code snippet correspond to sections of the Apache log record. In addition to these, the module understands a couple of others. Domain is the top level that the requesting host is in (e.g., .com, .uk, .org), which is calculated from the hostname. Hour is the hour of the day that the request took place. It is calculated from the date field.

Having created the Logfile object you can then start to produce reports with it. To list our files in order of popularity we can simply do this:

```
$log->report(Group => 'File');
```

which produces a report like this:

```
File                        Records
===================================
/                       11   2.53%
/examples                1   0.23%
/examples/index.html     1   0.23%
/images/graph            1   0.23%
/images/pix              1   0.23%
/images/sidebar          1   0.23%
/images/thumbnail        5   1.15%
/index                   1   0.23%
    .
    .
    .
[other lines snipped]
```

This is an alphabetized list of all of the files that were listed in the access log. We can make more sense if we sort the output by number of hits and perhaps just list the top ten files by changing the code like this:

```
$log->report(Group => 'File', Sort => 'Records', Top => 10);
```

We then get a more understandable report that looks like this:

```
File                        Records
===================================
/new/images            129 29.72%
/new/music              80 18.43%
/new/personal           52 11.98%
/new/friends            47 10.83%
/splash/splashes        28  6.45%
/new/pics               26  5.99%
/new/stuff              21  4.84%
/                       11  2.53%
/new/splash              6  1.38%
/images/thumbnail        5  1.15%
```

Perhaps instead of wanting to know the most popular files, you are interested in the most popular times of the day that people visit your site. You can do this using the Hour index. The following:

```
$log->report(Group => 'Hour');
```

will list all of the hours in chronological order and

```
$log->report(Group => 'Hour', Sort => 'Records');
```

will order them by the number of hits in each hour. If you want to find the quietest time of the day, simply reverse the order of the sort

```
$log->report(Group => 'Hour', Sort => 'Records', Reverse => 1);
```

There are a number of other types of reports that you can get using Logfile, but it would be impossible to cover them all here. Have a look at the examples in the README file and the test files to get some good ideas.

6.6   *Further information*

For more information about the $/, $, and $" variables (together with other useful Perl variables) see the `perldoc perlvar` manual pages.

For more information about the built-in date handling functions see the `perldoc perlfunc` manual pages.

For more information about the POSIX::strftime function see the `perldoc POSIX` manual page and your system's documentation for a list of supported character sequences.

Both the Date::Manip and Date::Calc modules are available from the CPAN. Having installed them you can read their full documentation by typing `perldoc Date::Manip` or `perldoc Date::Calc` at your command line.

6.7   *Summary*

- Record-oriented data is very easy to handle in Perl, particularly if you make appropriate use of the I/O control variables such as $/, $", and $,.
- The Text::CSV_XS CPAN module makes it very easy to read and write comma-separated values.
- Data caching can speed up your programs when used carefully, and using Memoize.pm can make adding caching to a program very easy.
- Perl has very powerful built-in date and time processing functions.
- More complex date and time manipulation can be carried out using modules from CPAN.

Fixed-width and binary data

7

In this chapter we will complete our survey of simple data formats by examining fixed-width and binary data. Many of the methods we have discussed in previous chapters will still prove to be useful, but we will also look at some new tricks.

7.1 *Fixed-width data*

Fixed-width data is becoming less common, but it is still possible that you will come across it, particularly if you are exchanging data with an older computer system that runs on a mainframe or is written in COBOL.

7.1.1 *Reading fixed-width data*

In a fixed-width data record, there is nothing to distinguish one data item from the next one. Each data item is simply written immediately after the preceding one, after padding it to a defined width. This padding can either be with zeroes or with spaces and can be before or after the data.[1] In order to interpret the data, we need more information about the way it has been written. This is normally sent separately from the data itself but, as we shall see later, it is also possible to encode this data within the files.

Here is an example of two fixed-width data records:

```
00374Bloggs & Co        19991105100103+00015000
00375Smith Brothers     19991106001234-00004999
```

As you can see, it's tricky to understand exactly what is going on here. It looks as though there is an ascending sequence number at the start and perhaps a customer name. Some of the data in the middle looks like it might be a date—but until we get a full definition of the data we can't be sure even how many data fields there are.

Here is the definition of the data:

- *Columns 1 to 5*—Transaction number (numeric)
- *Columns 6 to 25*—Customer name (text)
- *Columns 26 to 33*—Date of transaction (YYYYMMDD)
- *Columns 34 to 39*—Customer's transaction number (numeric)
- *Column 40*—Transaction direction (+/-)
- *Columns 41 to 48*—Amount of transaction (numeric with two implied decimal places)

---

[1] Although it is most common to find numerical data prepadded with zeroes and text data postpadded with spaces.

Now we can start to make some sense of the data. We can see that on November 5, 1999, we received a check (number 100103) for $150.00 from Bloggs & Co. and on November 6, 1999, we paid $49.99 to Smith Brothers in response to their invoice number 1234.

Example: extracting fixed-width data fields with substr

So how do we go about extracting that information from the data? Here's a first attempt using the substr function to do the work:

```
my @cols = qw(5 25 33 39 40 48);

while (<STDIN>) {
  my @rec;

  my $prev = 0;
  foreach my $col (@cols) {
    push @rec, substr($_, $prev, $col - $prev);
    $prev = $col;
  }
  print join('|', @rec);
  print "\n";
}
```

While this code works, it's not particularly easy to understand. We use an array of column positions to tell us where each column ends. Notice that we've actually used the positions where the columns begin rather than end. This is because the column definitions that we were given start from column one, whereas Perl arrays start from zero—all in all, not the most maintainable piece of code.

Example: extracting fixed-width data with regular expressions

Perhaps we'd do better if we used regular expressions:

```
my @widths = qw(5 20 8 6 1 8);

my $regex;

$regex .= "(.{$_})" foreach @widths;

while (<STDIN>) {
  my @rec = /$regex/;
  print join('|', @rec);
  print "\n";
}
```

In this case we've switched from using column start (or end) positions to using column widths. It's not very difficult to build this list given our previous list. We then use the list of widths to construct a regular expression which we can match against each row of our data file in turn. The regular expression that we build looks like this:

```
(.{5})(.{20})(.{8})(.{6})(.{1})(.{8})
```

which is really a very simple regular expression. For each column in the data record, there is an element of the form `(.{x})`, where x is the width of the column. This element will match any character x times and the parentheses will save the result of the match. Matching this regular expression against a data record and assigning the result to an array will give us a list containing all of the $1, $2, ... $n variables in order.

This isn't a very interesting use of regular expressions. There must be a better way.

Example: extracting fixed-width data with unpack

In this case the best way is to use Perl's unpack function. unpack takes a scalar expression and breaks it into a list of values according to a template that it is given. The template consists of a sequence of characters which define the type and size of the individual fields. A simple way to break apart our current data would be like this:

```
my $template = 'a5a20a8a6aa8';

while (<STDIN>) {
  my @rec = unpack($template, $_);
  print join('|', @rec);
  print "\n";
}
```

which returns exactly the same set of data that we have seen in all of the examples above. In this case our template consists of the letter a for each field followed by the length of the field (the length is optional on single-character fields like our +/- field). The a designates each field as an ASCII string, but the template can contain many other options. For reference, here is one of the data lines that was produced by the previous example:

```
00374|Bloggs & Co        |19991105|100103|+|00015000
```

Notice that the numbers are still prepadded with zeroes and the string is still post-padded with spaces. Now see what happens if we replace each a in the template with an A.

```
00374|Bloggs & Co|19991105|100103|+|00015000
```

The spaces at the end of the string are removed. Depending on your application, this may or may not be what you want. Perl gives you the flexibility to choose the most appropriate route.

There are a number of other options that can be used in the unpack template and we'll see some more of them when we look at binary data in more detail. For ASCII data, only a and A are useful.

Multiple record types

One slight variation of the fixed-width data record has different sets of data fields for different types of data within the same file. Consider a system that maintains a product list and, at the end of each day, produces a file that lists all new products added and old products deleted during the day. For a new product, you will need a lot of data (perhaps product code, description, price, stock count and supplier identifier). For the deleted product you only need the product code (but you might also list the product description to make the report easier to follow). Each record will have some kind of identifier and the start of the line denoting which kind of record it is. In our example they will be the strings ADD and DEL. Here are some sample data:

```
ADD0101Super Widget  00999901000SUPP01
ADD0102Ultra Widget  01499900500SUPP01
DEL0050Basic Widget
DEL0051Cheap Widget
```

On the day covered by this data, we have added two new widgets to our product catalogue. The Super Widget (product code 0101) costs $99.99 and we have 1000 in stock. The Ultra Widget (product code 0102) costs $149.99 and we have 500 in stock. We purchase both new widgets from the same supplier. At the same time we have discontinued two older products, the Basic Widget (Product Code 0050) and the Cheap Widget (Product Code 0051).

Example: reading multiple fixed-width record types

A program to read a file such as the previous example might look like this:

```perl
my %templates = (ADD => 'a4A14a6a5a6',
                 DEL => 'a4A14');

while (<STDIN>) {
  my ($type, $data) = unpack('a3a*', $_);
  my @rec = unpack($templates{$type}, $data);
  print "$type - ", join('|', @rec);
  print "\n";
}
```

In this case we are storing the two possible templates in a hash and unpacking the data in two stages. In the first stage we separate the record type from the main part of the data. We then use the record type to choose the appropriate template to unpack the rest of the data. One thing that we haven't seen before is the use of * as a field length to mean "use all characters to the end of the string." This is very useful when we don't know how long our string will be.

Data with no end-of-record marker

Another difference that you may come across with fixed-width data is that sometimes it comes without a defined end-of-record marker. As both the size of each field in a record and the number of fields in a record are well defined, we know how long each record will be. It is, therefore, possible to send the data as a stream of bytes and leave it up to the receiving program to split the data into individual records.

Perl, of course, has a number of ways to do this. You could read the whole file into memory and split the data using substr or unpack, but for many tasks the amount of data to process makes this unfeasible.

The most efficient way is to use a completely different method of reading your data. In addition to the <FILE> syntax that reads data from file handles one record at a time, Perl supports a more traditional syntax using the read and seek functions. The read function takes three or four arguments. The first three are: a file handle to read data from, a scalar variable to read the data into, and the maximum number of bytes to read. The fourth, optional, argument is an offset into the variable where you want to start writing the data (this is rarely used). read returns the number of bytes read (which can be less than the requested number if you are near the end of a file) and zero when there is no more data to read.

Each open file handle has a current position associated with it called a file pointer and read takes its data from the file pointer and moves the pointer to the end of the data it has read. You can also reposition the file pointer explicitly using the seek function. seek takes three arguments: the file handle, the offset you wish to move to, and a value that indicates how the offset should be interpreted. If this value is 0 then the offset is calculated from the start of the file, if it is 1 the offset is calculated from the current position, and if it is 2 the offset is calculated from the end of the file. You can always find out the current position of the file pointer by using tell, which returns the offset from the start of the file in bytes. seek and tell are often unnecessary when handling ASCII fixed-width data files, as you usually just read the file in sequential order.

Example: reading data with no end-of-record markers using read

As an example, if our previous data file were written without newlines, we could use code like this to read it (obviously we could use any of the previously discussed techniques to split the record up once we have read it):

```
my $template = 'A5A20A8A6AA8';

my $data;

while (read STDIN, $data, 48) {
  my @rec = unpack($template, $data);
```

```
    print join('|', @rec);
    print "\n";
}
```

Example: reading multiple record types without end-of-record markers

It is also possible to handle variable length, fixed-width records using a method similar to this. In this case we read 3 bytes first to get the record type and then use this to decide how many more bytes to read on a further pass.

```
my %templates = (ADD => {len => 35,
                         tem => 'a4A14a6a5a6'},
                 DEL => {len => 18,
                         tem => 'a4A14'});
my $type;
while (read STDIN, $type, 3) {
  read STDIN, $data, $templates{$type}->{len};
  my @rec = unpack($templates{$type}->{tem}, $data);
  print "$type - ", join('|', @rec);
  print "\n";
}
```

Defining record structure within the data file

I mentioned earlier that it is possible that the structure of the data could be defined in the file. You could then write your script to be flexible enough that it handles any changes in the structure (assuming that the definition of the structure remains the same).

There are a number of ways to encode this metadata, most of them based around putting the information in the first row of the file. In this case you would read the first line separately and parse it to extract the data. You would then use this information to build the format string that you pass to unpack. Here are a couple of the encoding methods that you might find—and how to deal with them.

Fixed-width numbers indicating column widths

In this case, the first line will be a string of numbers. You will be told how long each number is (probably two or three digits). You can unpack the record into an array of numbers. Each of these numbers is the width of one field. You can, therefore, build up an unpack format to use on the rest of the file.

```
my $line = <STDIN>;    # The metadata line

my $width = 3;         # The width of each number in $line;

my $fields = length($line) / $width;

my $meta_fmt = 'a3' x $fields;

my @widths = unpack($meta_fmt, $line);
```

```
my $fmt = join('', map { "A$_" } @widths);

while (<STDIN>) {
  my @data = unpack($fmt, $_);
  # Do something useful with the fields in @data
}
```

Notice that we can calculate the number of fields in each record by dividing the length of the metadata record by the width of each number in it. It might be useful to add a sanity check at that point to ensure that this calculation gives an integer answer as it should.

Using this method our financial data file would look like this:

```
005020008006001008
00374Bloggs & Co        19991105100103+00015000
00375Smith Brothers     19991106001234-00004999
```

The first line contains the field widths (5, 20, 8, 6, 1, and 8), all padded out to three digit numbers.

Field-end markers

In this method, the first row in the file is a blank row that contains a marker (perhaps a | character) wherever a field will end in the following rows. In other words, our example file would look like this:

```
     |                  |       |   ||        |
00374Bloggs & Co        19991105100103+00015000
00375Smith Brothers     19991106001234-00004999
```

To deal with this metadata, we can split the row on the marker character and use the length of the various elements to calculate the lengths of the fields:

```
my $line = <STDIN>; # The metadata line
chomp $line;
my $mark = '|'; # The field marker
my @fields = split($mark, $line);

my @widths = map { length($_) + 1 } @fields;

my $fmt = join('', map { "A$_" } @widths);

while (<STDIN>) {
  chomp;
  my @data = unpack($fmt, $_);
  # Do something useful with the fields in @data
}
```

Notice that we add one to the length of each element to get the width. This is because the marker character is not included in the array returned by the split, but it should be included in the width of the field.

These are just two common ways to encode field structures in a fixed-width data file. You will come across others, but it is always a case of working out the best way to extract the required information from the metadata record. Of course, if you have any influence in the design of your input file, you might like to suggest that the first line contains the format that you need to pass to unpack—let your source system do the hard work!

7.1.2 Writing fixed-width data

If you have to read fixed-width data there is, of course, a chance that eventually you will need to write it. In this section we'll look at some common ways to do this.

Writing fixed-width data using pack

Luckily, Perl has a function which is the opposite of unpack and, logically enough, it is called pack. pack takes a template and a list of values and returns a string containing the list packed according to the rules given by the template. Once again the full power of pack will be useful when we look at binary data, but for ASCII data we will just use the A and a template options. These options have slightly different meanings in a pack template than the ones they have in an unpack template. Table 7.1 summarizes these differences.

Table 7.1 Meanings of A and a in pack and unpack templates

	A	**a**
pack	Pad string with spaces	Pad string with null characters
unpack	Strip trailing nulls and spaces	Leave trailing nulls and spaces

Therefore, if we have a number of strings and wish to pack them into a fixed-width data record, we can do something like this:

```
my @strings = qw(Here are a number of strings);
my $template = 'A6A6A3A8A4A10';

print pack($template, @strings), "\n";
```

and our strings will all be space padded to the sizes given in the pack template. There is, however, a problem padding numbers using this method, as Perl doesn't know the difference between text fields and numerical fields, so you end up with numbers postpadded with spaces (or nulls, depending on the template you use). This may, of course, be fine for your data, but if you want to prepad numbers with spaces then you should use the sprintf or printf functions.

Writing fixed-width data using printf and sprintf

These two functions do very similar things. The only difference is that `sprintf`
returns its results in a scalar variable, whereas `printf` will write them directly to a
file handle. Both of the functions take a format description followed by a list of values which are substituted into the format string. The contents of the format string
control how the values appear in the final result. At each place in the format string
where you want a value to be substituted you place a format specifier in the format
`%m.nx`, where m and n control the size of the field and x controls how the value
should be interpreted. Full details of the syntax for format specifiers can be found in
your Perl documentation but, for our current purposes, a small subset will suffice.

To put integers into the string, use the format specifier `%d`;[2] to force the field to
be five characters wide, use the format specifier `%5d`; and to prepad the field with
zeroes, use `%05d`. Here is an example which demonstrates these options:

```
my @formats = qw(%d %5d %05d);

my $num = 123;

foreach (@formats) {
  printf "|$_|\n", $num;
}
```

Running this code produces the following results:

```
|123|
|  123|
|00123|
```

You can do similar things with floating point numbers using `%f`. In this case you can
control the total width of the field and also the number of characters after the decimal point by using notation such as `%6.2f` (for a 6 character field with two characters after the decimal point). Here is an example of this:

```
my @formats = qw(%f %6.2f %06.2f);

my $num = 12.3;

foreach (@formats) {
  printf "|$_|\n", $num;
}
```

which gives the following results (notice that the default number of decimal places
is six):

```
|12.300000|
| 12.30|
|012.30|
```

---

[2] `%d` is actually for a signed integer. If you need an unsigned value, use `%u`.

For strings we can use the format specifier %s. Again, we can use a number within the specifier to define the size of the field. You'll notice from the previous examples that when the data was smaller than the field it was to be used in, the data was right justified within the field. With numbers, that is generally what you want (especially when you are going to prepad the number with zeroes) but, as we've seen previously, text is often left justified and postpadded with spaces. In order to left justify the text we can prepend a minus sign to the size specifier. Here are some examples:

```perl
my @formats = qw(%s %10s %010s %-10s %-010s);

my $str = 'Text';

foreach (@formats) {
  printf "|$_|\n", $str;
}
```

which gives the following output:

```
|Text|
|      Text|
|000000Text|
|Text      |
|Text      |
```

Notice that we can prepad strings with zeroes just as we can for numbers, but it's difficult to think of a situation where that would be useful.

Example: writing fixed-width data with sprintf

Putting this all together, we can produce code which can output fixed-width financial transaction records like the ones we were reading earlier.

```perl
my %rec1 = ( txnref => 374,
             cust   => 'Bloggs & Co',
             date   => 19991105,
             extref => 100103,
             dir    => '+',
             amt    => 15000 );

my %rec2 = ( txnref => 375,
             cust   => 'Smith Brothers',
             date   => 19991106,
             extref => 1234,
             dir    => '-',
             amt    => 4999 );

my @cols = (
            { name  => 'txnref',
              width => 5,
              num   => 1 },
            { name  => 'cust',
```

```
                       width => 20,
                       num   => 0 },
                   { name  => 'date',
                     width => 8,
                     num   => 1 },
                   { name  => 'extref',
                     width => 6,
                     num   => 1 },
                   { name  => 'dir',
                     width => 1,
                     num   => 0 },
                   { name  => 'amt',
                     width => 8,
                     num   => 1 } );

my $format = build_fmt(\@cols);

print fixed_rec(\%rec1, \@cols, $format);
print fixed_rec(\%rec2, \@cols, $format);

sub build_fmt {

  my $cols = shift;
  my $fmt;

  foreach (@$cols) {

    if ($_->{num}) {
      $fmt .= "%0$_->{width}s";
    } else {
      $fmt .= "%-$_->{width}s";
    }
  }

  return $fmt;
}

sub fixed_rec {

  my ($rec, $cols, $fmt) = @_;

  my @vals = map { $rec->{$_->{name}} } @$cols;

  sprintf("$fmt\n", @vals);
}
```

In this program, we use an array of hashes (@cols) to define the characteristics of each data field in our record. These characteristics include the name of the column together with the width that we want it to be in the output, and a flag indicating whether or not it is a numeric field. We then use the data in this array to build a suitable sprintf format string in the function build_fmt. The fixed_rec function then extracts the relevant data from the record (which is stored in a hash) into an array and feeds that array to `sprintf` along with the format. This creates our fixed-width record. As expected, the results of running this program are the records that we started with at the beginning of this chapter.

7.2   *Binary data*

All of the data that we have looked at so far has been ASCII data. That is, it has been encoded using a system laid down by the American Standards Committee for Information Interchange. In this code, 128 characters[3] have been given a numerical equivalent value from 0 to 127. For example, the space character is number 32, the digits 0 to 9 have the numbers 48 to 57, and the letters of the alphabet appear from 65 to 90 in upper case and from 97 to 122 in lower case. Other numbers are taken up by punctuation marks and various control characters.

When an ASCII character is written to a file, what is actually written is the binary version of the ASCII code for the given character. For example the number 123 would be written to the file as 00110001 00110010 00110011 (the binary equivalents of 49, 50, and 51). The advantage of this type of data is that it is very easy to write software that allows users to make sense of the data. All you need to do is convert each byte of data into its equivalent ASCII character. The major disadvantage is the amount of space used. In the previous example we used 3 bytes of data to store a number, but if we had stored the binary number 01111011 (the binary equivalent of 123) we could have used a third of the space.

For this reason, there are a number of applications which store data in binary format. In many cases these are proprietary binary formats which are kept secret so that one company has a competitive advantage over another. A good example of this is spreadsheets. Microsoft and Lotus have their own spreadsheet file format and, although Lotus 123 can read Microsoft Excel files, each time a new feature is added to Excel, Lotus has to do more work to ensure that its Excel file converter can handle the new feature. Other binary file formats are in the public domain and can therefore be used easily by applications from many different sources. Probably the best example of this is in graphics files, where any number of applications across many different platforms can happily read and write each other's files.

We'll start by writing a script that can extract useful data from a graphics file. The most ubiquitous graphics file format (especially across the Internet) is the CompuServe *Graphics Interchange Format* (or GIF). Unfortunately for us, this file format uses a patented data compression technique and the owners of the patent (Unisys) are trying to

---

[3]   There are a number of extensions to the ASCII character set which define 256 characters, but the fact that they are nonstandard can make dealing with them problematic.

ensure that only properly licensed software is used to create GIF files.[4] As Perl is Open Source, it does not fall into this category, and you shouldn't use it to create GIFs. I believe that using Perl to read GIFs would not violate the licensing terms, but to be sure we'll look at the *Portable Network Graphics* (PNG) format instead.

7.2.1 Reading PNG files

In order to read any binary file, you will need a definition of the format. I'm using the definition in *Programming Web Graphics with Perl & GNU Software* by Shawn P. Wallace (O'Reilly), but you can get the definitive version from the PNG group home page at http://www.cdrom.com/pub/png/.

Reading the file format signature

Most binary files start with a *signature*, that is a few bytes that identify the format of the file. This is so that applications that are reading the file can easily check that the file is in a format that they can understand. In the case of PNG files, the first 8 bytes always contain the hex value 0x89 followed by the string PNG\cM\cJ\cZ\cM. In order to check that a file is a valid PNG file, you should do something like this:

```
my data;

read(PNG, $data, 8);

die "Not a valid PNG\n" unless $data eq '\x89PNG\cM\cJ\cZ\cM';
```

Note that we use \x89 to match the hex number 0x89 and \cZ to match Control-Z.

Reading the data chunks

After this header sequence, a PNG file is made up of a number of *chunks*. Each chunk contains an 8-byte header, some amount of data, and a 4-byte trailer. Each header record contains the length in a 4-byte integer followed by four characters indicating the type of the chunk. The length field gives you the number of bytes that you should read from the file and the type tells you how to process it. There are a number of different chunk types in the PNG specification, but we will look only at the IHDR (header) chunk, which is always the first chunk in the file and defines certain global attributes of the image.

Example: reading a PNG file

A complete program to extract this data from a PNG file (passed in via STDIN) looks like this:

---

[4] You can read more about this dispute in Lincoln Stein's excellent article at: http://www.webtechniques.com/archives/1999/12/webm/.

```
binmode STDIN;
my $data;

read(STDIN, $data, 8);
die "Not a PNG file" unless $data eq "\x89PNG\cM\cJ\cZ\cM";

while (read(STDIN, $data, 8)) {
  my ($size, $type) = unpack('Na4', $data);
  print "$type ($size bytes)\n";
  read(STDIN, $data, $size);

  if ($type eq 'IHDR') {
    my ($w, $h, $bitdepth, $coltype, $comptype, $filtype, $interlscheme) =
      unpack('NNCCCCC', $data);
    print << "END";
  Width: $w, Height: $h
  Bit Depth: $bitdepth, Color Type: $coltype
  Compression Type: $comptype, Filtering Type: $filtype
  Interlace Scheme: $interlscheme
END
  }
  read(STDIN, $data, 4);
}
```

The first thing to do when dealing with binary data is to put the file handle that you will be reading into binary mode by calling `binmode` on it. This is necessary on operating systems which differentiate between binary and text files (these include DOS and Windows). On these operating systems, a `\cM\cJ` end-of-line marker in a text file gets translated to `\n` as it is read in. If this sequence appears in a binary file, it needs to be left untouched. UNIX, like most operating systems, doesn't make this binary/text differentiation, so under them `binmode` has no effect. For reasons of portability it is advisable to always call this function.

Having called `binmode`, we can then start reading our binary data. As we saw before, the first thing that we do is to read the first 8 bytes and check them against the signature for PNG files. If it matches we continue, otherwise we terminate the program.

We then go into a `while` loop, reading the header of each chunk in the file. We read 8 bytes of raw data and convert it into something easier to understand using `unpack`. Notice that we use `N` to extract the 4-byte integer and `a4` to extract the 4-character string. The full set of options that you can use in an `unpack` format string is given in the documentation that came with your Perl distribution. It is in the `perlfunc` manual page (and notice that the full set of options is listed under the `pack` function). Having established the type of the chunk and the amount of data that it contains, we can read in that amount of data from the file. In our program we also display the information to the user.

The type of the chunk determines how we process the data we have read. In our case, we are only dealing with the IHDR chunk, and that is defined as two 4-byte integers followed by five single-character strings. We can, therefore, split the data apart using the unpack format NNCCCCC. The definition of these fields is in the PNG documentation but there is a *précis* in table 7.2.

Table 7.2   Elements of a PNG IHDR chunk

Field	Type	Description
Width	4-byte integer	The width of the image in pixels
Height	4-byte integer	The height of the image in pixels
Bit Depth	1-byte character	The number of bits used to represent the color of each pixel
Color Type	1-byte character	Code indicating how colors are encoded within the image. Valid values are: 0: A number from 0–255 indicating the greyscale value 2: Three numbers from 0–255 indicating the amount of red, green, and blue 3: A number which is an index into a color table 4: A greyscale value (0–255) followed by an alpha mask 6: An RGB triplet (as is 2, above) followed by an alpha mask
Compression Type	1-byte character	The type of compression used (always 0 in PNG version 1.0)
Filtering Type	1-byte character	The type of filtering applied to the data (always 0 in PNG version 1.0)
Interlacing Scheme	1-byte character	The interlacing scheme used to store the data. For PNG version 1.0 this is either 0 (for no interlacing) or 1 (for Adam7 interlacing)

Having unpacked this data into more useable chunks we can display it. It may be more useful to translate some of the numbers to descriptive strings, but we won't do that in this example.

After reading and processing the chunk data, we need only to read in the 4 bytes which make up the chunk footer. This value can be used as a checksum against the data in the chunk to ensure that it has not been corrupted. In this simple example we will throw it away.

Our program then goes on to read all of the other chunks in turn. It doesn't process them, it simply displays the type and size of each chunk it finds. A more complex program would need to read the PNG specification and work out how to process each type of chunk.

Testing the PNG file reader

To test this program I created a simple PNG file that was 100 pixels by 50 pixels, containing some simple text on a white background. As the program expects to read the PNG file from STDIN, I ran the program like this:

```
read_png.pl < test.png
```

and the output I got looked like this:

```
IHDR (13 bytes)
  Width: 100, Height: 50
  Bit Depth: 8, Color Type: 2
  Compression Type: 0, Filtering Type: 0
  Interlace Scheme: 0
tEXt (21 bytes)
tIME (7 bytes)
pHYs (9 bytes)
IDAT (1135 bytes)
IEND (0 bytes)
```

From this we can see that my file was, indeed, 100 pixels by 50 pixels. There were 8 bits per pixel and they were in RGB triplets. No compression, filtering, or interlacing was used. After the IHDR chunk, you can see various other chunks. The important one is the IDAT chunk which contains the actual image data.

CPAN modules

There are, of course, easier ways to get to this information than by writing your own program. In particular, Gisle Aas has written a module called Image::Info which is available from the CPAN. Currently (version 0.04) the module supports PNG, JPG, TIFF, and GIF file formats, and no doubt more will follow. Reading the source code for this module will give you more useful insights into reading binary files using Perl.

7.2.2 Reading and writing MP3 files

Another binary file format that has been getting a lot of publicity recently is the MP3[5] file. These files store near-CD quality sound in typically a third of the space required by raw CD data. This has led to a whole new drain on Internet bandwidth as people upload their favorite tracks to their web sites.

We won't look at reading or writing the actual audio data in an MP3 file (encoding audio data is a large enough field to deserve several books of description), but we will look at the ID3 data which is stored at the end of an MP3 file. The ID3 tags allow you to store useful information about the sounds contained in the file within

---

[5] Short for MPEG3 or Motion Pictures Experts Group—Audio Level 3.

the file itself. This includes obvious fields such as the artist, album, track name, and year of release, together with more obscure data like the genre of the track and the copyright and distribution information.

Chris Nandor has written a module which allows you to read and write these data fields. The module is called MPEG::MP3Info and it is available from the CPAN. Using the module is very simple. Here is a sample program which displays all of the ID3 data that it can find in a given MP3 file:

```
use MPEG::MP3Info;

my $file = shift;

my $tag = get_mp3tag($file);
my $info = get_mp3info($file);

print "Filename: $file\n";
print "MP3 Tags\n";
foreach (sort keys %$tag) {
  print "$_ : $tag->{$_}\n";
}

print "MP3 Info\n";
foreach (sort keys %$info) {
  print "$_ : $info->{$_}\n";
}
```

Notice that there are two separate parts of the ID3 data. The data returned in $tag is the data about the sound contained in the file—like track name, artist, and year of release. The data returned in $info tend to be more physical data about the actual data in the file—the bit-rate, frequency, and whether the recording is stereo or mono. For this reason, the module currently (and I'm looking at version 0.71) contains a set_mp3tag function, but not a set_mp3info function. It is likely that you'll have good reasons to change the ID3 tags which defined the track and artist, but less likely that you'll ever need to change the physical recording parameters. There is also a remove_mp3tag function which removes the ID3 data from the end of the file.

As with Image::Info which we discussed earlier, it is very instructive to read the code of this module as it will give you many useful ideas on the best way to read and write your binary data.

7.3 *Further information*

This chapter has discussed a number of built-in Perl functions. These include pack, unpack, read, printf, and sprintf. For more information about any built-in Perl function see the perldoc perlfunc manual page. The list of type specifiers supported by `sprintf` and `printf` is system-dependent, so you can get this information from your system documentation.

The `Image::Info` and `MPEG::MP3Info` modules are both available from the CPAN. Having installed them, you will be able to read their full documentation by typing `perldoc Image::Info` or `perldoc MPEG::MP3Info` at your command line.

7.4   *Summary*

- The easiest way to split apart a fixed-width data record is by using the `unpack` function.
- Conversely, the easiest way to create a fixed-width data record is by using the `pack` function.
- If your data doesn't have distinct end-of-record markers, you can read a certain number of bytes from your input data stream using the `read` function.
- Once you have used the `binmode` function on a binary data stream it can be processed using exactly the same techniques as a text data stream.

Part III

Simple data parsing

As this part of the tale commences, our heroes begin to realize that there are very good reasons for the beast to appear in more complex forms, and they see that their current techniques will be of limited use against these new forms. They begin to discuss more powerful techniques to attack them.

The beast then appears in a new, hierarchical format. Luckily, our heroes find a source of ready-made tools for defeating this form.

The beast appears once again in a more complex (and yet, in some ways, simplified) guise and our heroes once more find ready-built tools for defeating this form.

At the end of this part of the tale, our heroes develop techniques which let them build their own tools to tackle the beast whenever it appears in forms of arbitrary complexity.

Complex data formats

8

What this chapter covers:

- Using and processing more complex data formats
- Limitations in data parsing
- What are parsers and why should I use them?
- Parsers in Perl

We have now completed our survey of the simple data formats that you will come across. There is, however, a whole class of more complex data formats that you will inevitably be called upon to munge at some point. The increased flexibility that these formats give us for data storage comes at a price, as they will take more time to process. In this chapter we take a look at these types of data, how you discern when to use them, and how you go about processing them.

8.1 Complex data files

A lot of the data that we have seen up to now has used one line to represent each record in the data set. There have been exceptions; some of the records that we saw in chapter 6 used more than one row for each record, and most of the binary data that we discussed in chapter 7 had no record-based structure at all. Even going back to the very first chapter, the first sample CD data set that we saw consisted largely of a record-based middle section, but it also has header and footer records which would have made processing it slightly more complex.

8.1.1 Example: metadata in the CD file

Let's take another look at that first sample data file.

```
Dave's CD Collection
16 Sep 1999

Artist         Title            Label          Released
-----------------------------------------------------------
Bragg, Billy   Workers' Playtime  Cooking Vinyl  1987
Bragg, Billy   Mermaid Avenue     EMI            1998
Black, Mary    The Holy Ground    Grapevine      1993
Black, Mary    Circus             Grapevine      1996
Bowie, David   Hunky Dory         RCA            1971
Bowie, David   Earthling          EMI            1987

6 Records
```

As you can see, the data consists of three clearly delimited sections. The main body of the file contains the meat of the report—a list of the CDs in my record collection, giving information on artist, title, recording label, and year of release. However, the header and footer records also contain important data.

The header contains information about the data file as a whole, telling us whose CD collection it is and the date on which this snapshot is valid. It would be inappropriate to list this information for each record in the file, so the header is a good place to put it.[1]

---

[1] There are other places where the information could be stored. One common solution is to store this kind of information in the name of the data file, so that a file containing this data might be called something like 19990916_dave.txt.

The information in the footer is a little different. In this case we are describing the actual shape of the data rather than where (or when) it comes from. At first glance it might seem that this information is unnecessary, as we can find out the number of records in the file simply by counting them as we process them. The reason that it is useful for the file to contain an indication of the number of records is that it acts as a simple check that the file has not been corrupted between the time it was created and the time we received it. By simply comparing the number of records that we processed against the number that the file claims to contain, we can easily tell if any went missing in transmission.[2]

This then demonstrates one important reason for having more complex data files. They allow us to include *metadata*—data about the data we are dealing with.

Adding subrecords

Another good reason for using more complex formats is that you are dealing with data that doesn't actually fit very well into a simpler format. Staying with the CD example, perhaps your data file needs to contain details of the tracks on the CDs as well as the data that we already list. At this point our line-per-record approach falls down and we are forced to look at something more complicated. Perhaps we will indent track records with a tab character or prefix the track records with a + character. This would give us a file that looked something like this (listing only the first two tracks):

```
Dave's CD Collection
16 Sep 1999

Artist          Title             Label          Released
----------------------------------------------------------
Bragg, Billy  Workers' Playtime  Cooking Vinyl  1988
+She's Got A New Spell
+Must I Paint You A Picture
Bragg, Billy  Mermaid Avenue     EMI            1998
+Walt Whitman's Niece
+California Stars
Black, Mary    The Holy Ground   Grapevine      1993
+Summer Sent You
+Flesh And Blood
Black, Mary    Circus            Grapevine      1995
+The Circus
+In A Dream
Bowie, David  Hunky Dory         RCA            1971
+Changes
```

---

[2] As with the header information, including this data within the file isn't the only way to do it. Another common method is to send a second file with a similar name that contains the number of records. In the example of my CDs, we might have another file called 19990916_dave.rec which contains only the number 6.

```
+Oh You Pretty Things
Bowie, David  Earthling          EMI              1997
+Little Wonder
+Looking For Satellites

6 Records
```

8.1.2 *Example: reading the expanded CD file*

This file is more complicated to process than just about any other that we have seen. Here is one potential way to read the data into a data structure.

```
 1: my %data;
 2:
 3: chomp($data{title} = <STDIN>);
 4: chomp($data{date} = <STDIN>);
 5: <STDIN>;
 6: my ($labels, @labels);
 7: chomp($labels = <STDIN>);
 8: @labels = split(/\s+/, $labels);
 9: <STDIN>;
10:
11: my $template = 'A14 A19 A15 A8';
12:
13: my %rec;
14: while (<STDIN>) {
15:    chomp;
16:
17:    last if /^\s*$/;
18:
19:    if (/^\+/) {
20:      push @{$rec{tracks}}, substr($_, 1);
21:    } else {
22:      push @{$data{CDs}}, {%rec} if keys %rec;
23:      %rec = ();
24:      @rec{@labels} = unpack($template, $_);
25:    }
26: }
27:
28: push @{$data{CDs}}, {%rec} if keys %rec;
29:
30: ($data{count}) = (<STDIN> =~ /(\d+)/);
31:
32: if ($data{count} == @{$data{CDs}}) {
33:   print "$data{count} records processed successfully\n";
34: } else {
35:   warn "Expected $data{count} records but received ",
36:        scalar @{$data{CDs}}, "\n";
37: }
```

This code is not the best way to achieve this. We'll see a far better way when we examine the module `Parse::RecDescent` in chapter 11, but in the meantime let's take a look at the code in more detail to see where it's a bit kludgy.

Line 1 defines a hash where we will store the data that we read in.

Lines 3 and 4 read in the first two lines of data and store them in `$data{title}` and `$data{date}`, respectively.

Line 5 ignores the next line in the file (which is blank).

Lines 6 to 8 get the list of labels from the header line in the file and create an array containing the labels.

Line 9 ignores the next line in the file (which is the line of dashes).

Line 11 creates a template for extracting the data from the CD lines using `unpack`. Note that it would have been possible to create this template automatically by calculating the lengths of the fields from the header line.

Line 13 defines a hash that will store the details of each CD as we read it in.

Line 14 starts a `while` loop which will read in all of the CD data a line at a time.

Line 15 removes the end-of-line character from data record.

Line 17 terminates the loop when a blank line is found. This is because there is a blank line between the CD records and the footer data.

Line 19 checks to see if we have a CD record or a track record by examining the first character of the data. If it is a + then we have a track record, otherwise we assume we have a CD record.

Line 20 deals with the track record by removing the leading + and pushing the remaining data onto a list of tracks on our current CD.

Line 22 starts to deal with a new CD. First we need to push the previous CD record onto our list of CDs (which is stored in `$data{CDs}`). Notice that we also get to this line of code at the start of the first CD record. In this case there is no previous CD record to store. We take care of this by only storing the record if it contains data. Notice also that as we reuse the same `%rec` variable for each CD, we make an anonymous copy of it each time.

Line 23 resets the `%rec` hash to be empty, and line 24 gets the data about the new CD using `unpack`.

Having found the blank line at the end of the data section, we exit from the `while` loop at line 26. At this point the final CD is still stored in `$rec`, but hasn't been added to `$data{CDs}`. We put that right on line 28.

Line 30 grabs the number of records from the footer line in the file and then, as a sanity check, we compare that number with the number of records that we have processed and stored in `$data{CDs}`.

Figure 8.1 shows the data structure that we store the album details in.

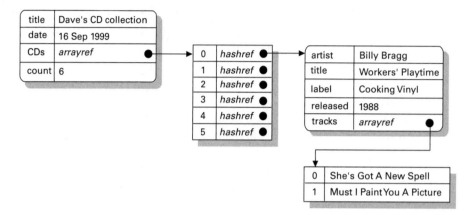

Figure 8.1   Data structure modeling the complex CD data file

As you can see, while this approach gets the job done, it is far from elegant. A better way to achieve this would be using a real parser. We will take a look at simple parsers later in this chapter, but first let's look at more limitations of our current methods.

8.2   *How not to parse HTML*

HTML and its more flexible sibling XML have become two of the most common data formats over recent years, and there is every reason to believe that they will continue to grow in popularity in the future. They are so popular, in fact, that the next two chapters are dedicated to ways of dealing with them using dedicated modules such as HTML::Parser and XML::Parser. In this section, however, I'd like to give you some idea of why these modules are necessary by pointing out the limitations in the data parsing methods that we have been using up to now.

8.2.1   *Removing tags from HTML*

A common requirement when processing HTML is to remove the HTML tags from the input, leaving only the plain text. We will, therefore, use this as our example. Let's take a simple piece of HTML and examine how we might remove the tags. Here is the sample HTML that we will use:

```
<!DOCTYPE HTML PUBLIC "-//IETF//DTD HTML//EN">
<html>
  <head>
    <title>Sample HTML</title>
  </head>

  <body>
    <h1>Sample HTML</h1>
```

```
    <p>This is a sample piece of HTML.</p>

    <ul>
      <li>It</li>
      <li>Has</li>
      <li>A</li>
      <li>List</li>
    </ul>

    <p>And links to the <a href="prev.html">Previous</a> and
      <a href="next.html">Next</a> pages.</p>
  </body>
</html>
```

Example: a first attempt

Here is a first attempt to write code that removes all of the HTML tags. I should reiterate here that all of this code is here to demonstrate the *wrong* way to do it, so you shouldn't be using this code in your programs.

```
# WARNING: This code doesn't work
use strict;

while (<STDIN>) {
  s/<.*>//;
  print;
}
```

Nothing too difficult there. Just read in the file a line at a time and remove everything that is between an opening < and a closing >. Let's see what output we get when we run that against our sample file.

and

That's probably not quite what we were hoping for. So what has gone wrong? In this case we have made a simple beginner's mistake. By default, Perl regular expressions are *greedy.* That is, they consume as much of the string as possible. What this means is that where we have a line like:

```
<h1>Sample HTML</h1>
```

our regular expression will consume all the data between the first < and the last >, effectively removing the whole line.

Example: another attempt using nongreedy regular expressions

We can, of course, correct this by making our regular expression nongreedy. We do this by placing a ? after the greedy part of the regular expression (.*), meaning our code will now look like this:

```
# WARNING: This code doesn't work either
use strict;

while (<STDIN>) {
  s/<.*?>//;
  print;
}
```

and our output looks like this:

```
Sample HTML</title>



Sample HTML</h1>

This is a sample piece of HTML.</p>


  It</li>
  Has</li>
  A</li>
  List</li>


And links to the <a href="prev.html">Previous</a> and
  Next</a> pages.</p>
```

Example: adding the g modifier

The preceding output is obviously an improvement, but instead of removing too much data we are now removing too little. We are removing only the first tag that appears on each line. We can correct this by adding the g modifier to our text replacement operator so that the code looks like this:

```
# WARNING: This code works, but only on very simple HTML
use strict;
```

```
while (<STDIN>) {
  s/<.*?>//g;
  print;
}
```

And the output will look like this:

```
Sample HTML



Sample HTML

This is a sample piece of HTML.


   It
   Has
   A
   List


And links to the Previous and
   Next pages.
```

That does look a lot better.

8.2.2 *Limitations of regular expressions*

At this point you might be tempted to think that I was exaggerating when I said that HTML parsing was difficult as we seem to have achieved it in four lines of Perl. The problem is that while we have successfully parsed this particular piece of HTML, we are still a long way from dealing with the problem in general. The HTML we have dealt with is very simple and almost certainly any real world HTML will be far more complex.

The first assumption that we have made about HTML is that all tags start and finish on the same line. You only need to look at a few web pages to see how optimistic that is. Many HTML tags have a number of attributes and can be spread out over a number of lines. Take this tag for example:

```
<img src="http://www.mag-sol.com/images/logo.gif"
     height="25" width="100"
     alt="Magnum Solutions Ltd.">
```

Currently our program will leave this tag untouched. There are, of course, ways around this. We could read the whole HTML file into a single scalar variable and run our text replacement on that variable.[3] The downside of this approach is that,

---

[3] We would have to add the s modifier to the operator, to get the . to match newline characters.

while it is not a problem for a small file like our example, there may be good reasons for not reading a larger document into memory all at once.

We have seen a number of reasons why our approach to parsing HTML is flawed. We can provide workarounds for all of the problems we have come across so far, but the next problem is a little more serious. Basically, our current methods don't understand the structure of an HTML document and don't know that different rules apply at different times. Take a look at the following piece of valid HTML:

```
<img src="/images/prev.gif" alt="<-">
<img src="/images/next.gif" alt="->">
```

In this example, the web page has graphics that link to the previous and next pages. In case the user has a text-only browser or has images switched off, the author has provided `alt` attributes which can be displayed instead of the images. Unfortunately, in the process he has completely broken our basic HTML parsing routine. The `>` symbol in the second `alt` attribute will be interpreted by our code as the end of the `img` tag. Our code doesn't know that it should ignore `>` symbols if they appear in quotes. Building regular expressions to deal with this is possible, but it will make your code much more complex and just when you've added that you'll find another complication that you'll need to deal with.

The point is that while you can solve all of these problems, there are always new problems around the corner and there comes a point when you have to stop looking for new problems to address and put the code into use. If you can be sure of the format of your HTML, you can write code which processes the subset of HTML that you know you will be dealing with, but the only way to deal with all HTML is to use an HTML parser. We'll see a lot more about parsing HTML (and also XML) in the following chapters.

8.3 Parsers

We've seen in the previous section that for certain types of data, our usual regular expression-based approach is not guaranteed to work. We must therefore find a new approach. This will involve the use of parlance.

8.3.1 An introduction to parsers

As I have hinted throughout this chapter, the solution to all of these problems is to use a parser. A *parser* is a piece of software that takes a piece of input data and looks for recognizable patterns within it. This is, of course, what all of our parsing routines have been doing, but we are now looking at a far more mathematically rigorous way of splitting up our input data.

Before I go into the details of parsing, I should point out that this is a very complex field and there is a lot of very specific jargon which I cannot address here in detail. If you find your interest piqued by this high-level summary you might want to look at the books recommended at the end of this chapter.

An introduction to parsing jargon

I said that parsers look for recognizable patterns in the input data. The first question, therefore, should be: how do parsers know what patterns to recognize? Any parser works on a grammar that defines the allowable words in the input data and their allowed relationships with each other. Although I say words, obviously in the kinds of data that we are dealing with these words can, in fact, be any string of characters. In parsing parlance they are more accurately known as *tokens*.

The grammar therefore defines the tokens that the input data should contain and how they should be related. It does this by defining a number of rules. A rule has a name and a definition. The definition contains the list of items that can be used to match the rule. These items can either be *subrules* or a definition of the actual text that makes up the token. This may all become a bit clearer if we look at a simple grammar. Figure 8.2 shows a grammar which defines a particular type of simple English sentence.

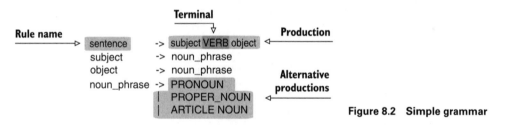

Figure 8.2 Simple grammar

This grammar says that a sentence is made up of a subject followed by a verb and an object. The verb is a *terminal* (in capital letters) which means that no further definition is required. Both the subject and the object are noun phrases and a noun phrase is defined as either a pronoun, a proper noun, or an article followed by a noun. In the last rule, pronouns, proper nouns, articles, and nouns are all terminals. Notice that the vertical bars in the definition of a noun_phrase indicate alternatives, i.e., a noun phrase rule can be matched by one of three different forms. Each of these alternatives is called a *production*.

Matching the grammar against input data

Having defined the grammar, the parser now has to match the input data against the grammar. First it will break up the input text into tokens. A separate process called a lexer often does this. The parser then examines the stream of tokens and compares it with the grammar. There are two different ways that a parser will attempt this.

Bottom-up parsers

An LR (scan left, expand rightmost subrule) parser will work like a finite state machine. Starting in a valid start state, the parser will compare the next token with the grammar to see if it matches a possible successor state. If so, it moves to the successor state and starts the process again. Figure 8.3 shows how this process works for our simple grammar. The parser begins at the Start node and takes the first token from the input stream. The parser is allowed to move to any successor state which is linked to its current state by an arrow (but only in the direction of the arrow). If the parser gets to the end of the stream of tokens and is at the Finish node, then the parse was successful; otherwise the parse has failed. If at any point the parser finds a token which does not match the successor states of its current state, then the parse also fails.

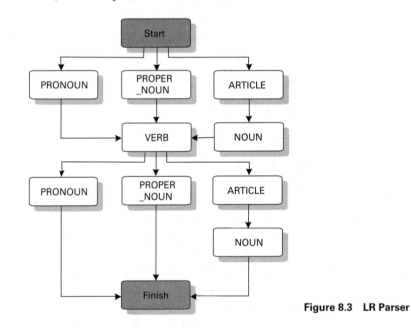

Figure 8.3   LR Parser

At any point, if the finite state machine cannot find a matching successor state, it will go back a state and try an alternative route. If it gets to the end of the input data and finds itself in a valid end state, then the parse has succeeded; if not it has failed. This type of parser is also known as a *bottom-up* parser.

Top-down parsers

An LL (scan left, expand leftmost subrule) parser will start by trying to match the highest level rule first (the sentence rule in our example). To do that, it needs to match the subrules within the top-level rule, so it would start to match the subject rule and so on down the grammar. Once it has matched all of the terminals in a rule, it knows that has matched that rule. Figure 8.4 shows the route that an LL parser would take when trying to match an input stream against out sample grammar.

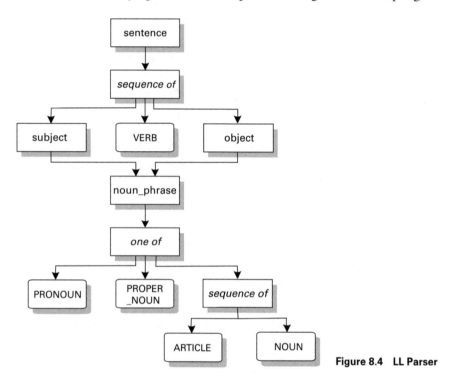

Figure 8.4 LL Parser

Matching all of the subrules in a production means that it has matched the production and, therefore, the rule that the production is part of. If the parser matches all of the subrules and terminals in one of the productions of the top-level rule, then the parse has succeeded. If the parser runs out of productions to try before matching the top-level rule, then the parse has failed. For obvious reasons, this type of parser is also known as a *top-down* parser.

8.3.2 *Parsers in Perl*

Parsers in Perl come in two types: prebuilt parsers such as HTML::Parser and XML::Parser, which are designed to parse a particular type of data, and modules such as `Parse::Yapp` and `Parse::RecDescent` which allow you to create your own parsers from a grammar which you have defined.

In the next two chapters we will take a longer look at the `HTML::Parser` and `XML::Parser` families of modules; and in chapter 11 we will examine `Parse::RecDescent`, in detail, which is the most flexible tool for creating your own parsers in Perl.

8.4 Further information

More information about parsing HTML can be found in the next chapter of this book.

For additional information about parsing in general: *Compilers: Principles, Techniques and Tools* (a.k.a. "The Dragon Book") by Aho, Sethi, and Ullman (Addison-Wesley) is the definitive guide to the field; *The Art of Compiler Design* by Pittman and Peters (Prentice Hall) is, however, a far gentler introduction.

8.5 Summary

- There are often very good reasons for having data that is not strictly in a record-based format. These reasons can include:
  - Including metadata about the data file.
  - Including subsidiary records.
- When parsing hierarchical data such as HTML our usual regular expression-based approach can break down and we need to look for more powerful techniques.
- Parsers work by examining a string of tokens to see if they match the rules defined in a grammar.
- Parsers can either be bottom-up (scan left, expand rightmost subrule) or top-down (scan left, expand leftmost subrule).

HTML

Since the explosion in interest in the World Wide Web in the 1990s, HTML has become one of the most popular file formats that we can use for the purpose of extracting data. At the end of the 1990s it seemed more and more likely that HTML would be overtaken in terms of popularity by its younger cousin, XML.

In this chapter we will look at HTML and see how to extract the data that we need from HTML documents.

9.1 *Extracting HTML data from the World Wide Web*

Perl has a set of modules which can be used to read data from the World Wide Web. This set of modules is called LWP (for Library for WWW Programming in Perl) and you can find it on the CPAN under the name libwww.[1] LWP contains modules for gleaning data from the WWW under a large number of conditions. Here we will look at only the simplest module that it contains. If these methods don't work for you then you should take a close look at the documentation that comes with LWP.

The simplest method to use when pulling data down from the web is the LWP::Simple module. This module exports a number of functions which can send an HTTP request and handle the response. The simplest of these is the get function. This function takes a URL as an argument and returns the data that is returned when that URL is requested. For example:

```
use LWP::Simple;

my $page = get('http://www.mag-sol.com/index.html');
```

will put the contents of the requested page into the variable $page. If there is an error, then get will return undef.

Two of the most common steps that you will want to take with the data returned will be to print it out or to store it in a file. LWP::Simple has functions that carry out both of these options with a single call:

```
getprint('http://www.mag-sol.com/index.html');
```

will print the page directly to STDOUT and

```
getstore('http://www.mag-sol.com/index.html', 'index.html');
```

will store the data in the (local) file index.html.

---

[1] If, however, you are using ActiveState's ActivePerl for Windows, you'll find that LWP is part of the standard installation.

9.2 Parsing HTML

Parsing HTML in Perl is all based around the HTML::Parser CPAN module.[2] This module takes either an HTML file or a chunk of HTML in a variable and splits it into individual tokens. To use HTML::Parser we need to define a number of *handler* subroutines which are called by the parser whenever it encounters certain constructions in the document being parsed.

The HTML that you want to parse can be passed to the parser in a couple of ways. If you have it in a file you can use the parse_file method, and if you have it in a variable you can use the parse method.

9.2.1 Example: simple HTML parsing

Here is a very simple HTML parser that displays all of the HTML tags and attributes it finds in an HTML page.

```
use HTML::Parser;
use LWP::Simple;

sub start {
  my ($tag, $attr, $attrseq) = @_;

  print "Found $tag\n";
  foreach (@$attrseq) {
    print " [$_ -> $attr->{$_}]\n";
  }
}

my $h = HTML::Parser->new(start_h => [\&start, 'tagname,attr,attrseq']);

my $page = get(shift);
$h->parse($page);
```

In this example, we define one handler, which is called whenever the parser encounters the start of an HTML tag. The subroutine start is defined as being a handler as part of the HTML::Parser->new call. Notice that we pass new a hash of values. The keys to the hash are the names of the handlers and the values are references to arrays that define the associated subroutines. The first element of the referenced array is a reference to the handler subroutine and the second element is a string that defines the parameters that the subroutine expects. In this case we require the name of the tag, a hash of the tag's attributes, and an array which contains the sequence

---

[2] Note that what I am describing here is HTML::Parser version 3. In this version, the module was rewritten so that it was implemented in C for increased performance. The interface was also changed. Unfortunately, the version available for ActivePerl on Win32 platforms still seems to be the older, pure Perl version, which doesn't support the new interface.

in which the attributes were originally defined. All parameters are passed to the handler as scalars. This means that the attribute hash and the attribute sequence array are actually passed as references.

In the `start` subroutine, we simply print out the type of the HTML element that we have found, together with a list of its attributes. We use the `@$attrseq` array to display the attributes following the same order in which they were defined in the original HTML. Had we relied on `keys %$attr`, we couldn't have guaranteed the attributes appearing in any particular order.

Testing the simple HTML parser

In order to test this, here is a simple HTML file:

```
<!DOCTYPE HTML PUBLIC "-//IETF//DTD HTML//EN">
<html>
<head><title>Test HTML Page</title></head>
<body bgcolor="#FFDDDD">
<h1 ALIGN=center>test HTML Page</h1>
<p>This is the first paragraph</p>
<p><font color="#0000FF">This</font> is the 2nd paragraph</p>
<p>Here is a list</p>
<ol><li>Item one</li>
<li>Item two</li></ol>
</body>
</html>
```

and here is the output we get from running it through our parser:

```
Found html
Found head
Found title
Found body
 [bgcolor -> #FFDDDD]
Found h1
 [align -> center]
Found p
Found p
Found font
 [color -> #0000FF]
Found p
Found ol
Found li
Found li
```

Each time the parser finds an HTML element, it calls `start`, which displays information about the element and its attributes. Notice that none of the actual text of the document appears in our output. For that to happen we would need to define a text handler. You would do that by declaring a `text_h` key/value pair in the call to `HTML::Parser->new`. You would define the handler in the same way, but in this case you might choose a different set of parameters. Depending on what your script was doing, you would probably choose the `text` or `dtext` parameters. Both of these parameters give you the text found, but in the `dtext` version any HTML entities are decoded.

You can see how easy it is to build up a good idea of the structure of the document. If you wanted a better picture of the structure of the document, you could also define an `end` handler and display information about closing tags as well. One option might be to keep a global variable, which was incremented each time a start tag was found, and decremented each time a close tag was found. You could then use this value to indent the data displayed according to how deeply nested the element was.

9.3 *Prebuilt HTML parsers*

`HTML::Parser` gives you a great deal of flexibility to parse HTML files in any way that you want. There are, however, a number of tasks that are common enough that someone has already written an `HTML::Parser` subclass to carry them out.

9.3.1 *HTML::LinkExtor*

One of the most popular is `HTML::LinkExtor` which is used to produce a list of all of the links in an HTML document. There are two ways to use this module. The simpler way is to parse the document and then run the `links` function, which returns an array of the links found. Each of the elements in this array is a reference to another array. The first element of this second-level array is the type of element in which the link is found. The subsequent elements occur in pairs. The first element in a pair is the name of an attribute which denotes a link, and the second is the value of that attribute. This should become a bit clearer with an example.

Example: listing links with HTML::LinkExtor

Here is a program which simply lists all of the links found in an HTML file.

```
use HTML::LinkExtor;

my $file = shift;

my $p = HTML::LinkExtor->new;

$p->parse_file($file);

my @links = $p->links;

foreach (@links) {
  print 'Type: ', shift @$_, "\n";
```

```
while (my ($name, $val) = splice(@$_, 0, 2)) {
    print "  $name -> $val\n";
  }
}
```

and here is a sample HTML file which contains a number of links of various kinds:

```
<!DOCTYPE HTML PUBLIC "-//IETF//DTD HTML//EN">
<html>
<head><title>Test HTML Page</title>
<link rel=stylesheet type='text/css' href='style.css'></head>
<body background="back.gif">
<h1 ALIGN=center>test HTML Page</h1>
<p>This is the first paragraph.
It contains a <a href="http://www.perl.com/">link</a></p>
<p><font color="#0000FF">This</font> is the 2nd paragraph.
It contains an image - <img src="test.gif"></p>
<p>Here is an image used as a link<br>
<a href="http://www.pm.org"><img src="pm.gif" lowsrc="pmsmall.gif"></a></p>
</body>
</html>
```

When we run this program on this HTML file, the output is as follows:

```
Type: link
  href -> style.css
Type: body
  background -> back.gif
Type: a
  href -> http://www.perl.com/
Type: img
  src -> test.gif
Type: a
  href -> http://www.pm.org
Type: img
  src -> pm.gif
  lowsrc -> pmsmall.gif
```

Example: listing specific types of links with HTML::LinkExtor

As you can see, there are a number of different types of links that HTML:LinkExtor returns. The complete list changes as the HTML specification changes, but basically any element that can refer to an external file is examined during parsing. If you only want to look at, say, links within an a tag, then you have a couple of options. You can either parse the file as we've just discussed and only use the links you are interested in when you iterate over the list of links (using code something like: next unless $_->[0] eq 'a'), or you can use the second, more complex, interface to HTML::LinkExtor. For this interface, you need to pass the new function a reference to a function which the parser will call each time it encounters a link. This function will be passed the name of the element containing the link together with pairs of parameters indicating the names and values of attributes which contain the actual links. Here is an example which displays only the a links within a file:

```
use HTML::LinkExtor;

my $file = shift;

my $p = HTML::LinkExtor->new(\&check);

$p->parse_file($file);

my @links;

foreach (@links) {
  print 'Type: ', shift @$_, "\n";
  while (my ($name, $val) = splice(@$_, 0, 2)) {
    print "  $name -> $val\n";
  }
}
sub check {
  push @links, [@_] if $_[0] eq 'a';
}
```

Running our test HTML file through this program gives us the following output:

```
Type: a
  href -> http://www.perl.com/
Type: a
  href -> http://www.pm.org
```

which only lists the links that we are interested in.

9.3.2 HTML::TokeParser

Another useful prebuilt HTML parser module is HTML::TokeParser. This parser effectively turns the standard HTML::Parser interface on its head. HTML::TokeParser parses the file and stores the contents as a stream of tokens. You can request the next token from the stream using the get_tag method. This method takes an optional parameter which is a tag name. If this argument is used then the parser will skip tags until it reaches a tag of the given type. There is also a get_text function which returns the text at the current position in the stream.

Example: extracting <h1> elements with HTML::TokeParser

For example, to extract all of the <h1> elements from an HTML file you could use code this way:

```
use HTML::TokeParser;

my $file = shift;
```

```
my $p = HTML::TokeParser->new($file);

while ($p->get_tag('h1')) {
  print $p->get_text(), "\n";
}
```

We will use the following HTML file to test this program:

```
<!DOCTYPE HTML PUBLIC "-//IETF//DTD HTML//EN">
<html>
<head><title>Test HTML Page</title>
</head>
<body>
<h1>The first major item</h1>
<h2>Section 1.1</h2>
<p>Some text<p>
<h2>Section 1.2</h2>
<h3>Section 1.2.1</h3>
<p>blah</p>
<h3>Section 1.2.2</h3>
<p>blah</p>
<h1>Another major header</h1>
<h2>Section 2.1</h2>
<h3>Section 2.1.1</h3>
<h3>Section 2.1.2</h3>
<h2>Section 2.2</h2>
</body>
</html>
```

and here is the output:

```
The first major item
Another major header
```

Example: listing all header tags with HTML::TokeParser

A more sophisticated approach might be to look at the structure of the document by examining all of the headers in the document. In this case we need to look a little more closely at the return value from get_tag. This is a reference to an array, the elements of which are different for start tags and close tags. For start tags the elements are: the tag name, a reference to a hash containing attribute names and values, a reference to an array indicating the original order of the attributes, and the original HTML text. For an end tag the array contains the name of the tag prefixed with the character / and the original HTML text.

We can therefore iterate over all of the tags in a document, checking them to see which ones are headers and displaying the structure of the document using code like this:

```
use HTML::TokeParser;

my $file = shift;
```

```
my $p = HTML::TokeParser->new($file);

my $tag;
while ($tag = $p->get_tag()) {
  next unless $tag->[0] =~ /^h(\d)/;

  my $level = $1;

  print ' ' x $level, "Head $level: ", $p->get_text(), "\n";
}
```

Notice that we only process tags where the name matches the regular expression
/^h(\d)/. This ensures that we only see HTML header tags. We put brackets
around the \d to capture this value in $1. This value indicates the level of the header
we have found and we can use it to calculate how far to indent the output. Running
this program on our previous sample HTML file gives the following output:

```
Head 1: The first major item
  Head 2: Section 1.1
  Head 2: Section 1.2
   Head 3: Section 1.2.1
   Head 3: Section 1.2.2
 Head 1: Another major header
  Head 2: Section 2.1
   Head 3: Section 2.1.1
   Head 3: Section 2.1.2
  Head 2: Section 2.2
```

which is a very useful outline of the structure of the document.

9.3.3 *HTML::TreeBuilder and HTML::Element*

Another very useful subclass of HTML::Parser is HTML::TreeBuilder. As you can
probably guess from its name, this class builds a parse tree that represents an HTML
document. Each node in the tree is an HTML::Element object.

Example: parsing HTML with HTML::Treebuilder

Here is a simple script which uses HTML::TreeBuilder to parse an HTML document.

```
#!/usr/bin/perl -w
use strict;
use HTML::TreeBuilder;

my $h = HTML::TreeBuilder->new;

$h->parse_file(shift);

$h->dump;

print $h->as_HTML;
```

In this example we create a new parser object using the `HTML::Treebuilder->new` method. We then parse our file using the new object's `parse_file` method.[3] Notice that, unlike some other tree-based parsers, this function doesn't return a new tree object, rather the parse tree is built within the parser object itself.

As the example demonstrates, this class has a couple of ways to display the parse tree. Both of these are, in fact, inherited from the `HTML::Element` class. The `dump` method prints a simple representation of the element and its descendents and the `as_HTML` method prints the element and its descendents as HTML. This might seem a little less than useful given that we have just created the parse tree *from* an HTML file, but there are at least three reasons why this might be useful. First, a great many HTML files aren't strictly valid HTML. `HTML::TreeBuilder` does a good job of parsing invalid HTML and the `as_HTML` method can then be used to output valid HTML. Second, the `HTML::Element` has a number of methods for changing the parse tree, so you can alter your page and then use the `as_HTML` method to produce the altered page. And third, the tree can be scanned in ways that would be inconvenient or impossible with just a token stream.

Notice that I've been saying that you can call `HTML::Element` methods on an `HTML::TreeBuilder` object. This is because `HTML::TreeBuilder` inherits from both `HTML::Parser` and `HTML::Element`. An HTML document should always start with an `<HTML>` and end with a `</HTML>` tag and therefore the whole document can be viewed as an HTML element, with all of the other elements contained within it. It is, therefore, valid to call `HTML::Element` methods on our `HTML::TreeBuilder` object.

Both `HTML::TreeBuilder` and `HTML::Element` are part of the HTML-Tree bundle of modules which can be found on the CPAN.

9.4 *Extended example: getting weather forecasts*

To finish this section, here is an example demonstrating the extraction of useful data from web pages. We will get a weather forecast for the Central London area from Yahoo! The front page to Yahoo!'s U.K. weather service is at weather.yahoo.co.uk and by following a couple of links we can find that the address of the page containing the weather forecast for London is at http://uk.weather.yahoo.com/1208/index_c.html. In order to extract the relevant data from the file we need to examine the HTML source for the page. You can either use the View Source menu option of your browser or write a quick Perl script using LWP and `getstore` to store the page in a file.

---

[3] Note that `HTML::Treebuilder` supports the same parsing interface as `HTML::Parser`, so you could just as easily call `$h->parse`, passing it a variable containing HTML to parse.

Having retrieved a copy of the page we can examine it to find out where in the page we can find the data that we want. Looking at the Yahoo! page I found that the description of the weather outlook was within the first <font> tag after the sixth <table> tag. The high and low temperature measurements were within the following two <b> tags.[4] Armed with this knowledge, we can write a program which will extract the weather forecast and display it to the user. The program looks like this:

```
use HTML::TokeParser;
use LWP::Simple;

my $addr = 'http://uk.weather.yahoo.com/1208/index_c.html';

my $page = get $addr;

my $p = HTML::TokeParser->new(\$page)
  || die "Parse error\n";

$p->get_tag('table') || die "Not enough table tags!" foreach (1 .. 6);

$p->get_tag('font');
my $desc = $p->get_text, "\n";

$p->get_tag('b');
my $high = $p->get_text;
$p->get_tag('b');
my $low = $p->get_text;

print "$desc\nHigh: $high, Low: $low\n";
```

You will notice that I've used HTML::TokeParser in this example. I could have also chosen another HTML::Parser subclass or even written my own, but HTML::TokeParser is a good choice for this task as it is very easy to target specific elements, such as the sixth <table> tag, and then move to the next <font> tag.

In the program we use LWP::Simple to retrieve the required page from the web site and then parse it using HTML::TokeParser. We then step through the parsed document looking for <table> tags, until we find the sixth one. At this point we find the next <font> tag and extract the text within it using the get_text method. This gives us the brief weather outlook. We then move in turn to each of the next two <b> tags and for each one extract the text from it. This gives us the forecast high and low temperatures. We can then format all of this information in a nice way and present it to the user.

This has been a particularly simple example, but similar techniques can be used to extract just about any information that you can find on the World Wide Web.

---

[4] You should, of course, bear in mind that web pages change very frequently. By the time you read this, Yahoo! may well have changed the design of this page which will render this program useless.

9.5   *Further information*

LWP and `HTML::Parser` together with all of the other modules that we have discussed in this section are not part of the standard Perl distribution. You will need to download them from the CPAN (at www.cpan.org).

A very good place to get help with these modules is the LWP mailing list. To subscribe, send a blank email to libwww-subscribe@perl.org (but please make sure that you have read all of the documentation that comes with the module before posting a question).

9.6   *Summary*

- HTML is one of the most common data formats that you will come across because of its popularity on the World Wide Web.

- You can retrieve HTML documents from the Internet using the LWP bundle of modules from the CPAN.

- The main Perl module used for parsing HTML is `HTML::Parser`, but you may well never need to use it, because subclasses like `HTML::LinkExtor`, `HTML::TokeParser`, and `HTML::TreeBuilder` are often more useful for particular tasks.

XML

What this chapter covers:

- What is XML and what's wrong with HTML?
- Parsing XML
- Using handlers to control the parser
- Parsing XML using the Document
  Object Model
- Converting an XML document to POD,
  HTML, or plain text

175

Over the next few years, it looks as though XML will become the data exchange format of choice for a vast number of computer systems. In this chapter we will take a look at some of the tools available for parsing XML with Perl.

10.1 XML overview

One of the problems we had when extracting the weather information from the web page in the previous chapter was that it was difficult to know where in the page to find the data we needed. The only way to do it was to closely examine the HTML file and work out which tags surrounded our required data. This also meant that each time the design of the page was changed, we would have to rework our program.

10.1.1 What's wrong with HTML?

The reason this was so difficult was that HTML was designed to model the logical structure of a document, not the meaning of the various elements. For example, an HTML document makes it easy to recognize headings at various levels, paragraphs, lists, and various other publishing elements. You can tell when an element should be printed in bold, but the problem is that you don't know *why* that particular element was bold. It could be purely for emphasis, it could be because it is a row heading in a table, or it could be because it is the temperature on a weather page.

Our task would be a lot easier if the mark-up in a document told us more about the actual meaning of the data. In our weather example, it would be nice if there was a <FORECAST> ... </FORECAST> element that surrounded the actual forecast description and perhaps a <TEMPERATURE> ... </TEMPERATURE> element which surrounded each of the temperature figures in which we were interested. Even better, the <TEMPERATURE> element could have attributes which told us whether it was a maximum or minimum temperature and whether it was in degrees Fahrenheit or Celsius.

10.1.2 What is XML?

This is exactly the kind of problem that XML was designed to solve. XML is the *Extensible Mark-up Language*. In fact it isn't really a mark-up language at all, it is a method to define new mark-up languages which are better suited to particular tasks. The way it works is by defining a syntax for *Document Type Definitions* (DTDs). A DTD defines the set of elements that are allowed in a document, together with their attributes and relationships to each other. It will define which elements are mandatory or optional, whether there is any defined order, and which elements can (or must) contain other elements. The exact syntax of DTDs is beyond the scope of this book, but there are a number of specialized books which cover it in some detail (for example *XML Pocket Reference* by Robert Eckstein and published by O'Reilly).

Sample XML file

Going back to our weather forecast example, we could design a DTD that defined a file format for weather forecasts. Let's keep it very simple and say that a sample would look like this:

```
<FORECAST>
  <OUTLOOK>
    Partly Cloudy
  </OUTLOOK>
  <TEMPERATURE TYPE="MAX" DEGREES="C">12</TEMPERATURE>
  <TEMPERATURE TYPE="MIN" DEGREES="C">6</TEMPERATURE>
</FORECAST>
```

If Yahoo! (or any other information provider) made a file available in this format then we could download it from the Internet and parse it using Perl to extract the relevant information. If the parser that we wrote was sophisticated enough, Yahoo! could reorder the contents of the source file and we would still be able to access the data. This is because the file is marked up to show what each data element is, not how it should be displayed.[1]

Valid vs. well-formed

It's worth stopping at this point to discuss a couple of XML concepts. There are two levels of XML correctness. A correct XML document can be said to be *valid* or it can be said to be *well-formed*. Well-formed is the easier criterion to adhere to. This means that the document is syntactically correct or, in other words, it follows all of the general rules for XML documents. Basically, these rules say this:

- The document must have one top-level element.
- All elements must have opening and closing tags (except in the special case of empty tags where the opening tag is also used as the closing tag).
- Opening and closing tags must be nested correctly (i.e., nested tags must be closed in the reverse of the order in which they were opened).
- All attributes must be quoted and cannot contain a < or an & (except as the first character of a reference).

Our sample weather document fulfills all of these constraints and is, therefore, well-formed. It cannot, however, be described as valid. A valid document is one that

---

[1] XML fans have been known to disparage HTML by describing it as a "What You See Is *All* You Get" language.

follows the rules laid down in a DTD. This means that it must have all of the correct elements in the right order and any nesting of elements must also be in combinations sanctioned by the DTD. If we wrote a weather DTD and wrote our weather document to conform with that DTD then we could call it valid. Currently, we don't have such a DTD so there is no way that our document can be valid.

XML parsers fall into two types. Validating parsers will check the document's structure against its DTD and nonvalidating parsers only check that the document is well-formed.

10.2 *Parsing XML with XML::Parser*

Of course there are Perl XML parsers available. The most generalized one is the CPAN module XML::Parser. This module is based on an XML parser called Expat. Expat is a nonvalidating parser, so in Perl you will generally only be interested in the well-formedness of documents.[2]

XML::Parser works in a similar way to HTML::Parser, but as XML is more complex than HTML, XML::Parser needs to be more complex than HTML::Parser.

10.2.1 *Example: parsing weather.xml*

As an example of using XML::Parser, here is a simple script to parse our weather XML file:

```
use strict;
use XML::Parser;

my %forecast;
my @curr;
my $type;

my $p = XML::Parser->new(Style => 'Stream');

$p->parsefile(shift);

print "Outlook: $forecast{outlook}\n";
foreach (keys %forecast) {
  next if /outlook/;
  print "$_: $forecast{$_}->{val} $forecast{$_}->{deg}\n";
}

sub StartTag {
  my ($p, $tag) = @_;

    push @curr, $tag;
```

---

[2] I hope this explains my reluctance to go into the details of DTDs—XML::Parser makes no use of them. There is, however, an experimental subclass of XML::Parser, called XML::Checker::Parser, which does validate an XML document against a DTD.

```
        if ($tag eq 'TEMPERATURE') {
        $type = $_{TYPE};
        $forecast{$type}->{deg} = $_{DEGREES};
    }
}
sub EndTag {
  pop @curr;
};

sub Text {
  my ($p) = shift;

  return unless /\S/;

  s/^\s+//;
  s/\s+$//;

  if ($curr[-1] eq 'OUTLOOK') {
    $forecast{outlook} .= $_;
  } elsif ( $curr[-1] eq 'TEMPERATURE') {
    $forecast{$type}->{val} = $_;
  }
}
```

Running this script against our sample weather XML document gives the following result:

```
Outlook: Partly Cloudy
MAX: 12 C
MIN: 6 C
```

10.2.2 Using XML::Parser

There are a number of different ways to use XML::Parser. In this example we are using it in a very similar manner to HTML::Parser. When we create the parser object we pass it a hash containing various configuration options. In this case, the hash consists of one key (Style) and an associated value, which is the string Stream. The Style parameter tells XML::Parser that we want to use one of a number of built-in parsing methods. The one that we want to use in this example is called Stream. In this mode XML::Parser works very similarly to HTML::Parser. There are a number of predefined methods which the parser will call when encountering various parts of the XML document. For this example we need to define three of these methods. StartTag is called when the start of an XML tag is found, EndTag is called when the end of a tag is seen, and Text is called when text data is encountered. In each case the first parameter to the function will be a reference to the underlying Expat object which is doing the parsing. In the StartTag and EndTag functions the second parameter is the name of the tag which is being started or ended. The complete original tag is stored in $_. Additionally, in the StartTag function, the list of attributes is stored in %_. In the Text function, the text that has been found is stored in $_.

This may all make a bit more sense if we look at the example code in more detail.

The main part of the program defines some global variables, creates the parser, parses the file, and displays the information which has been extracted. The global variables which it defines are: %forecast, which will store the forecast data that we want to display, @curr which is a list of all of the current elements that we are in, and $type which stores the current temperature type. All of the real work goes on in the parsing functions which are called by the parser as it processes the file.

The StartTag function pushes the new tag on to the end of the @curr array, and if the tag starts a TEMPERATURE element, it stores the values of the TYPE and DEGREES attributes (which it finds in %_).

The EndTag function simply pops the last element from the @curr array. You might think that we should check whether the tag that we are ending is of the same type as the current end of this list but, if it wasn't the case, the document wouldn't be well-formed and would, therefore, fail the parsing process.[3]

The Text function checks whether there is useful data in the text string (which is stored in $_) and returns if it can't find at least one nonspace character. It then strips leading and trailing spaces from the data. If the current element we are processing (given by $curr[-1]) is the OUTLOOK element, then the text must be the outlook description and we store it in the appropriate place in the %forecast variable. If the current element is a TEMPERATURE element, then the text will be the temperature data and that is also stored in the %forecast hash (making use of the current temperature type which is stored in the global $type variable).

Once the parsing is complete the data is all stored in the %forecast hash and we can traverse the hash to display the required data. Notice that the method that we use for this makes no assumptions about the list of temperature types used. If we were to add average temperature data to the weather document, our program would still display this.

Parsing failures

XML::Parser (and the other parsers which are based on it) have a somewhat harsh approach to non-well-formed XML documents. They will always throw a fatal exception when they encounter non-well-formed XML. Unfortunately, this behavior is defined in the XML specifications, so they have no choice about this, but it can

---

[3] This always throws a fatal exception, but there are ways to prevent your program from dying if you give it non-well-formed XML, as we will see later.

still take beginners by surprise as they often expect the `parse` or `parsefile` method to return an error code, but instead their entire program is halted.

It's difficult to see what processing you might want to proceed with if your XML document is incorrect, so in many cases dying is the correct approach for a program to take. If, however, you have a case where you want to recover a little more gracefully you can catch the fatal exception. You do this using `eval`. If the code that is passed to `eval` causes an exception, the program does not die, but the error message is put in the variable `$@`. You can therefore parse your XML documents using code like this:

```
eval { $p->parsefile($file) };

if ($@) {
  die "Bad XML Document: $file\n";
} else {
  print "Good XML!\n";
}
```

10.2.3 *Other XML::Parser styles*

The Stream style is only one of a number of styles which `XML::Parser` supports. Depending on your requirements, another style might be better suited to the task.

Debug

The Debug style simply prints out a stylized version of your XML document. Parsing our weather example file using the Debug style gives us the following output:

```
\\ ()
FORECAST || #10;
FORECAST ||
FORECAST \\ ()
FORECAST OUTLOOK || #10;
FORECAST OUTLOOK ||        Partly Cloudy
FORECAST OUTLOOK || #10;
FORECAST OUTLOOK ||
FORECAST //
FORECAST || #10;
FORECAST ||
FORECAST \\ (TYPE MAX DEGREES C)
FORECAST TEMPERATURE || 12
FORECAST //
FORECAST || #10;
FORECAST ||
FORECAST \\ (TYPE MIN DEGREES C)
FORECAST TEMPERATURE || 6
FORECAST //
FORECAST || #10;
  //
```

If you look closely, you will see the structure of our weather document in this display. A line containing the opening tag of a new element contains the character sequence \\ and the attributes of the element appear in brackets. A line containing the character sequence // denotes an element's closing tag, and a line containing the character sequence || denotes the text contained within an element. The #10 sequences denote the end of each line of text in the original document.

Subs

The Subs style works in a very similar manner to the Stream style, except that instead of the same functions being called for the start and end tags of each element, a different pair of functions is called for each element type. For example, in our weather document, the parser would expect to find functions called FORECAST and OUTLOOK that it would call when it found <FORECAST> and <OUTLOOK> tags. For the closing tags, it would look for functions called _FORECAST and _OUTLOOK. This method prevents the program from having to check which element type is being processed (although this information is still passed to the function as the second parameter).

Tree

All of the styles that we have seen so far have been *stream-based*. That is, they move through the document and call certain functions in your code when they come across particular events in the document. The Tree style does things differently. It parses the document and builds a data structure containing a logical model of the document. It then returns a reference to this data structure.

The data structure generated by our weather document looks like this:

```
[ 'FORECAST', [ {}, 0, "\n  ",
  'OUTLOOK', [ {}, 0, "\n    Partly Cloudy\n  "], 0, "\n  ",
  'TEMPERATURE', [ { 'DEGREES' => 'C', 'TYPE' => 'MAX' }, 0, '12' ], 0, "\n ",
  'TEMPERATURE', [ { 'DEGREES' => 'C', 'TYPE' => 'MAX' }, 0, '6'  ], 0, "\n"
] ]
```

It's probably a little difficult to follow, so let's look at it in detail.

Each element is represented by a list. The first item is the element type and the second item is a reference to another list which represents the contents of the element. The first element of this second level list is a reference to a hash which contains the attributes for the element. If the element has no attributes then the reference to the hash still exists, but the hash itself is empty. The rest of the list is a series of pairs of items, which represent the text, and elements that are contained within the element. These pairs of items have the same structure as the original two-item list, with the exception that a text item has a special element type of 0.

If you're the sort of person who thinks that a picture is worth a thousand words, then figure 10.1 might have saved me a lot of typing.

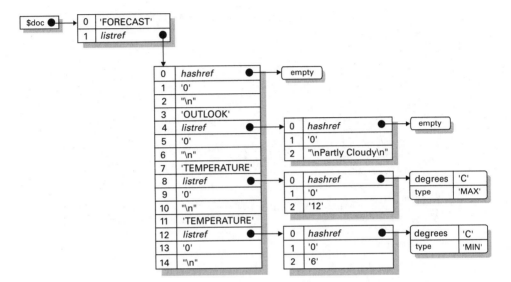

Figure 10.1 Output from XML::Parser **Tree style**

In the figure the variable $doc is returned from the parser. You can also see the arrays which contain the definitions of the XML content and the hashes which contain the attributes.

Example: using XML::Parser in Tree style

This may become clearer still if we look at some sample code for dealing with one of these structures. The following program will print out the structure of an XML document. Using it to process our weather document will give us the following output:

```
FORECAST []

OUTLOOK []
  Partly Cloudy

TEMPERATURE [DEGREES: C, TYPE: MAX]
  12

TEMPERATURE [DEGREES: C, TYPE: MIN]
  6
```

Here is the code:

```
use strict;
use XML::Parser;
```

```perl
my $p = XML::Parser->new(Style => 'Tree');

my $doc = $p->parsefile(shift);

my $level = 0;

process_node(@$doc);

sub process_node {
  my ($type, $content) = @_;

  my $ind = ' ' x $level;

  if ($type) { # element
    my $attrs = shift @$content;

    print $ind, $type, ' [';
    print join(', ', map { "$_: $attrs->{$_}" } keys %{$attrs});
    print "]\n";

    ++$level;
    while (my @node = splice(@$content, 0, 2)) {
      process_node(@node); # Recursively call this subroutine
    }
    --$level;

  } else { # text
    $content =~ s/\n/ /g;
    $content =~ s/^\s+//;
    $content =~ s/\s+$//;
    print $ind, $content, "\n";
  }
}
```

Let's look at the code in more detail.

The start of the program looks similar to any number of other parsing programs that we've seen in this chapter. The only difference is that we create our XML:Parser object with the Tree style. This means that the `parsefile` method returns us a reference to our tree structure.

As we've seen above, this is a reference to a list with two items in it. We'll call one of these two-item lists a *node* and write a function called `process_node` which will handle one of these lists. Before calling `process_node`, we initialize a global variable to keep track of the current element nesting level.

In the `process_node` function, the first thing that we do is determine the type of node we are dealing with. If it is an element, then the first item in the node list will have a `true` value. Text nodes have the value 0 in this position, which will evaluate as `false`.

If we are dealing with an element, then `shifting` the first element off of the content list will give us a reference to the attribute hash. We can then print out the element type and attribute list indented to the correct level.

Having dealt with the element and its attributes we can process its contents. One advantage of using `shift` to get the attribute hash reference is that it now leaves the content list with an even number of items in it. Each pair of items is another node. We can simply use `splice` to pull the nodes off the array one at a time and pass them recursively to `process_node`, pausing only to increment the level before processing the content and decrementing it again when finished.

If the node is text, then the second item in the node list will be the actual text. In this case we just clean it up a bit and print it out.

Example: parsing weather.xml using the Tree style

This program will work with any tree structure that is generated by XML::Parser using the Tree style. However, more often you will want to do something a little more specific to the document with which you are dealing. In our case, this will be printing out a weather forecast. Here is a Tree-based program for printing the forecast in our usual format.

```perl
use strict;
use XML::Parser;

my $p = XML::Parser->new(Style => 'Tree');

my $doc = $p->parsefile(shift);

process_node(@$doc);

sub process_node {
  my ($type, $content) = @_;

  if ($type eq 'OUTLOOK') {
    print 'Outlook: ', trim($content->[2]), "\n";
  } elsif ($type eq 'TEMPERATURE') {
    my $attrs = $content->[0];

    my $temp = trim($content->[2]);
    print "$attrs->{TYPE}: $temp $attrs->{DEGREES}\n";
  }

  if ($type) {
    while (my @node = splice @$content, 1, 2) {
      process_node(@node)
    }
  }
}

sub trim {
```

```
local $_ = shift;

s/\n/ /g;
s/^\s+//;
s/\s+$//;

return $_;
}
```

The basic structure of this program is quite similar to the previous one. All of the work is still done in the `process_node` function. In this version, however, we are on the lookout for particular element types which we know we want to process. When we find an OUTLOOK element or a TEMPERATURE element we know exactly what we need to do. All other elements are simply ignored. In the case of an OUTLOOK element we simply extract the text from the element and print it out. Notice that the text contained within the element is found at `$content->[2]`, the third item in the content array. This is true for any element that only contains text, as the first two items in the content list will always be a reference to the attribute hash and the character 0.

The processing for the TEMPERATURE element type is only slightly more complex as we need to access the attribute hash to find out the type of the temperature (minimum or maximum) and the kind of degrees in which is it measured.

Notice that we still need to process any child elements and that this is still done in the same way as in the previous program—by removing nodes from the `@$content` list. In this case we haven't removed the attribute hash from the front of the list, so we start the `splice` from the second item in the list (the second item has the index 0).

Objects

The Objects style works very much like the Tree style, except that instead of arrays and hashes, the document tree is presented as a collection of objects. Each element type becomes a different object class. The name of the class is created by appending main:: to the front of the element's name.[4] Text data is turned into an object of class main::Characters. The value that is returned by the `parse` method is a reference to an array of such objects. As a well-formed XML object can only have one top-level element, this array will only have one element.

---

[4] This is the default behavior. You can create your objects within other packages by using the Pkg option to XML::Parser->new. For example:

```
my $p = XML::Parser->new(Style => 'Objects', Pkg => 'Some_Other_Package');
```

Attributes of the element are stored in the element hash. This hash also contains a special key, Kids. The value associated with this key is a reference to an array which contains all of the children of the element.

Example: parsing XML with XML::Parser using the Objects style

Here is a program that displays the structure of any given XML document using the Objects style:

```perl
use strict;
use XML::Parser;

my $p = XML::Parser->new(Style => 'Objects');

my $doc = $p->parsefile(shift);

my $level = 0;

process_node($doc->[0]);

sub process_node {
  my ($node) = @_;

  my $ind = ' ' x $level;

  my $type = ref $node;
  $type =~ s/^.*:://;

  if ($type ne 'Characters') {
    my $attrs = {%$node};
    delete $attrs->{Kids};

    print $ind, $type, ' [';
    print join(', ', map { "$_: $attrs->{$_}" } keys %{$attrs});
    print "]\n";

    ++$level;
    foreach my $node (@{$node->{Kids}}) {
      process_node($node);
    }
    --$level;
  } else {
    my $content = $node->{Text};
    $content =~ s/\n/ /g;
    $content =~ s/^\s+//;
    $content =~ s/\s+$//;
    print $ind, $content, "\n" if $content =~ /\S/;
  }
}
```

This program is very similar to the example that we wrote using the Tree style. Once again, most of the processing is carried out in the process_node function. In this case each node is represented by a single reference rather than a two-item list. The first thing that we do in `process_node` is to work out the type of element with which we are dealing. We do this by using the standard Perl function `ref`. This function takes one parameter, which is a reference, and returns a string containing the type of object that the reference refers to. For example, if you pass it a reference to an array, it will return the string `ARRAY`. This is a good way to determine the object type a reference has been `blessed` into. In our case, each reference that we pass to it will be of type `main::Element`, where `Element` is the name of one of our element types. We remove the `main::` from the front of the string to leave us with the specific element with which we are dealing.

If we are dealing with an element (rather than character data) we then take a copy of the object hash which we will use to get the list of attributes. Notice that we don't use the more obvious `$attrs = $node` as this only copies the reference and still leaves it pointing to the same original hash. As the next line of the code deletes the `Kids` array reference from this hash, we use the slightly more complex `$attrs = {%$node}` as this takes a copy of the original hash and returns a reference to the new copy. We can then delete the `Kids` reference without doing any lasting damage to the original object.

Having retrieved the attribute hash, we display the element type along with its attributes. We then need to process all of the element's children. We do this by iterating across the `Kids` array (which is why it's a good idea that we didn't delete the original earlier), passing each object in turn to `process_node`.

If the object with which we are dealing is of the class Characters then it contains character data and we can access the actual text by using the special `Text` key.

Choosing between Tree and Object styles

The Tree and Object styles can both be used to address the same set of problems. You would usually use one of these two styles when your document processing requires multiple passes over the document structure. Whether you choose the Tree or Objects style for your tree-based parsing requirements is simply a matter of personal taste.

10.2.4 *XML::Parser handlers*

The `XML::Parser` styles that we have been discussing are a series of prebuilt methods for parsing XML documents in a number of popular ways. If none of these styles meet your requirements, there is another way that you can use `XML::Parser` which gives even more control over the way it works. This is accomplished by setting up a series of *handlers* which can respond to various events that are triggered while parsing a document. This is very similar to the way we used `HTML::Parser` or the Stream style of `XML::Parser`.

Handlers can be set to process a large number of XML constructs. The most obvious ones are the start and end of an XML element or character data, but you can also set handlers for the XML declaration, various DTD definitions, XML comments, processing instructions, and any other construct that you find in an XML document.

You set handlers either by using the `Handlers` parameter when you create a parser object, or by using the `setHandlers` method later on. If you use the `Handlers` parameter then the value associated with the parameter should be a reference to a hash. In this hash the keys will be handler names, and each value will be a reference to the appropriate function.

Different handler functions receive different sets of parameters. The full set of handlers and their parameters can be found in the `XML::Parser` documentation, but here is a brief summary of the most frequently used ones:

- *Init*—Called before parsing of a document begins. It is passed a reference to the Expat parser object.

- *Final*—Called after parsing of a document is complete. It is passed a reference to the Expat parser object.

- *Start*—Called when the opening tag of an XML element is encountered. It is passed a reference to the Expat parser object, the name of the element, and a series of pairs of values which represents the name and value of the element's attributes.

- *End*—Called when the closing tag of an XML element is encountered. It is passed a reference to the Expat parser object and the name of the element.

- *Char*—Called when character data is encountered. It is passed a reference to the Expat parser object and the string of characters that has been found.

All of these subroutines are passed a reference to the Expat parser object. This is the actual object that `XML::Parser` uses to parse your XML document. It is useful in some more complex parsing techniques, but at this point you can safely ignore it.

Example: parsing XML using XML::Parser handlers

Here is an example of our usual program for displaying the document structure, rewritten to use handlers.

```
use strict;
use XML::Parser;

my $p = XML::Parser->new(Handlers => {Init  => \&init,
                                      Start => \&start,
                                      End   => \&end,
                                      Char  => \&char});

my ($level, $ind);
```

```
my $text;

$p->parsefile(shift);

sub init {
  $level = 0;
  $text = '';
}

sub start {
  my ($p, $tag) = (shift, shift);

  my %attrs = @_ if @_;

  print $ind, $tag, ' [';
  print join ', ', map { "$_: $attrs{$_}" } keys %attrs;
  print "]\n";

  $level++;
  $ind = ' ' x $level;
}

sub end {
  print $ind, $text, "\n";
  $level--;
  $ind = ' ' x $level;
  $text = '';
}

sub char {
  my ($p, $str) = (shift, shift);

  return unless $str =~ /\S/;

  $str =~ s/^\s+//;
  $str =~ s/\s+$//;

  $text .= $str;
}
```

In this case we only need to define four handlers for Init, Start, End, and Char. The Init handler only exists to allow us to set $level and $text to initial values.

In the Start handler we do very similar processing to the previous examples. That is, we print the element's name and attributes. In this case it is very easy to get these values as they are passed to us as parameters. We also increment $level and use the new value to calculate an indent string which we will print before any output.

In the End handler we print out any text that has been built up in $text, decrement $level, recalculate $ind, and reset $text to an empty string.

In the Char handler we do the usual cleaning that strips any leading and trailing white space and appends the string to $text. Notice that it is possible that because of the way the parser works, any particular sequence of character data can be split up and processed in a number of calls to this handler. This is why we build up the string and print it out only when we find the closing element tag. This would be even more important if we were applying some kind of formatting to the text before displaying it.

10.3 *XML::DOM*

As we have seen, XML::Parser is a very powerful and flexible module, and one that can be used to handle just about any XML processing requirement. However, it's well known that one of the Perl mottoes is that there's more than one way to do it, and one of the cardinal virtues of a programmer is laziness.[5] It should not therefore come as a surprise that there are many other XML parser modules available from the CPAN. Some of these are specialized to deal with XML that conforms to a particular DTD (we will look at one of these a bit later), but many others present yet more ways to handle general XML parsing tasks. Probably the most popular of these is XML::DOM. This is a tree-based parser which returns a radically different view of an XML document.

XML::DOM implements the Document Object Model. DOM is a way to access arbitrary parts of an XML document. DOM has been defined by the World Wide Web Consortium (W3C), and is rapidly becoming a standard method to parse and access XML documents.

XML::DOM is a subclass of XML::Parser, so all XML::Parser methods are still available, but on top of these methods, XML::DOM implements a whole new set of methods which allow you to walk the document tree.

10.3.1 *Example: parsing XML using XML::DOM*

As an example of XML::DOM in use, here is our usual document structure script rewritten to use it.

```
use strict;
use XML::DOM;

my $p = XML::DOM::Parser->new;

my $doc = $p->parsefile(shift);

my $level = 0;

process_node($doc->getFirstChild);
```

---

[5] The other two being impatience and hubris, according to Larry Wall.

```
sub process_node {
  my ($node) = @_;

    my $ind = ' ' x $level;;

  my $nodeType = $node->getNodeType;
  if ($nodeType == ELEMENT_NODE) {
    my $type = $node->getTagName;

    my $attrs = $node->getAttributes;

    print $ind, $type, ' [';
    my @attrs;
    foreach (0 .. $attrs->getLength - 1) {
      my $attr = $attrs->item($_);
      push @attrs, $attr->getNodeName . ': ' . $attr->getValue;
    }
    print join (', ', @attrs);

      print "]\n";

    my $nodelist = $node->getChildNodes;

    ++$level;
    for (0 .. $nodelist->getLength - 1) {
      process_node($nodelist->item($_));
    }
    --$level;
  } elsif ($nodeType == TEXT_NODE) {
    my $content = $node->getData;
    $content =~ s/\n/ /g;
    $content =~ s/^\s+//;
    $content =~ s/\s+$//;
    print $ind, $content, "\n" if $content =~ /\S/;
  }
}
```

A lot of the structure of this program will be very familiar by now, so we will look at only the differences between this version and the Tree style version.

You should first notice that the value returned by parsefile is a reference to an object that represents the whole document. To get the single element which contains the whole document, we need to call this object's getFirstChild method. We can then pass this reference to the process_node function.

Within the process_node function we still do exactly the same things that we have been doing in previous versions of this script; it is only the way that we access the data which is different. To work out the type of the current node, we call its getNodeType method. This returns an integer defining the type. The XML::DOM module exports constants which make these values easier to interpret. In this simplified example we only check for ELEMENT_NODE or TEXT_NODE, but there are a number of other values listed in the module's documentation.

Having established that we are dealing with an element node, we get the tag's name using the getTagName method and a reference to its list of attributes using the getAttributes method. The value returned by getAttributes is a reference to a NodeList object. We can get the number of nodes in the list with the getLength method and retrieve each node in the list in turn, using the item method. For each of the nodes returned we can get the attribute name and value using the getNodeName and getValue methods, respectively.

Having retrieved and displayed the node attributes we can deal with the node's children. The getChildNodes method returns a NodeList of child nodes which we can iterate over (using getLength and item again), recursively passing each node to process_node.

If the node that we are dealing with is a text node, we get the actual text using the getData method, and process the text in exactly the same way we have before.

This description has barely scratched the surface of XML::DOM, but it is something that you will definitely come across if you process XML data.

10.4 Specialized parsers—XML::RSS

Some of the subclasses of XML::Parser are specialized to deal with particular types of XML documents, i.e., documents which conform to a particular DTD. As an example we will look at one of the most popular of these parsers, XML::RSS.

10.4.1 What is RSS?

As you can probably guess, XML::RSS parses rich site summary (RSS) files. The RSS format has become very popular among web sites that want to exchange ideas about the information they are currently displaying. This is most often used by news-based sites, as they can create an RSS file containing their current headlines and other sites can grab the file and create a list of the headlines on a web page.

Quite a community of RSS-swapping has built up around these files. My Netscape and Slashdot are two of the biggest sites using this technology. Chris Nandor has built a web site called My Portal which demonstrates a web page which users can configure to show news stories from the sources which interest them.

10.4.2 A sample RSS file

Here is an example of an RSS file for a fictional news site called Dave's news.

```
<?xml version="1.0" encoding="UTF-8"?>

<!DOCTYPE rss PUBLIC "//Netscape Communications//DTD RSS 0.91//EN"
```

```
                 "http://my.netscape.com/publish/formats/rss-0.91.dtd">
<rss version="0.91">

  <channel>
    <title>Dave's News</title>
    <link>http://daves.news</link>
    <description>All the news that's unfit to print!</description>
    <language>en</language>
    <pubDate>Wed May 10 21:06:38 2000</pubDate>
    <managingEditor>ed@daves.news</managingEditor>
    <webMaster>webmaster@daves.news</webMaster>

    <image>
      <title>Dave's News</title>
      <url>http://daves.news/images/logo.gif</url>
      <link>http://daves.news</link>
    </image>

    <item>
      <title>Data Munging Book tops best sellers list</title>
      <link>http://daves.news/cgi-bin/read.pl?id=1</link>
    </item>

    <item>
      <title>Microsoft abandons ASP for Perl</title>
      <link>http://daves.news/cgi-bin/read.pl?id=2</link>
    </item>

    <item>
      <title>Gates offers job to Torvalds</title>
      <link>http://daves.news/cgi-bin/read.pl?id=3</link>
    </item>

  </channel>
</rss>
```

I hope you can see that the structure is very simple. The first thing to notice is that because the file could potentially be processed using a validating parser, it needs a reference to a DOCTYPE (or DTD). This is given on the second line and points to version 0.91 of the DTD (which, you'll notice, was defined by Netscape). After the DOCTYPE definition, the next line opens the top-level element, which is called <rss>. Within one RSS file you can define multiple channels; however, most RSS files will contain only one channel.

With the channel element you can define a number of data items which define the channel. Only a subset of the possible items is used in this example. The next complex data item is the <image> element. This element defines an image which a client program can display to identify your channel. You can define a URL to fetch the image from, a title, and a link. It is obviously up to the client program how this information is used, but if the channel was being displayed in a browser, it might be useful to display the image as a hot link to the given URL and to use the title as the ALT text for the image.

After the image element comes a list of the items which the channel contains. Once more, the exact use of this information is up to the client application, but browsers often display the title as a hot link to the given URL. Notice that the URLs in the list of items are to individual news stories, whereas the earlier URLs were to the main page of the site.

10.4.3 *Example: creating an RSS file with XML::RSS*

XML::RSS differs from other XML parsers that we have seen as it can also be used to create an RSS file. Here is the script that I used to create the file given above:

```perl
#!/usr/bin/perl -w

use strict;
use XML::RSS;

my $rss = XML::RSS->new;

$rss->channel(title => "Dave's News",
              link => 'http://daves.news',
              language => 'en',
              description => "All the news that's unfit to print!",
              pubDate => scalar localtime,
              managingEditor => 'ed@daves.news',
              webMaster => 'webmaster@daves.news');

$rss->image(title => "Dave's News",
            url => 'http://daves.news/images/logo.gif',
            link => 'http://daves.news');

$rss->add_item(title=>'Data Munging Book tops best sellers list',
               link=>'http://daves.news/cgi-bin/read.pl?id=1');

$rss->add_item(title=>'Microsoft abandons ASP for Perl',
               link=>'http://daves.news/cgi-bin/read.pl?id=2');

$rss->add_item(title=>'Gates offers job to Torvalds',
               link=>'http://daves.news/cgi-bin/read.pl?id=3');

$rss->save('news.rss');
```

As you can see, XML::RSS makes the creation of RSS files almost trivial. You create an RSS object using the class's new method and then add a channel using the channel method. The named parameters to the channel method are the various subelements of the <channel> element in the RSS file. I'm only using a subset here. The full set is described in the documentation for the XML::RSS which you can access by typing `perldoc XML::RSS` from your command line once you have installed the module.

The `image` method is used to add image information to the RSS object. Once more, the various subelements of the `<image>` element are passed as named parameters to the method. For each item that you wish to add to the RSS file, you call the `add_item` method. Finally, to write the RSS object to a file you use the `save` method. You could also use the `as_string` method, which will return the XML that your RSS object generates.

10.4.4 *Example: parsing an RSS file with XML::RSS*

Interpreting an RSS file using `XML::RSS` is just as simple. Here is a script which displays some of the more useful data from an RSS file.

```
use strict;

use XML::RSS;

my $rss = XML::RSS->new;

$rss->parsefile(shift);

print $rss->channel('title'), "\n";
print $rss->channel('description'), "\n";
print $rss->channel('link'), "\n";
print 'Published: ', $rss->channel('pubDate'), "\n";
print 'Editor: ', $rss->channel('managingEditor'), "\n\n";

print "Items:\n";

foreach (@{$rss->items}) {
  print $_->{title}, "\n\t<", $_->{link}, ">\n";
}
```

The file is parsed using the `parsefile` method (which `XML::RSS` overrides from its parent `XML::Parser`). This method adds data structures modeling the RSS file to the RSS parser object. This data can be accessed using various accessor methods. The `channel` method gives you access to the various parts of the `<channel>` element, and the `items` method returns a list of the items in the file. Each element in the items list is a reference to a hash containing the various attributes of one item from the file.

If we run this script on our sample RSS file, here is the output that we get.

```
Dave's News
All the news that's unfit to print!
http://daves.news
Published: Wed May 10 21:06:38 2000
Editor: ed@daves.news

Items:
```

```
Data Munging Book tops best sellers list
        <http://daves.news/cgi-bin/read.pl?id=1>
Microsoft abandons ASP for Perl
        <http://daves.news/cgi-bin/read.pl?id=2>
Gates offers job to Torvalds
        <http://daves.news/cgi-bin/read.pl?id=3>
```

This example script only displays very basic information about the RSS file, but it should be simple to expand it to display more details and to produce an HTML page instead of text. There are a number of example scripts in the XML::RSS distribution which you can use as a basis for your scripts.

10.5 *Producing different document formats*

One of the best uses of XML is producing different outputs from the same input file. As an example of this kind of processing, in this section we will look at producing a number of different document formats from a single XML document. The example that we will look at is the documentation for Perl modules. Traditionally, when a Perl module is released to the CPAN the accompanying documentation is written in *plain old documentation* (POD). POD is a very simple markup language which can be embedded within Perl code. The Perl interpreter knows to ignore it, and there are a number of documentation tools which can be used to extract the POD from a Perl script and present it in a number of formats.[6]

In this example we will put the documentation for a Perl module in an XML file and use a Perl script to convert this XML document to POD, HTML, or plain text.

10.5.1 *Sample XML input file*

Here is an example of the XML document we will use.

```
<?xml version="1.0" encoding="UTF-8"?>
<README>
  <NAME>Test README File</NAME>

  <SYNOPSIS>
    This is a summary of the file.
    It should appear in PRE tags
  </SYNOPSIS>

  <DESCRIPTION>
    <TEXT>This is the full description of the file</TEXT>
    <SUBSECTION>
      <HEAD>Subsection Title</HEAD>
      <TEXT>Subsection text</TEXT>
```

---

[6] You can find out a lot more about POD by reading the *perlpod* manual page.

```
      </SUBSECTION>
      <SUBSECTION>
        <HEAD>Another Subsection Title</HEAD>
        <TEXT>More Subsection text</TEXT>
        <LIST TYPE='bullet'>
          <ITEM>List item 1</ITEM>
          <ITEM>List item 2</ITEM>
        </LIST>
      </SUBSECTION>
    </DESCRIPTION>

    <AUTHOR>
      <ANAME>Dave Cross</ANAME>
      <EMAIL>dave@mag-sol.com</EMAIL>
    </AUTHOR>

    <SEE_ALSO>
      <LIST TYPE='bullet'>
        <ITEM>Something</ITEM>
        <ITEM>Something else</ITEM>
      </LIST>
    </SEE_ALSO>
  </README>
```

This file supports most of the headings that you will see in a Perl module's README file.

10.5.2 *XML document transformation script*

Here is the script that we will use to transform it into other formats.

```
 1: #!/usr/bin/perl -w
 2:
 3: use strict;
 4:
 5: use XML::Parser;
 6: use Getopt::Std;
 7: use Text::Wrap;
 8:
 9: my %formats = (h => {name => 'html'},
10:                p => {name => 'pod'},
11:                t => {name => 'text'});
12:
13: my %opts;
14: (getopts('f:', \%opts) && @ARGV)
15:   || die "usage: format_xml.pl -f h|p|t xml_file\n";
16:
17: die "Invalid format: $opts{f}\n" unless exists $formats{$opts{f}};
18:
19: warn "Formatting file as $formats{$opts{f}}->{name}\n";
20:
```

```
21:  my $p = XML::Parser->new(Style => 'Tree');
22:  my $tree = $p->parsefile(shift);
23:
24:  my $level = 0;
25:  my $ind = '';
26:  my $head = 1;
27:
28:  top($tree);
29:
30:  process_node(@$tree);
31:
32:  bot();
33:
34:  sub process_node {
35:     my ($type, $content) = @_;
36:
37:     $ind = ' ' x $level;
38:
39:     if ($type) {
40:
41:        local $_ = $type;
42:
43:        my $attrs = shift @$content;
44:
45:        /^NAME$/ && name($content);
46:        /^SYNOPSIS$/ && synopsis($content);
47:        /^DESCRIPTION$/ && description();
48:        /^TEXT$/ && text($content);
49:        /^CODE$/ && code($content);
50:        /^HEAD$/ && head($content);
51:        /^LIST$/ && do {list($attrs, $content); @$content = ()};
52:        /^AUTHOR$/ && author();
53:        /^ANAME$/ && aname($content);
54:        /^EMAIL$/ && email($content);
55:        /^SEE_ALSO$/ && see_also($content);
56:
57:        while (my @node = splice @$content, 0, 2) {
58:           ++$level;
59:           ++$head if $type eq 'SUBSECTION';
60:           process_node(@node);
61:           --$head if $type eq 'SUBSECTION';
62:           --$level;
63:        }
64:     }
65:  }
66:
67:  sub top {
68:     $tree = shift;
69:
70:     if ($opts{f} eq 'h') {
71:        print "<html>\n";
```

```
72:        print "<head>\n";
73:        print "<title>$tree->[1]->[4]->[2]</title>\n";
74:        print "</head>\n<body>\n";
75:    } elsif ($opts{f} eq 'p') {
76:        print "=pod\n\n";
77:    } elsif ($opts{f} eq 't') {
78:        print "\n", $tree->[1]->[4]->[2], "\n";
79:        print '-' x length($tree->[1]->[4]->[2]), "\n\n";
80:    }
81: }
82:
83: sub bot {
84:    if ($opts{f} eq 'h') {
85:        print "</body>\n</html>\n";
86:    } elsif ($opts{f} eq 'p') {
87:        print "=cut\n\n";
88:    } elsif ($opts{f} eq 't') {
89:        # do nothing
90:    }
91: }
92:
93: sub name {
94:    my $content = shift;
95:
96:    if ($opts{f} eq 'h') {
97:        print "<h1>NAME</h1>\n";
98:        print "<p>$content->[1]</p>\n"
99:    } elsif ($opts{f} eq 'p') {
100:        print "=head1 NAME\n\n";
101:        print "$content->[1]\n\n";
102:    } elsif ($opts{f} eq 't') {
103:        print "NAME\n\n";
104:        print $ind, "$content->[1]\n\n";
105:    }
106: }
107:
108: sub synopsis {
109:    my $content = shift;
110:
111:    if ($opts{f} eq 'h') {
112:        print "<h1>SYNOPSIS</h1>\n";
113:        print "<pre>$content->[1]</pre>\n"
114:    } elsif ($opts{f} eq 'p') {
115:        print "=head1 SYNOPSIS\n\n";
116:        print "$content->[1]\n";
117:    } elsif ($opts{f} eq 't') {
118:        print "SYNOPSIS\n";
119:        print "$content->[1]\n";
120:    }
121: }
122:
```

```
123: sub description {
124:
125:     if ($opts{f} eq 'h') {
126:       print "<h1>DESCRIPTION</h1>\n";
127:     } elsif ($opts{f} eq 'p') {
128:       print "=head1 DESCRIPTION\n\n";
129:     } elsif ($opts{f} eq 't') {
130:       print "DESCRIPTION\n\n";
131:     }
132: }
133:
134: sub text {
135:     my $content = shift;
136:
137:     if ($opts{f} eq 'h') {
138:       print "<p>$content->[1]</p>\n"
139:     } elsif ($opts{f} eq 'p') {
140:       print wrap('', '', trim($content->[1])), "\n\n";
141:     } elsif ($opts{f} eq 't') {
142:       print wrap($ind, $ind, trim($content->[1])), "\n\n";
143:     }
144: }
145:
146: sub code {
147:     my $content = shift;
148:
149:     if ($opts{f} eq 'h') {
150:       print "<pre>$content->[1]</pre>\n"
151:     } elsif ($opts{f} eq 'p') {
152:       print "$content->[1]\n";
153:     } elsif ($opts{f} eq 't') {
154:       print "$content->[1]\n";
155:     }
156: }
157:
158: sub head {
159:     my $content = shift;
160:
161:     if ($opts{f} eq 'h') {
162:       print "<h$head>", trim($content->[1]), "</h$head>\n"
163:     } elsif ($opts{f} eq 'p') {
164:       print "=head$head ", trim($content->[1]), "\n\n";
165:     } elsif ($opts{f} eq 't') {
166:       print trim($content->[1]), "\n\n";
167:     }
168: }
169:
170: sub list {
171:     my ($attrs, $content) = @_;
172:
173:     my %list = (bullet => 'ul', numbered => 'ol');
```

```
174:
175:    my $type = $attrs->{TYPE};
176:
177:    if ($opts{f} eq 'h') {
178:      print "<$list{$type}>\n";
179:      while (my @node = splice @$content, 0, 2) {
180:        if ($node[0] eq 'ITEM') {
181:          print "<li>$node[1]->[2]</li>\n";
182:        }
183:      }
184:      print "</$list{$type}>\n";
185:    } elsif ($opts{f} eq 'p') {
186:      print "=over 4\n";
187:      while (my @node = splice @$content, 0, 2) {
188:        my $cnt = 1;
189:        if ($node[0] eq 'ITEM') {
190:          print "=item *\n$node[1]->[2]\n\n";
191:        }
192:      }
193:      print "=back\n\n";
194:    } elsif ($opts{f} eq 't') {
195:      while (my @node = splice @$content, 0, 2) {
196:        my $cnt = 1;
197:        if ($node[0] eq 'ITEM') {
198:          print $ind, "* $node[1]->[2]\n";
199:        }
200:      }
201:      print "\n";
202:    }
203: }
204:
205: sub author {
206:    if ($opts{f} eq 'h') {
207:      print "<h1>AUTHOR</h1>\n";
208:    } elsif ($opts{f} eq 'p') {
209:      print "=head1 AUTHOR\n\n";
210:    } elsif ($opts{f} eq 't') {
211:      print "AUTHOR\n\n";
212:    }
213: }
214:
215: sub aname {
216:    my $content = shift;
217:
218:    if ($opts{f} eq 'h') {
219:      print "<p>$content->[1]\n"
220:    } elsif ($opts{f} eq 'p') {
221:      print trim($content->[1]), ' ';
222:    } elsif ($opts{f} eq 't') {
223:      print $ind, trim($content->[1]), ' ';
224:    }
```

```
225: }
226:
227: sub email {
228:   my $content = shift;
229:
230:   if ($opts{f} eq 'h') {
231:     print '&lt;', trim($content->[1]), "&gt;</p>\n"
232:   } elsif ($opts{f} eq 'p') {
233:     print '<', trim($content->[1]), ">\n\n";
234:   } elsif ($opts{f} eq 't') {
235:     print '<', trim($content->[1]), ">\n\n";
236:   }
237: }
238:
239: sub see_also {
240:
241:   if ($opts{f} eq 'h') {
242:     print "<h1>SEE ALSO</h1>\n";
243:   } elsif ($opts{f} eq 'p') {
244:     print "=head1 SEE ALSO\n\n";
245:   } elsif ($opts{f} eq 't') {
246:     print "SEE ALSO\n\n";
247:   }
248: }
249:
250: sub trim {
251:   local $_ = shift;
252:
253:   s/\n/ /g;
254:   s/^\s+//;
255:   s/\s+$//;
256:
257:   $_;
258: }
```

This is the longest script that we have looked at so far, so let's review it a section at a time.

Lines 1 to 3 should be the standard way that you start a Perl script.

Lines 5 to 7 bring in the modules which we will be using. XML::Parser will be used to parse the XML input, Getopt::Std is used to process command line options, and Text::Wrap is used to reformat lines of text.

Lines 9 to 11 define the types of formatting that the script can handle in a hash. Each value is another hash containing information about the format. Currently, it only lists the name of the format, but if there are other attributes of a format that are useful, this would be a good place to store them.

Lines 13 to 19 use the function `getops` from `Getopt::Std` to process the command line flags. In this case there is just one flag that indicates the chosen output type. This is stored in `$opts{f}`. If we are passed an unknown format we warn the user and `die`. On line 19 we let the user know what format we are using.

Line 21 creates an XML parser using the Tree style and line 22 uses this object to parse the XML document, returning the document tree data structure which we store in `$tree`.

Lines 24 to 26 define some global variables: `$level` will store the nesting level of the current element, `$ind` will store a string of spaces which will be used to indent text, and `$head` will store the current header level.

Line 28 calls the `top` function which is defined in lines 67 to 81. This function prints header information for the chosen format. For HTML, this is all of the `<HEAD>` ... `</HEAD>` section, for POD it is simply the text `=pod`, and for text it is the title of the document underlined. Notice that we use the expression `$tree->[1]->[4]->[2]` to get the title of the document. We can take this kind of shortcut because we know the structure of our document. `$tree->[1]` is the content of the first node in the tree (i.e., everything within the `<README>` element). `$tree->[1]->[4]` is the content of the second node contained within the `<README>` element. The first node within this element is the text node containing the newline character immediately after the `<README>` tag.[7] The second node is the `<NAME>` element. `$tree->[1]->[4]->[2]` is the content of the first node within the `<NAME>` element, i.e., the name text, which we will use as a title.

Line 30 calls the `process_node` function which is defined in lines 34 to 65. This function is where most of the work goes on. The basic structure should be familiar from the previous tree-based parsing scripts that we have discussed. The function is passed the type of a node together with a reference to its content. If the node is an element (remember the value of `$type` is the name of the element or zero if it is a text node), we extract the attributes and call the relevant subroutine to process each type of element. In most cases we pass the element content to the subroutine, but there are two exceptions. The `<DESCRIPTION>` element has no useful content (other than, of course, its contained elements, which will be handled elsewhere). The `<LIST>` element is more complex. First, it is the only element with an attribute list which needs to be passed on to the subroutine and, second, as the `list` subroutine processes all of the element's content, we need to set the content to an empty list to prevent it being processed again.

---

[7] Of course, the script now relies on this newline character always being there. Relying on the presence of this ignorable white space is a serious limitation of this script, and if you wanted to use a script like this in earnest you would need to design something a little more robust.

Having processed the element, we need to process any child elements. This is accomplished in much the same way as we have in previous examples. We simply walk the `@$content` list a node at a time (where a node is represented by two items in the array), passing the nodes one at a time to `process_node`. We pause only to increment the `$level` and `$head` variables before starting to process the list and to decrement them after we have finished.

Once the script returns from the main call to `process_node`, the final action (line 32) is to call the function `bot`. The function is defined in lines 83 to 91 and simply finishes off the file in that same way that `top` started it (except that in this case the processing is much simpler).

The rest of the script consists of definitions of the functions which handle the various element types. Most of these are very similar and simple. All they do is print out the content of the element surrounded by various fixed strings. It is, however, worth taking a closer look at the `head` and `list` functions.

`head` is the function which prints out header sections. In its POD and HTML sections it needs to know which level of header to display. It accomplishes this by using the global `$head` variable which is incremented each time a `<SUBSECTION>` element is encountered. Like many of the other element functions, `head` also makes use of a helper function called `trim` which removes all of the excess white space from a text string.

`list` is the most complex of the element functions as it builds up a complete list rather than relying on the usual subelement handling which we have used for other elements. This is because in the future we may well want to support numbered lists, and it will be far easier if the list numbers can all be calculated within the same function. This function therefore traverses the `@$content` array in much the same way as the `process_node` function.

10.5.3 *Using the XML document transformation script*

Having described the script in detail, let's run it in the various modes on our sample document and see what output we get. The script takes the input file as an argument and writes its output to STDOUT. We can, therefore, call the script like this:

```
format_xml.pl -f p doc.xml > doc.pod
format_xml.pl -f h doc.xml > doc.html
format_xml.pl -f t doc.xml > doc.txt
```

to get the POD, HTML, and text outputs. Here are the results.

POD file

```
=pod

=head1 NAME
```

```
Test README File

=head1 SYNOPSIS

    This is a summary of the file.
    It should appear in PRE tags

=head1 DESCRIPTION

This is the full description of the file

=head2 Subsection Title

Subsection text

=head2 Another Subsection Title

More Subsection text

=over 4

=item *
List item 1

=item *
List item 2

=back
=head1 AUTHOR

Dave Cross <dave@mag-sol.com>

=head1 SEE_ALSO

=over 4

=item *
Something

=item *
Something else

=back

=cut
```

HTML file

```html
<html>
<head>
<title>Test README File</title>
</head>
<body>
<h1>NAME</h1>
<p>Test README File</p>
<h1>SYNOPSIS</h1>
<pre>
```

```
        This is a summary of the file.
        It should appear in PRE tags
</pre>
<h1>DESCRIPTION</h1>
<p>This is the full description of the file</p>
<h2>Subsection Title</h2>
<p>Subsection text</p>
<h2>Another Subsection Title</h2>
<p>More Subsection text</p>
<ul>
<li>List item 1</li>
<li>List item 2</li>
</ul>
<h1>AUTHOR</h1>
<p>Dave Cross
&lt;dave@mag-sol.com&gt;</p>
<h1>SEE_ALSO</h1>
<ul>
<li>Something</li>
<li>Something else</li>
</ul>
</body>
</html>
```

Text file

```
Test README File
----------------

NAME

 Test README File

SYNOPSIS

     This is a summary of the file.
     It should appear in PRE tags

DESCRIPTION

  This is the full description of the file

Subsection Title

   Subsection text

Another Subsection Title

   More Subsection text

    * List item 1
    * List item 2

AUTHOR
```

```
Dave Cross <dave@mag-sol.com>
```

```
SEE_ALSO
```

```
 * Something
 * Something else
```

10.6 *Further information*

The XML and Perl world is a very exciting place at the moment. Things are changing all the time. The best way to keep abreast of the latest news is to read the Perl-XML mailing list. You can subscribe via the web interface at:

http://listserv.ActiveState.com/mailman/listinfo/perl-xml.

None of the modules that we have discussed in this chapter are installed as part of the standard Perl installation. You will need to get them from the CPAN and install them yourself.

10.7 *Summary*

- XML is becoming a very common data format, particularly for exchanging data between different computer systems.

- XML documents can be either valid or well-formed. Currently, no Perl XML parser checks for validity.

- XML parsing in Perl is very easy using XML::Parser and its various subclasses.

- XML::Parser has a number of different styles which can be used to solve particular types of parsing tasks. If none of the standard styles suit your requirements, you can use handlers for even more control over how the parser works.

- XML::DOM brings the industry-standard Document Object Model to the Perl/XML community.

- Specialized parsers such as XML::RSS can be used to parse documents conforming to specific DTDs.

Building your own parsers

The prebuilt parsers that we have looked at in the two previous chapters are, of course, very useful, but there are many times when you need to parse data in a format for which a prebuilt parser does not exist. In these cases you can create your own parser using a number of Perl modules. The most flexible of these is `Parse::RecDescent`, and in this chapter we take a detailed look at its use.

11.1 *Introduction to Parse::RecDescent*

`Parse::RecDescent` is a tool for building top-down parsers which was written by Damian Conway. It doesn't form a part of the standard Perl distribution, so you will need to get it from the CPAN. It can be found at http://www.cpan.org/modules/by-module/Parse/. The module comes with copious documentation and more example code than anyone would ever want to read.

Using `Parse::RecDescent` is quite simple. In summary you define a grammar for the parser to use, create a parser object to process the grammar, and then pass the text to be parsed to the parser. We'll see more specific examples later, but all the programs will have a basic structure which looks like this:

```
use Parse::RecDescent;

my $grammar = q(
                # Text that define your grammar
                );

my $parser = Parse::RecDescent->new($grammar);

my $text = q(
             # Scalar which contains the text to be parsed
             );

# top_rule is the name of the top level rule in you grammar.
$parser->top_rule($text);
```

11.1.1 *Example: parsing simple English sentences*

For example, if we go back to the example of simple English sentences which we used in chapter 8, we could write code like this in order to check for valid sentences.

```
use Parse::RecDescent;

my $grammar = q(
                sentence: subject verb object
                subject: noun_phrase
                object: noun_phrase
                verb: 'wrote' | 'likes' | 'ate'
                noun_phrase: pronoun | proper_noun | article noun
                article: 'a' | 'the' | 'this'
                pronoun: 'it' | 'he'
                proper_noun: 'Perl' | 'Dave' | 'Larry'
```

```
                noun: 'book' | 'cat'
              );
my $parser = Parse::RecDescent->new($grammar);

while (<DATA>) {
  chomp;
  print "'$_' is ";
  print 'NOT ' unless $parser->sentence($_);
  print "a valid sentence\n";
}

__END__
Larry wrote Perl
Larry wrote a book
Dave likes Perl
Dave likes the book
Dave wrote this book
the cat ate the book
Dave got very angry
```

Notice that we have expanded the terminals to actually represent a (very limited) subset of English words. The output of this script is a follows:

```
'Larry wrote Perl' is a valid sentence
'Larry wrote a book' is a valid sentence
'Dave likes Perl' is a valid sentence
'Dave likes the book' is a valid sentence
'Dave wrote this book' is a valid sentence
'the cat ate the book' is a valid sentence
'Dave got very angry' is NOT a valid sentence
```

Which shows that "Dave got very angry" is the only text in our data, which is not a valid sentence.[1]

Explaining the code

The only complex part of this script is the definition of the grammar. The syntax of this definition is similar to one that we used in chapter 8. The only major difference is that we have replaced the arrow -> with a colon. If you read the rules, replacing the colon with the phrase "is made up of" and the vertical bar with the word "or", then these rules are easy to understand.

In this example all of our terminals are fixed strings. As we shall see later in the chapter, it is quite possible to match Perl regular expressions instead.

Having defined our grammar, we simply create a parser object using this grammar and use that object to see if our sentences are valid. Notice that we use the

---

[1] By the rules of our grammar of course—not by the real rules of English.

method `sentence` to validate each sentence in turn. This method was created by the `Parse::RecDescent` object as it read our grammar. The `sentence` method returns `true` or `false` depending on whether or not the parser object successfully parsed the input data.

11.2 Returning parsed data

The previous example is all very well if you just want to know whether your data meets the criteria of a given grammar, but it doesn't actually produce any useful data structures which represent the parsed data. For that we have to look a little deeper into `Parse::RecDescent`.

11.2.1 Example: parsing a Windows INI file

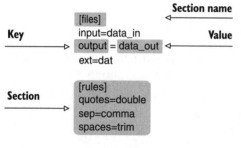

Figure 11.1 INI file structure.

Let's look at parsing a Windows INI file. These files contain a number of named sections. Each of these sections contain a number of assignment statements. Figure 11.1 shows an example INI together with the various parts that make up the file structure.

In this example we have sections called "files" and "rules." The files section lists the names of the input and output files together with their extension; the rules section lists a number of configuration options. This file might be used to control the configuration of a text-processing program.

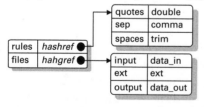

Figure 11.2 INI file data structure.

Before looking at how we would get the data out, it is a good idea to decide what data structure we are going to use to store the parsed data. In this case it seems fairly obvious that a hash of hashes would be most useful. Each key within the first hash would be a section name and the value would be a reference to another hash. Within these second-level hashes the keys would be the left-hand side of the assignment statement and the values would be the right-hand side. Figure 11.2 shows this data structure.

This means that you can get an individual value very easily using code like:

```
$input_file = $Config{files}{input};
```

11.2.2 Understanding the INI file grammar

Let's take a look at a grammar that defines an INI file. We'll use the syntax found in `Parse::RecDescent`.

```
file: section(s)
section: header assign(s)
header: '[' /\w+/ ']'
assign: /\w+/ '=' /\w+/
```

The grammar can be explained in English like this:

- An INI file consists of one or more sections.
- Each section consists of a header followed by one or more assignments.
- The header consists of a [character, one or more word characters, and a] character.
- An assignment consists of a sequence of one or more word characters, an = character, and another sequence of one or more word characters.

Using subrule suffixes

There are a couple of new features to notice here. First, we have used (s) after the names of some of our subrules. This means that the subrule can appear one or more times in the rule. There are a number of other suffixes which can control the number of times that a subrule can appear, and the full list is in table 11.1. In this case we are saying that a file can contain one or more sections and that each section can contain one or more assignment statements.

Table 11.1 Optional and repeating subrules

Subrule suffix	Meaning
(?)	Optional subrule. Appears zero or one time.
(s)	Mandatory repeating subrule. Appears one or more times.
(s?)	Optional repeating subrule. Appears zero or more times.
(N)	Repeating subgroup. Must appear exactly N times.
(N..M)	Repeating subgroup. Must appear between N and M times.
(..M)	Repeating subgroup. Must appear between 1 and M times.
(N..)	Repeating subgroup. Must appear at least N times.

Using regular expressions

The other thing to notice is that we are using regular expressions in many places to match our terminals. This is useful because the names of the sections and the keys and values in each section can be any valid word. In this example we are saying that they must all be a string made up of Perl's word characters.[2]

11.2.3 Parser actions and the @item array

0	header
1	[
2	files
3	]

**Figure 11.3
The @item array
after matching
the header rule
for the first time**

In order to extract data, we can make use of parser actions. These are pieces of code that you write and then attach to any rule in a grammar. Your code is then executed whenever that rule is matched. Within the action code a number of special variables are available. The most useful of these is probably the `@item` array which contains a list of the values that have been matched in the current rule. The value in `$item[0]` is always the name of the rule which has matched. For example, when our `header` rule is matched, the `@item` array will contain "header", "[", the name of the section, and "]" with elements 0 to 3[3] (figure 11.3).

In order to see what values are being matched, you could put action code on each of the rules in the grammar like the following code. All this code does is print out the contents of the `@item` array each time a rule is matched.

```
file: section(s) { print "$item[0]: $item[1]\n"; }
section: header assign(s) { print "$item[0]: $item[1] $item[2]\n"; }
header: '[' /\w+/ ']' { print "$item[0]: $item[1] $item[2] $item[3]\n"; }
assign: /\w+/ '=' /\w+/  { print "$item[0]: $item[1] $item[2] $item[3]\n"; }
```

However, Parse::RecDescent provides an easier way to achieve the same result, by providing a way to assign a default action to all rules in a grammar. If you assign a string containing code to the variable `$::RD_AUTOACTION`, then that code will be assigned to every rule which doesn't have an explicit action.

11.2.4 Example: displaying the contents of @item

Here is a sample program which reads an INI file and displays the contents of `@item` for each matched rule.

```
use Parse::RecDescent;

my $grammar = q(
```

---

[2] That is, alphanumeric characters and the underbar character.

[3] The same information is also available in a hash called `%item`, but I'll use `@item` in these examples. For more details on `%item` see `perldoc Parse::RecDescent`.

```
            file: section(s)
            section: header assign(s)
            header: '[' /\w+/ ']'
            assign: /\w+/ '=' /\w+/
            );

$::RD_AUTOACTION = q { print "$item[0]: @item[1..$#item]\n"; 1 } ;

$parser = Parse::RecDescent->new($grammar);

my $text;

{
  $/ = undef;
  $text = <STDIN>;
}

$parser->file($text);
```

The general structure of the code and the grammar should be familiar. The only thing new here is the code assigned to $::RD_AUTOACTION. This code will be run whenever a rule that doesn't have its own associated action code is matched. When you run this program using our earlier sample INI file as input, the resulting output is as follows:

```
header: [ files ]
assign: input = data_in
assign: output = data_out
assign: ext = dat
section: 1 ARRAY(0x8adc868)
header: [ rules ]
assign: quotes = double
assign: sep = comma
assign: spaces = trim
section: 1 ARRAY(0x8adc844)
file: ARRAY(0x8adc850)
```

How rule matching works

The previous example shows us a couple of interesting things about the way that Parse::RecDescent works. Look at the order in which the rules have been matched and recall what we saw about the workings of top-down parsers in chapter 8. Here you can clearly see that a rule doesn't match until all of its subrules have been matched successfully.

Secondly, look at the output for the section and file rules. Where you have matched a repeating subrule, @item contains a reference to an array, and where you have matched a nonrepeating subrule, @item contains the value 1. This shows us something about what a matched rule returns. Each matched rule returns a true value. By default this is the number 1, but you can change this in the associated action code. Be sure that your code has a `true` return value, or else the parser will think that the match has failed.

11.2.5 *Returning a data structure*

The value that is returned from the top-level rule will be the value returned by the top-level rule method when called by our script. We can use this fact to ensure that the data structure that we want is returned. Here is the script that will achieve this:

```perl
use Parse::RecDescent;

my $grammar = q(
                file: section(s)
                  { my %file;
                    foreach (@{$item[1]}) {
                      $file{$_->[0]} = $_->[1];
                    }
                    \%file;
                  }
                section: header assign(s)
                  { my %sec;
                    foreach (@{$item[2]}) {
                      $sec{$_->[0]} = $_->[1];
                    }
                    [ $item[1], \%sec]
                  }
                header: '[' /\w+/ ']' { $item[2] }
                assign: /\w+/ '=' /\w+/
                  { [$item[1], $item[3]] }
              );

$parser = Parse::RecDescent->new($grammar);

my $text;

{
  $/ = undef;
  $text = <STDIN>;
}

my $tree = $parser->file($text);

foreach (keys %$tree) {
  print "$_\n";
  foreach my $key (keys %{$tree->{$_}}) {
    print "\t$key: $tree->{$_}{$key}\n";
  }
}
```

The code that has been added to the previous script is in two places. First (and most importantly) in the parser actions and, secondly, at the end of the script to display the returned data structure and demonstrate what is returned.

The action code might look a little difficult, but it's probably a bit easier if you read it in reverse order and see how the data structure builds up.

The `assign` rule now returns a reference to a two-element list. The first element is the left-hand side of the assignment and the second element is the right-hand side. The `header` rule simply returns the name of the section.

The `section` rule creates a new hash called `%sec`. It then iterates across the list returned by the `assign` subrule. Each element in this list is the return value from one `assign` rule. As we saw in the previous paragraph, this is a reference to a two-element list. We convert each of these lists to a key/value pair in the `%sec` hash. Finally, the rule returns a reference to a two-element hash. The first element of this list is the return value from the `header` rule (which is the section name), and the second element is a reference to the section hash.

The file rule uses a very similar technique to take the list of sections and convert them into a hash called `%file`. It then returns the `%file` hash.

This means that the file method returns a reference to a hash. The keys to the hash are the names of the sections in the file and the values are references to hashes. The keys to the second level hashes are the text from the left-hand side of the assignments, and the values are the associated strings from the right-hand side of the assignment.

The code at the end of the script prints out the values in the returned data structure. Running this script against our sample INI file gives us the following result:

```
rules
        quotes: double
        sep: comma
        spaces: trim
files
        input: data_in
        ext: dat
        output: data_out
```

which demonstrates that we have built up the data structure that we wanted.

11.3 Another example: the CD data file

Let's take a look at another example of parsing a data file with `Parse::RecDescent`. We'll take a look at how we'd parse the CD data file that we discussed in chapter 8. What follows is the data file we were discussing:

```
Dave's CD Collection
16 Sep 1999

Artist          Title              Label        Released
---------------------------------------------------------
Bragg, Billy  Workers' Playtime  Cooking Vinyl  1988
+She's Got A New Spell
+Must I Paint You A Picture
Bragg, Billy  Mermaid Avenue     EMI            1998
+Walt Whitman's Niece
+California Stars
Black, Mary    The Holy Ground   Grapevine      1993
+Summer Sent You
+Flesh And Blood
Black, Mary    Circus            Grapevine      1995
+The Circus
+In A Dream
Bowie, David   Hunky Dory        RCA            1971
+Changes
+Oh You Pretty Things
Bowie, David   Earthling         EMI            1997
+Little Wonder
+Looking For Satellites

6 Records
```

In chapter 8 we came up with a rather unsatisfying way to extract the data from this file and put it into a data structure. Now that `Parse::RecDescent` is in our toolkit, we should be able to come up with something far more elegant.

As with the last example, the best approach is to start with a grammar for the data file.

11.3.1 Understanding the CD grammar

Here is the grammar that I have designed for parsing the CD data file.

```
file: header body footer
header: /.+/ date
date: /\d\d?\s+\w+\s+\d{4}/
body: col_heads /-+/ cd(s)
col_heads: col_head(s)
col_head: /\w+/
cd: cd_line track_line(s)
cd_line: /.{14}/ /.{19}/ /.{15}/ /\d{4}/
track_line: '+' /.*/
footer: /\d+/ 'Records'
```

Let's take a closer look at the individual rules. Like the parser, we'll take a top-down approach.

- A data file is made up of three sections—a header, a body, and a footer.
- The file header is made up of a string of any characters followed by a date.

- A date is one or two digits followed by at least one space, any number of word characters, at least one space and four digits. Note that we are assuming that all dates will appear in the same format as the one in our sample file.

- The file body contains the column headers followed by a number of - characters and one or more CD records.

- The column headers are made up of one or more headers per individual column.

- A column header consists of a number of word characters.

- A CD record consists of a CD line followed by at least one track record.

- A CD line consists of a number of records, each of which is a particular number of characters long. We have to match in this way, as the CD record is in fixed width format.

- A track record contains a + character followed by at least one other character.

- A footer record consists of at least one digit followed by the text "CDs".

11.3.2 *Testing the CD file grammar*

Having defined our grammar, one of the best ways to test it is to write a brief program like the one that we used to test the English sentences. The program would look like this:

```
use Parse::RecDescent;

use vars qw(%datas @cols);

my $grammar = q(
                file: header body footer
                header: /.+/ date
                date: /\d+\s+\w+\s+\d{4}/
                body: col_heads /-+/ cd(s)
                col_heads: col_head(s)
                col_head: /\w+/
                cd: cd_line track_line(s)
                cd_line: /.{14}/ /.{19}/ /.{15}/ /\d{4}/
                track_line: '+' /.+/ { $item[2] }
                footer: /\d+/ 'CDs'
               );

$parser = Parse::RecDescent->new($grammar);

my $text;
{
  local $/ = undef;

  $text = <STDIN>;
}

print $parser->file($text) ? "valid" : "invalid";
```

This program will print `valid` or `invalid` depending on whether or not the file passed to it on STDIN parses correctly against the given grammar. In this case it does, but if it doesn't and you want to find out where the errors are, there are two useful variables which `Parse::RecDescent` uses to help you follow what it is doing.

Debugging the grammar with $::RD_TRACE and $::RD_HINT

Setting `$::RD_TRACE` to `true` will display a trace of the parsing process as it progresses, allowing you to see where your grammar and the structure of the file disagree. If the problems are earlier in the process and there are syntax errors in your grammar, then setting `$::RD_HINT` to `true` will provide hints on how you could fix the problems. Setting `$::RD_AUTOACTION` to a snippet of code which prints out the values in `@item` can also be a useful debugging tool.

11.3.3 Adding parser actions

Having established that our grammar does what we want, we can proceed with writing the rest of the program. As previously, most of the interesting code is in the parser actions. Here is the complete program:

```perl
use strict;
use Parse::RecDescent;
use Data::Dumper;

use vars qw(@cols);

my $grammar = q(
            file: header body footer
              {
                my %rec =
                  (%{$item[1]}, list => $item[2], %{$item[3]});
                \%rec;
              }
            header: /.+/ date
              { { title => $item[1], date => $item[2] } }
            date: /\d+\s+\w+\s+\d{4}/ { $item[1] }
            body: col_heads /-+/ cd(s) { $item[3] }
            col_heads: col_head(s) { @::cols = @{$item[1]} }
            col_head: /\w+/ { $item[1] }
            cd: cd_line track_line(s)
              { $item[1]->{tracks} = $item[2]; $item[1] }
            cd_line: /.{14}/ /.{19}/ /.{15}/ /\d{4}/
              { my %rec; @rec{@::cols} = @item[1 .. $#item]; \%rec }
            track_line: '+' /.+/ { $item[2] }
            footer: /\d+/ 'CDs'
              { { count => $item[1] } }
            );

my $parser = Parse::RecDescent->new($grammar);
```

```
my $text;

{
  local $/ = undef;

  $text = <DATA>;
}

my $CDs = $parser->file($text);

print Dumper($CDs);
```

As is generally the case, the parser actions will be easier to follow if we examine them bottom up.

The `footer` rule returns a reference to a hash with only one value. The key to this hash is `count` and the value is `$item[1]`, which is the number that is matched on the footer line. As we'll see when we get to the `file` rule, I chose to return this as a hash reference since it makes it easier to combine parts into a data structure.

The `track` rule returns the name of the track.

The `cd_line` rule builds a hash where the keys are the column headings and the values are the associated values from the CD line in the file. In order to do this, it makes use of the global `@cols` array which is created by the `col_heads` rule.

The `cd` rule takes the hash reference which is returned by the `cd_line` rule and creates another element in the same hash where the key is `tracks`, and the value is a reference to the array of multiple track records which is returned by the `track(s)` subrule. The rule then returns this hash reference.

The `col_head` rule matches one individual column heading and returns that value.

The `col_heads` rule takes the array which is returned by the `col_head(s)` subrule and assigns this array to the global array `@cols`, so that it can later be used by the `cd_line` rule.

The `body` rule returns the array returned by the `cd(s)` subrule. Each element of this array is the hash returned by one occurrence of the `cd` rule.

The `date` rule returns the date that was matched.

The `header` rule works similarly to the footer rule. It returns a reference to a two-element hash. The keys in this hash are "title" and "date" and the values are the respective pieces of matched text.

The `file` rule takes the three pieces of data returned by the `header`, `body`, and `footer` rules and combines them into a single hash. It then returns a reference to this hash.

Checking the output with Data::Dumper

The program uses the `Data::Dumper` module to print out a data dump of the data structure that we have built. For our sample CD data file, the output from this program look like this:

```
$VAR1 = {
          'list' => [
                     {
                       'Released' => '1988',
                       'Artist' => 'Bragg, Billy ',
                       'Title' => 'Workers\' Playtime ',
                       'Label' => 'Cooking Vinyl ',
                       'tracks' => [
                                     'She\'s Got A New Spell',
                                     'Must I Paint You A Picture'
                                   ]
                     },
                     {
                       'Released' => '1998',
                       'Artist' => 'Bragg, Billy ',
                       'Title' => 'Mermaid Avenue     ',
                       'Label' => 'EMI            ',
                       'tracks' => [
                                     'Walt Whitman\'s Niece',
                                     'California Stars'
                                   ]
                     },
                     {
                       'Released' => '1993',
                       'Artist' => 'Black, Mary   ',
                       'Title' => 'The Holy Ground   ',
                       'Label' => 'Grapevine      ',
                       'tracks' => [
                                     'Summer Sent You',
                                     'Flesh And Blood'
                                   ]
                     },
                     {
                       'Released' => '1995',
                       'Artist' => 'Black, Mary   ',
                       'Title' => 'Circus          ',
                       'Label' => 'Grapevine      ',
                       'tracks' => [
                                     'The Circus',
                                     'In A Dream'
                                   ]
                     },
                     {
                       'Released' => '1971',
                       'Artist' => 'Bowie, David  ',
```

```
                        'Title' => 'Hunky Dory         ',
                        'Label' => 'RCA              ',
                        'tracks' => [
                                    'Changes',
                                    'Oh You Pretty Things'
                                    ]
                },
                {
                        'Released' => '1997',
                        'Artist' => 'Bowie, David  ',
                        'Title' => 'Earthling          ',
                        'Label' => 'EMI              ',
                        'tracks' => [
                                    'Little Wonder',
                                    'Looking For Satellites'
                                    ]
                }
            ],
    'title' => 'Dave\'s CD Collection',
    'count' => '6',
    'date' => '16 Sep 1999'
};
```

You can see that this structure is the same as the one that we built in chapter 8. The main part of the structure is a hash, the keys of which are "list," "title," "count," and "date." Of these, all but "list" is associated with a scalar containing data from the header or the footer of the file. The key "list" is associated with a reference to an array. Each element of that array contains the details of one CD in a hash. This includes a reference to a further list that contains the tracks from each CD.

11.4 *Other features of Parse::RecDescent*

That completes our detailed look at using Parse::RecDescent. It should give you enough information to parse some rather complex file formats into equally complex data structures. We have, however, only scratched the surface of what Parse::RecDescent can do. Here is an overview of some of its other features. For further details see the documentation that comes with the module.

- *Autotrees*—This is a method by which you can get the parser to automatically build a parse tree for your input data. If you don't have a specific requirement for your output data structure, then this functionality might be of use to you.

- *Lookahead rules*—Sometimes the data that you are parsing can be more complex than the examples that we have covered. In particular, if a token can change its meaning depending on what follows it, you should make use of lookahead rules. These allow you to specify text in the rule which must be matched, but is not consumed by the match. This is very similar to the (?= ...) construct in Perl regular expressions.

- *Error handling*—Parse::RecDescent has a powerful functionality to allow you to output error messages when a rule fails to match.

- *Dynamic rules*—Because terminals are either text strings or regular expressions and both of these can contain variables which are evaluated at run time, it is possible to create rules which change their meaning as the parse progresses.

- *Subrule argument*—It is possible for a rule to pass arguments down into its subrule and, therefore, alter the way that they work.

- *Incremental parsing*—It is possible to change the definition of a grammar which a program is running, using two methods called Extend and Replace.

- *Precompiling parsers*—Using the Precompile method it is possible to create a new module that will parse a particular grammar. This new module can then be used in programs without Parse::RecDescent being present.

11.5 *Further information*

The best place to get more information about Parse::RecDescent is in the manual pages that come with the module. Typing perldoc Parse::RecDescent at any command line will show you this documentation. The distribution also contains almost forty demo programs and an HTML version of Damian Conway's article for the Winter 1998 issue of *The Perl Journal* titled "The man of descent," which is a useful introduction to parsing in general and Parse::RecDescent in particular.

11.6 *Summary*

- Parse::RecDescent is a Perl module for building recursive descent parsers.
- Parsers are created by passing the new method the definition of a grammar.
- The parser is run by passing the text to be parsed to a method named after the top-level rule in the grammar.
- Parser action code can be associated with grammar rules. The associated code is called when the rule matches.
- The @item array contains details of the tokens which have matched in a given rule.
- Parser actions can change the value that will be returned by a rule. This is how you can build up parse tree data structures.

Part IV

The big picture

At the end of the tale, our heroes return home determined to spread the news to the general population about the tools and techniques they have learned. Nevermore will the people be terrified by the data munging beast.

This is obviously a cause for much celebration.

Looking back—
and ahead

227

The received wisdom for giving a presentation is that you should "tell them what you're going to tell them, tell them, and then tell them what you've told them." A book is no different in principle to a presentation, so in this chapter we'll review what we've covered and discuss where you can go for more information.

12.1 *The usefulness of things*

A brief reminder of why you munge data and, more importantly, why you should munge it using Perl.

12.1.1 *The usefulness of data munging*

In chapter 1 I said that data munging lived in the "interstices between computer systems." I hope that you can now see just how all-pervasive it is. There are very few computing tasks that don't involve munging data to some degree. From the run-once command line script which loads data files into a new database, to the many-thousand lines of code which run bank's accounting systems, they are all munging data in one way or another.

12.1.2 *The usefulness of Perl*

The next aim of the book was to demonstrate how well Perl fits into the data munging problem space. By allowing programmers to define a problem in a way that is closer to the way that their thought processes work and further from the way that computer CPUs work, many programmers find that using Perl makes them far more productive.

In a recent article on www.perl.com, Mark-Jason Dominus talks about the difference between "natural" code and "synthetic" code. Natural code is the code which is fundamentally tied in with solving the problem at hand. Synthetic code is code which is merely a side effect of the programming constructs that you use to solve the problem. A good example of synthetic code is a loop counter. In many programming languages, if you wanted to iterate across an array you would need to write code similar to this:

```
for ($i = 0; $i <= $#arr; $i++) {
  some_function($arr[$i]);
}
```

You can, of course, write code like this in Perl (as the sample demonstrates), but a far more Perlish way to write it is like this:

```
foreach (@arr) {
  some_function($_);
}
```

Because the second version removes all of the synthetic code required to iterate across an array, it is far easier for a programmer to follow exactly what is happening.

Synthetic code only gets in the way of a programmer's understanding of a program so the goal must always be to eliminate as much of it as possible. Because Perl is particularly good at allowing programmers to model the problem exactly, it follows that you end up with a far smaller amount of synthetic code than in many other languages.

If you're interested in reading more (and you *should* be), Dominus' article is at http://www.perl.com/pub/2000/06/commify.html.

12.1.3 *The usefulness of the Perl community*

One of the best things about using Perl is the community that goes with it. It seems to attract people who are only too happy to help others—whether by submitting their code to the CPAN, answering a technical question in a newsgroup such as comp.lang.perl.misc, or on a website like Perl Monks, or even writing articles for *The Perl Journal*.

If you are going to use Perl, I would certainly encourage you to become part of the Perl community. There are a number of ways to do this:

- Join your local Perl Mongers group. These are users' groups. You can find the contact for your local group at www.pm.org. If there isn't one for your area, why not form one?

- Visit comp.lang.perl.misc regularly. This is the main Perl newsgroup. As long as you follow the rules of Netiquette, you will be very welcome there.

- Read *The Perl Journal*. This is the only printed magazine dedicated to Perl. You can subscribe at www.tpj.com.

- Submit your code to the CPAN. If you have written code which could be of use to others, why not put it in a place where everyone can find it? Details on becoming a CPAN author can be found at www.cpan.org.

12.2 *Things to know*

A brief list of things that you should know to make your data munging work as easy as possible.

12.2.1 *Know your data*

When munging data, the more that you know about your source and your sink, the better you will be able to design your program and, perhaps more importantly, your intermediate data structures. You need to know as much as possible about not only the format of the data, but also what it will be used for, as this will help you to build flexibility into your program. Always design your program to be as flexible as possible. This includes designing intermediate data structures carefully and using the UNIX filter model to remove any assumptions about input and output channels.

Know whether your data inputs or outputs are liable to change. If so, can you design your program so that it makes no assumptions about input and output formats? Can your program work out the format from the actual input data? Or can the input and output formats be driven from configuration files? Can you have some input into the design of these formats? If so, can you make them flexible enough that one output format can go to more than one sink? Or can more than one source provide data in the same format? If not, can you munge the formats in a preprocessing program to make them all the same?

You may also need to know about the operating system that data was produced on or will be used on, as this may affect the format of the data. Is it in ASCII, EBCDIC or Unicode? Is binary data big-endian or little-endian? What is the line end character sequence?

12.2.2 *Know your tools*

Ensure that you are as comfortable as possible with Perl and its features. Buy and read Perl books. All Perl programmers should have read *Programming Perl, The Perl Cookbook, Mastering Regular Expressions,* and *Object Oriented Perl.* Read the documentation that comes with Perl—it will be more up-to-date than any book. Know what questions are answered in `perldoc perlfaq` (and know their answers). Subscribe to *The Perl Journal* (and consider buying a complete set of back issues).

Understand common Perl methods such as complex sorting techniques. Learn how to benchmark your programs. Find the best performing solution to the problem (but know when your solution is fast enough).

Visit the CPAN often enough to have an overview of what is there. If a module will solve your problem then install it and save yourself writing more code than is necessary. If a module will almost solve your problem then consider contacting the author and suggest improvements. Even better, supply patches.

12.2.3 *Know where to go for more information*

Here is a list of sources for information about Perl. Most of them have been mentioned at some point in the book, but I thought it would be useful to gather them together in one place.

- *The Perl Home Page*—Definitive source for all things Perl: www.perl.com
- *comp.lang.perl.misc*—The most active Perl newsgroup.

- *perldoc perl* *(and others)*—The best Perl documentation installed right on your computer.

- *Programming Perl* (O'Reilly), Larry Wall, Tom Christiansen, and Jon Orwant—The essential Perl book. Make sure you get the 3rd edition.

- *The Perl Cookbook* (O'Reilly), Tom Christiansen and Nathan Torkington—The essential Perl book (volume 2).

- *Mastering Regular Expressions* (O'Reilly), Jeffrey Friedl—Everything you ever wanted to know about regexes.

- *Object Oriented Perl* (Manning), Damian Conway—Everything you ever wanted to know about programming with objects in Perl.

- *The Perl Journal*—The only Perl magazine.

- *The Perl Mongers*—Friendly Perl people in your town. www.pm.org.

- *Perl Monks*—A web site where Perl programmers help each other with Perl problems. http://www.perlmonks.org.

Modules reference

In this book, we have looked at a number of Perl modules. Some of them are standard modules that come bundled with your Perl distribution; others can be obtained from the CPAN. Full instructions on how to install CPAN modules can be found in `perldoc perlmodinstall`.

In order to avoid interrupting the flow of the narrative chapters, I have not given detailed descriptions of the modules earlier in the book. Instead, I have gathered all of that information in this appendix. In all cases, this is not a complete reference for the module, but should be enough to take you beyond the examples in the book. Full references will come with the module and can be accessed by typing `perldoc <module_name>` at your command line. For example, typing

`perldoc DBI`

will give you a full description of `DBI.pm`.

A.1 DBI

The following is a brief list of the most useful DBI functions.

A.1.1 Functions called on the DBI class

These functions are called via the DBI class itself.

- `DBI->available_drivers`
  Returns a list of the available DBD modules.

- `DBI->connect($data_source, $user, $password [, \%attributes])`
  Creates a connection to a database and returns a handle which you use to carry out further actions on this connection.

  - `$data_source` will always start with "dbi:driver_name:". The rest of the string is driver dependent.

  - `$user` and `$password` are passed unchanged to the database driver. They will usually be a valid database user and associated password.

  - `\%attributes` is a reference to an optional hash of attribute values. Currently supported attributes are PrintError, RaiseError, and AutoCommit. These attributes are the keys of the hash and the associated values should be Boolean expressions (e.g., 0 or 1). The default values are the equivalents of setting the parameter to
    `{PrintError => 1, RaiseError => 0, AutoCommit => 1}`.

- `DBI->data_sources($driver)`
  Returns a list of data sources available for the given driver.

- `DBI->trace($level [, $file])`
  Controls the amount of trace information to be displayed (or written to the optional file). Calling trace via the DBI class will enable tracing on all handles. It is also possible to control trace levels at the handle level. The trace levels are described in detail in the DBI documentation.

A.1.2 Attributes of the DBI class

The following attribute can be accessed through the DBI class.

- `$DBI::err, $DBI::errstr`
  Returns the most recent database driver error encountered. A numeric error code is returned by `$DBI::err` and a text string is returned by `$DBI::errstr`.

A.1.3 Functions called on any DBI handle

The following functions are called via any valid DBI handle (usually a database handle or a statement handle).

- `$h->err, $h->errstr`
  Returns the most recent database driver error encountered by this handle. A numeric error code is returned by `$h->err` and a text string is returned by `$h->errstr`.

- `$h->trace($level [, $file])`
  Similar to `DBI->trace`, but works at the handle level.

A.1.4 Attributes of any DBI handle

The following attributes can be accessed via any DBI handle.

- `$h->{warn}`
  Set to a Boolean value which determines whether warnings are raised for certain bad practices.

- `$h->{Kids}`
  Returns the number of statement handles that have been created from it and not destroyed.

- `$h->{PrintError}`
  Set to a Boolean value which determines whether errors are printed to STDERR rather than just returning error codes. The default for this attribute is on.

- `$h->{RaiseError}`
  Set to a Boolean value which determines whether errors cause the program to die rather than just returning error codes. The default for this attribute is off.

- `$h->{Chopblanks}`
Set to a Boolean value which determines whether trailing blanks are removed from fixed-width character fields. The default for this value is off.

- `$h->{LongReadLen}`
Determines the amount of data that a driver will read when reading a large field from the database. These fields are often known by such names as text, binary, or blob. The default value is 0, which means that long data fields are not returned.

- `$h->{LongTruncOk}`
Set to a Boolean value which determines whether a fetch should fail if it attempts to fetch a long column that is larger than the current value of `LongReadLen`. The default value is 0 which means that truncated fetches raise an error.

A.1.5   *Functions called on a database handle*

The following functions are called on a valid database handle.

- `$dbh->selectrow_array($statement [, \%attr [, @bind_values]])`
Combines the `prepare`, `execute`, and `fetchrow_array` functions into one function call. When it is called in a list context it returns the first row of data returned by the query. When it is called in a scalar context it returns the first field of the first row. See the separate functions for more details on the parameters.

- `$dbh->selectall_arrayref($statement [, \%attr`
`[, @bind_values]])`
Combines the `prepare`, `execute`, and `fetchall_arrayref` functions into a single function call. It returns a reference to an array. Each element of the array contains a reference to an array containing the data returned. See the separate functions for more details on the parameters.

- `$dbh->prepare($statement [, \%attr])`
Prepares an SQL statement for later execution against the database and returns a statement handle. This handle can later be used to invoke the execute function. Most database drivers will, at this point, pass the statement to the database to ensure that it compiles correctly. If there is a problem, `prepare` will return `undef`.

- `$dbh->do($statement, \%attr, @bind_values)`
Prepares and executes an SQL statement. It returns the number of rows affected (–1 if the database driver doesn't support this) or `undef` if there is an error. This is useful for executing statements that have no return sets, such as updates or deletes.

- `$dbh->commit, $dbh->rollback`
  Will commit or rollback the current database transaction. They are only effective if the AutoCommit attribute is set to 0.

- `$dbh->disconnect`
  Disconnects the database handle from the database and frees any associated memory.

- `$dbh->quote`
  Applies whatever transformations are required to quote dangerous characters in a string, so that the string can be passed to the database safely. For example, many database systems use single quotes to delimit strings so that any apostrophes in a string can cause a syntax error. Passing the string through the quote function will escape the apostrophe in a database-specific manner.

A.1.6 *Database handle attributes*

The following attribute can be accessed through a database handle.

- `$dbh->{AutoCommit}`
  Set to a Boolean value which determines whether or not each statement is committed as it is executed. The default value is 1, which means that it is impossible to roll back transactions. If you want to be able to roll back database changes then you must change this attribute to 0.

A.1.7 *Functions called on a statement handle*

The following functions are all called via a valid statement handle.

- `$sth->bind_param($p_num, $bind_value[, $bind_type])`
  Used to bind a value to a placeholder in a prepared SQL statement. Placeholders are marked with the question mark character (?). The $p_num parameter indicates which placeholder to use (placeholders are numbered from 1) and the $bind_values is the actual data to use. For example:

```
my %data = (LON => 'London', MAN => 'Manchester', BIR => 'Birmingham');
my $sth = $dbh->prepare('insert into city (code, name) values (?, ?)');
foreach (keys %data) {
  $sth->bind_param(1, $_);
  $sth->bind_param(2, $data{$_});
  $sth->execute;
}
```

- `$sth->bind_param_inout($p_num, \$bind_value, $max_len`
  `[, $bindtype])`
  Like bind_param but it also enables variables to be updated by the results of the statement. This function is often used when the SQL statement is a call to

a stored procedure. Note that the `$bind_value` must be passed as a reference to the variable to be used. The `$max_len` parameter is used to allocate the correct amount of memory to store the returned value.

- `$sth->execute([@bind_values])`
  Executes the prepared statement on the database. If the statement is an `insert`, `delete`, or `update` then when this function returns, the insert, delete, or update will be complete. If the statement was a `select` statement, then you will need to call one of the fetch functions to get access to the result set. If any parameters are passed to this function, then `bind_param` will be run for each value before the statement is executed.

- `$sth->fetchrow_arrayref, $sth->fetch`
  (fetch is an alias for `fetchrow_arrayref`)
  Fetches the next row of data from the result set and returns a reference to an array that holds the data values. Any NULL data items are returned as `undef`. When there are no more rows to be returned, the function returns `undef`.

- `$sth->fetchrow_array`
  Similar to `fetchrow_arrayref`, except that it returns an array containing the row data. When there are no more rows to return, `fetchrow_array` returns an empty array.

- `$sth->fetchrow_hashref`
  Similar to `fetchrow_arrayref`, except that it returns a hash containing the row data. The keys of the hash are the column names and the values are the data items. When there are no more rows to return, this function returns `undef`.

- `$sth->fetchall_arrayref`
  Returns all of the data from a result set at one time. The function returns a reference to an array. Each element of the array is a reference to another. Each of these second-level arrays represents one row in the result set and each element contains a data item. This function returns an empty array if there is no data returned by the statement.

- `$sth->finish`
  Disposes of the statement handle and frees up any memory associated with it.

- `$sth->bind_col($column_number, \$var_to_bind)`
  Binds a column in a return set to a Perl variable. Note that you must pass a reference to the variable. This means that each time a row is fetched, the variable is automatically updated to contain the value of the bound column in the newly fetched row. See the code example under `bind_columns` for more details.

- `$sth->bind_columns(@list_of_refs_to_vars)`
  Binds each variable in the list to a column in the result set (the first variable in the list is bound to the first column in the result set, and so on). Note that the list must contain references to the variables. For example:

```
my ($code, $name);
my $sth = $dbh->prepare('select code, name from city');
$sth->execute;
$sth->bind_columns(\$code, \$name);

while ($sth->fetch) {
  print "$code: $name\n";
}
```

A.1.8 Statement handle attributes

The following attributes can be accessed through a statement handle.

- `$sth->{NUM_OF_FIELDS}`
  Contains the number of fields (columns) that the statement will return.

- `$sth->{NAME}`
  Contains a reference to an array which contains the names of the fields that will be returned by the statement.

- `$sth->{TYPE}`
  Contains a reference to an array which contains an integer for each field in the result set. This integer indicates the data type of the field using an international standard.

- `$sth->{NULLABLE}`
  Contains a reference to an array which contains a value for each field that indicates whether the field can contain NULL values. The valid values are 0 = no, 1 = yes, and 2 = don't know.

A.2 Number::Format

The following is a brief reference to `Number::Format`.

A.2.1 Attributes

These are the attributes that can be passed to the `new` method.

- `THOUSANDS_SEP`
  The character which is inserted between groups of three digits. The default is a comma.

- DECIMAL_POINT
  The character which separates the integer and fractional parts of a number. The default is a decimal point.

- MON_THOUSANDS_SEP
  The same as THOUSANDS_SEP, but used for monetary values (formatted using format_price). The default is a comma.

- MON_DECIMAL_POINT
  The same as DECIMAL_POINT, but used for monetary values (formatted using format_price). The default is a decimal point.

- INT_CURR_SYMBOL
  The character(s) used to denote the currency. The default is USD.

- DECIMAL_DIGITS
  The number of decimal digits to display. The default is two.

- DECIMAL_FILL
  A Boolean flag indicating whether or not the formatter should add zeroes to pad out decimal numbers to DECIMAL_DIGITS places. The default is off.

- NEG_FORMAT
  The format to use when displaying negative numbers. An 'x' marks where the number should be inserted. The default is -x.

- KILO_SUFFIX
  The letter to append when format_bytes is formatting a value in kilobytes. The default is K.

- MEGA_SUFFIX
  The letter to append when format_bytes is formatting a value in megabytes. The default is M.

A.2.2 Methods

These are the methods that you can call to format your data.

- round($number, $precision)
  Rounds the given number to the given precision. If no precision is given, then DECIMAL_DIGITS is used. A negative precision will decrease the precision before the decimal point. This method doesn't make use of the DECIMAL_POINT or THOUSANDS_SEP values.

- format_number($number, $precision, $trailing_zeroes)
  Formats the given number to the given precision and pads with trailing zeroes if $trailing_zeroes is true. If neither $precision nor $trailing_zeroes

are given then the values in DECIMAL_DIGITS and DECIMAL_FILL are used instead. This method inserts the value of THOUSANDS_SEP every three digits and replaces the decimal point with the value of DECIMAL_POINT.

- format_negative($number, $picture)
  Formats the given number using the given picture. If a picture is not given then the value of NEG_FORMAT is used instead. In the picture, the character "x" should be used to mark the place where the number should go.

- format_picture($number, $picture)
  Formats the given number using the given picture. The picture should contain the character # wherever you want a digit from $number to appear. If there are fewer digits in $number than there are # characters, then the output is left-padded with spaces and any occurrences of THOUSANDS_SEP to the left of the number are removed. If there are more digits in $number than there are # characters in $picture then all of the # characters are replaced with * characters.

- format_price($number, $precision)
  Works like format_number, except that the values of MON_THOUSANDS_SEP and MON_DECIMAL_POINT are used, and the value of INT_CURR_SYMBOL is prepended to the result.

- format_bytes($number, $precision)
  Works like format_number except that numbers larger than 1024 will be divided by 1024 and the value of KILO_SUFFIX will be appended and numbers larger than 1024^2 will be divided by 1024^2 and the value of MEGA_SUFFIX will be appended.

- unformat_number($formatted_number)
  The parameter $formatted_number must be a number that has been formatted by format_number, format_price or format_picture. The formatting is removed and an unformatted number is returned.

A.3 Date::Calc

The most useful functions in Date::Calc include:

- $days = Days_in_Month($year, $month)
  Returns the number of days in the given month in the given year.

- $days = Days_in_Year($year, $month)
  Returns the number of days in the given year up to the end of the given month.

Thus, `Days_in_Year(2000, 1)` returns 31, and `Days_in_Year(2000, 2)` returns 60.

- `$is_leap = leap_year($year)`
  Returns 1 if the given year is a leap year and 0 if it isn't.

- `$is_data = check_date($year, $month, $day)`
  Checks whether or not the given combination of year, month, and day constitute a valid date. Therefore `check_date(2000, 2, 29)` returns `true`, but `check_date(2000, 2, 2001)` returns `false`.

- `$doy = Day_of_Year($year, $month, $day)`
  Takes a given date in the year and returns the number of the day in the year that the date falls. Therefore `Day_of_Year(1962, 9, 7)` prints 250 as September 7 was the 250th day of 1962.

- `$dow = Day_of_Week($year, $month, $day)`
  Returns the day of the week that the given date fell on. This will be 1 for Monday and 7 for Sunday. Therefore `Day_of_Week(1962, 9, 7)` returns 5 as September 7, 1962, was a Friday.

- `$week = Week_Number($year, $month, $day)`
  Returns the week number of the year that the given date falls in. Week one is defined as the week that January 4 falls in, so it is possible for the number to be zero. It is also possible for the week number to be 53.

- `($year, $month, $day) = Monday_of_Week($week, $year)`
  Returns the date of the first day (i.e., Monday) of the given week in the given year.

- `($year, $month, $day) = Nth_Weekday_of_Month_Year($year,`
  `                                                   $month,`
  `                                                   $dow, $n)`
  Returns the *n*th week day in the given month in the given year. For example if you wanted to find the third Sunday (day seven of the week) in November 1999 you would call it as `Nth_Weekday_of_Month_Year(1999, 11, 7, 3)` which would return the November 21, 1999.

- `$days = Delta_Days($year1, $month1, $day1,`
  `                    $year2, $month2, $day2)`
  Calculates the number of days between the two given dates.

- `($days, $hours, $mins, $secs) =`
  `    Delta_DHMS($year1, $month1,$day1, $hour1, $min1, $sec1,`
  `               $year2, $month2, $day2, $hour2, $min2, $sec2)`
  Returns the number of days, hours, minutes, and seconds between the two given dates and times.

- ($year, $month, $day) = Add_Delta_Days($year, $month, $day, $days)

  Adds the given number of days to the given date and returns the resulting date. If $days is negative then it is subtracted from the given date. There are other functions that allow you to add days, hours, minutes, and seconds (Add_Delta_DHMS) and years, months, and days (Add_Delta_YMD).

- ($year, $month, $day, $hour, $min, $sec, $doy, $dow, $dst) =System_Clock

  Returns the same set of values as Perl's own internal localtime function, except that the values have been converted into the values recognized by Date::Calc. Specifically, this means the ranges of the month and day of week have been shifted and the year has had 1900 added to it. There are also functions to get the current date (Today), time (Now) and date and time (Today_and_Now).

- ($year, $month, $day) = Easter_Sunday($year)

  Calculates the date of Easter Sunday in the given year.

- $month = Decode_Month($string)

  Parses the string and attempts to recognize it as a valid month name. If a month is found then the corresponding month number is returned. There is a similar function (Decode_Day_of_Week) for working with days of the week.

- $string = Date_to_Text($year, $month, $day)

  Returns a string which is a textual representation of the data that was passed to the function. For example Date_to_Text(1999, 12, 25) returns Sat 25-Dec-1999. There is also a Date_to_Text_Long function which for the same input would return Saturday 25 December 1999.

This is only a sample of the most useful functions in the module. In particular, I have ignored the multilanguage support in the module.

A.4   Date::Manip

This is a brief list of some of the more important functions in Date::Manip.

- $date=ParseDateString($string)

  Takes a string and attempts to parse a valid date out of it. The function will handle just about all common date and time formats and many other surprising ones like "today," "tomorrow," or in "two weeks on Friday." This function returns the date in a standardized format, which is YYYYMMDDHH:MM:SS. You can convert it into a more user-friendly format using the UnixDate function described below. This is the most useful function in the module and you should think about installing this module simply to get access to this functionality.

- `$date = UnixDate($date, $format)`
  Takes the given date (which can be in any format that is understood by `ParseDateString`) and formats it using the value of `$format`. The format string can handle any of the character sequences used by `POSIX::strftime`, but it defines a number of new sequences as well. These are all defined in the `Date::Manip` documentation.

- `$delta = ParseDelta($string)`
  As well as dates (which indicate a fixed point in time), `Date::Manip` deals with date *deltas*. These are a number of years, months, days, hours, minutes, or seconds that you can add or subtract from a date in order to get another date. This function attempts to recognize deltas in the string that is passed to it and returns a standardized delta in the format `Y:M:W:D:H:MN:S`. The function recognizes strings like `+3Y 4M 2D` to add three years, four months and two days. It also recognizes more colloquial terms like "ago" (e.g., 4 years ago) and "in" (e.g., in three weeks).

- `@dates = ParseRecur($recur, [$base, $start, $end, $flags])`
  Returns a list of dates for a recurring event. The rules that govern how the event recurs are defined in `$recur`. The syntax is a little complex, but it is based loosely on the syntax of a UNIX crontab file and is defined in detail in the `Date::Manip` documentation.

- `$diff = Date_Cmp($date1, $date2)`
  Compares two dates and returns the same values as Perl's internal `Cmp` and `<=>` operators do for strings and numbers respectively; i.e., –1 if `$date` < `$date1`, 0 if `$date1` == `$date2`, and 1 if `$date1` > `$date2`. This means that this function can be used as a sort routine.

- `$d = DateCalc($d1, $d2)`
  Takes two dates (or two deltas or one of each) and performs an appropriate calculation with them. Two deltas yield a third delta; a date and a delta yield the result of applying the delta to the date; and two dates yield a delta which is the time between the two dates. There are additional parameters that give you finer control over the calculation.

- `$date = Date_GetPrev($date, $dow, $curr, $time)`
  Given a date, this function will calculate the previous occurrence of the given day of the week. If the given date falls on the given day of the week, then the behavior depends on the setting of the `$curr` flag. If `$curr` is non-zero then the current date is returned. If `$curr` is zero then the date a week earlier is

returned. If the optional parameter `$time` is passed to the function, then the time in the returned date is set to that value. There is also a very similar `Date_GetNext` function.

- `$day = Date_DayOfWeek($month, $day, $year)`
  Returns the day of the week that the given date fell on (1 for Monday, 7 for Sunday). Note the nonstandard order of the arguments to this function.

- `$day = Date_DayOfYear($month, $day, $year)`
  Returns the day of the year (1 to 366) that the given date falls on. Note the nonstandard order of the arguments to this function.

- `$days = Date_DaysInYear($year)`
  Returns the number of days in the given year.

- `$days = Date_DaysInMonth($month, $year)`
  Returns the number of days in the given month in the given year.

- `$flag = Date_LeapYear($year)`
  Returns 1 if the given year is a leap year and 0 otherwise.

- `$day = Date_DaySuffix($day)`
  Calculates the suffix that should be applied to the day number and appends it to the number; e.g., `Date_DaySuffix` returns "1st."

This only scratches the surface of what `Date::Manip` is capable of. In particular, it has very good support for working with business days and holidays and allows you to configure it to work with local holidays.

A.5   *LWP::Simple*

In chapter 9 we took a brief look at the `LWP::Simple` module. Here is a slightly less brief look at the functions that this module provides. For more information on using this module see the `lwpcook` manual page which comes with the LWP bundle of modules.

- `$page = get($url)`
  Returns the document which is found at the given URL. It returns only the document without any of the HTTP headers. Returns `undef` if the request fails.

- `($content_type, $document_len, $mod_time, $expiry_time, $server) = head($url)`
  Returns various information from the HTTP header that is returned when the given URL is requested. Returns an empty list if the request fails.

- `$http_code = getprint($url)`
  Gets the document from the given URL and prints it to STDOUT. If the request fails, it prints the status code and error message. The return value is the HTTP response code.

- `$http_code = getstore($url, $file)`
  Gets the document from the given URL and stores it in the given file. The return value is the HTTP response code.

- `$http_response = mirror($url, $file)`
  Mirrors the document at the given URL into the given file. If the document hasn't changed since the file was created then no action is taken. Returns the HTTP response code.

A.6   HTML::Parser

Here is a brief guide to the methods of the HTML::Parser object. As I mentioned briefly in chapter 9, this describes version 3.x of HTML::Parser. In older versions you had to subclass HTML::Parser in order to do any useful work with it. Unfortunately, as I write this, the version of HTML::Parser available from the ActiveState module repository for use with ActivePerl is still a 2.x version.[1] For further detail on using an older version, see the documentation that comes with the module.

- `$parser = HTML::Parser->new(%options_and_handlers)`
  Creates an instance of the HTML parser object. For details of the various options and handlers that can be passed to this method, see the description later in this section. Returns the new parser object or undef on failure.

- `$parser->parse($html)`
  Parses a piece of HTML text. Can be called multiple times.

- `$parser->eof`
  Tells the parser that you have finished calling parse.

- `$parser->parse_file($file_name)`
  Parses a file containing HTML.

- `$parser->strict_comment($boolean)`
  Many popular browsers (including Netscape Navigator and Microsoft Internet Explorer) parse HTML comments in a way which is subtly different than the HTML standard. Calling this function and passing it a true value will switch on strict (i.e., in line with the HTML specification) comment handling.

---

[1] As I was completing the final edits of this book, there were some moves towards correcting this discrepancy.

- `$parser->strict_names($boolean)`
  This method has similar functionality to `strict_comment`, but deals with certain browsers' ability to understand broken tag and attribute names.

- `$parser->xml_mode($boolean)`
  When `xml_mode` is switched on, the parser handles certain XML constructs which aren't allowed in HTML. These include combined start and end tags (e.g., `<br/>`) and XML processing instructions.

- `$parser->handler(%hash)`
  Allows you to change handler functions. The arguments are similar to those in the handler arguments optionally passed to the `new` method. These are discussed in the next section.

A.6.1 *Handlers*

To do anything useful with `HTML::Parser`, you need to define handlers which are called when the parser encounters certain constructs in the HTML document. You can define handlers for the events shown in table A.1.

Table A.1 `HTML::Parser` handlers

Handler	Called when ...
declaration	an HTML DOCTYPE declaration is found
start	the start of an HTML tag is found
end	the end of an HTML tag is found
text	plain text is found
comment	an HTML comment is found
process	a processing instruction is found

Each of these handlers can be defined in two ways. Either you can pass details of the handler to the `new` method or you can use the `handler` method after creating the parser object, but before parsing the document. Here are examples of both uses.

```
my $parser = HTML::Parser->new(start_h => [\&start, 'tagname,attr']);

$parser->handler(start => [\&start, 'tagname,attr']);
```

In both examples we have set the start handler to be a function called `start` which must be defined somewhere within our program. The only difference between the two versions is that when using `new`, the event name (i.e., `start`) must have the string `_h` appended to it. In both examples the actual subroutine to be called is defined in a two-element array. The first element of the array is a reference to the subroutine to be called and the second element is a string defining the arguments which the subroutine expects. The various values that this string can contain are listed in table A.2.

Table A.2 Argument specification strings

Name	Description	Data type
self	The current parser object	Reference to the object
tokens	The list of tokens which makes up the current event	Reference to an array
tokenpos	A list of the positions of the tokens in the original text. Each token has two numbers; the first is the offset of the start of the token, and the second is the length of the token.	Reference to an array
token0	The text of the first token (this is the same as `$tokens->[0]`)	Scalar value
tagname	The name of the current tag	Scalar value
attr	The name and values of the attributes of the current tag	Reference to a hash
attrseq	A list of the names of the attributes of the current tag in the order that they appear in the original document	Reference to an array
text	The source text for this event	Scalar value
dtest	The same as "text" but with any HTML entities (e.g., &) decoded	Scalar value
is_cdata	True if event is in a CDATA section	Scalar value
offset	The offset (in bytes) of the start of the current event from the start of the HTML document	Scalar value
length	Length (in bytes) of the original text which constitutes the event	Scalar value
event	The name of the current event	Scalar value
line	The number of the line in the document where this event started	Scalar value
' '	Any literal string is passed to the handler unchanged	Scalar value
undef	An `undef` value	Scalar value

A.7   *HTML::LinkExtor*

`HTML::LinkExtor` is a subclass of `HTML::Parser` and, therefore, all of that class's methods are available. Here is a list of extra methods together with methods that have a different interface.

- `$parser = $HTML::LinkExtor->new($callback, $base)`
  Creates an `HTML::LinkExtor` object. Both of its parameters are optional.
  The first parameter is a reference to a function which will be called each time
  a link is found in the document being parsed. This function will be called
  with the tag name in lower case as the first argument followed by a list of
  attributes and values. Only link attributes will be included. The second
  parameter is a base URL used to convert relative URLs to absolute ones (you
  will need the `URI::URL` module installed in order to use this functionality).

- `@links = $parser->links`
  Having parsed a document, this method returns a list of all of the links found.
  Each element of the array returned is a reference to another array. This second level array contains the same values as would have been passed to the
  links callback if you had defined one in the call to `new`. If you do provide a
  link callback function, then `links` will return an empty array.

A.8   HTML::TokeParser

`HTML::TokeParser` is another subclass of `HTML::Parser`; however, it is not recommended that you call any of the methods from the superclass. You should only
use the methods defined by `HTML::TokeParser`.

- `$parser = HTML::TokeParser->new($document)`
  Creates an `HTML::TokeParser` object. The single parameter defines the document to be parsed in one of a number of possible ways. If the method is
  passed a plain scalar then it is taken as the name of a file to open and read. If
  the method is passed a reference to a scalar then it assumes that the scalar
  contains the entire text of the document. If it is passed any other type of
  object (for example, a file handle) then it assumes that it can read data from
  the object as it is required.

- `$token = $parser->get_token`
  Returns the next token from the document (or `undef` when there are no
  more tokens). A token consists of a reference to an array. The first element in
  the array is a character indicating the type of the token (`S` for start tag, `E` for
  end tag, `T` for text, `C` for comment, and `D` for a declaration). The remaining
  elements are the same as the parameters to the appropriate method of the
  `HTML::Parser` object.

- `$parser->unget_token`
  You can't know what kind of token you will get next until you have received
  it. If you find that you don't need it yet, you can call this method to return it
  to the token stack to be given to you again the next time you call `get_token`.

- $tag = $parser->get_tag($tag)

  Returns the next start or end tag in the document. The parameter is optional and, if it is used, the method will return the next tag of the given type. The method returns undef if no more tokens (or no more tokens of the given type) are found. The tag is returned as a reference to an array. The elements of the array are similar to the elements in the array returned from the get_token method, but the character indicating the token type is missing and the name of an end tag will have a / character prepended.

- $text = $parser->get_text($endtag)

  Returns all text at the current position of the document. If the optional parameter is omitted it returns the text up to the next tag. If an end tag is given then it returns all text up to the next end tag of the given type.

- $text = $parser->get_trimmed_text($endtag)

  Works in the same way as the get_text method, except that any sequences of white space characters are collapsed to a single space, and any leading or trailing white space is removed.

A.9   *HTML::TreeBuilder*

HTML::TreeBuilder inherits all of the methods from HTML::Parser and HTML::Element. It builds an HTML parse tree when each node is an HTML::Element object. It only has a few methods of its own, and here is a list of them.

- $parser->implicit_tags($boolean)

  If the boolean value is true then the parser will try to deduce where missing elements and tags should be.

- $parser->implicit_body_p_tag($boolean)

  If the boolean value is true, the parser will force there to be a <p> element surrounding any elements which should not be immediately contained within a <body> tag.

- $parser->ignore_unknown($boolean)

  Controls what the parser does with unknown HTML tags. If the boolean value is true then they are simply ignored.

- $parser->ignore_text($boolean)

  If the boolean value is true then the parser will not represent any of the text of the document within the parser tree. This can be used (and save a lot of storage space) if you are only interested in the structure of the document.

- `$parser->ignore_ignorable_whitespace($boolean)`
  If the boolean value is `true` then the parser will not build nodes for white space which can be ignored without affecting the structure of the document.

- `$parser->p_strict($boolean)`
  If the boolean value is `true` then the parser will be very strict about the type of elements that can be contained within a `<p>` element and will insert a closing `</p>` tag if it is necessary.

- `$parser->store_comments($boolean)`,
  `$parser->store_declarations($boolean)`,
  `$parser->store_pis($boolean)`
  These control whether or not comments, declarations, and processing instructions are stored in the parser tree.

- `$parser->warn($boolean)`
  Controls whether or not warnings are displayed when syntax errors are found in the HTML document.

A.10 *XML::Parser*

`XML::Parser` is one of the most complex modules that is covered in this book. Here is a brief reference to its most commonly used methods.

- `$parser = XML::Parser->new(Style => $style,`
  `                            Handlers => \%handlers,`
  `                            Pkg => $package)`
  Creates an `XML::Parser` object. It takes a number of optional named parameters. The `Style` parameter indicates which of a number of canned parsing styles you would like to use. Table A.3 lists the available styles along with the results of choosing a particular style.

Table A.3 `XML::Parser` **Styles**

Style name	Results
Debug	Prints out a stylized version of the document outline.
Subs	When the start of an XML tag is found, the parser calls a subroutine with the same name as the tag. When the end of an XML tag is found, the parser calls a subroutine with the same names as the tag with an underscore character prepended. Both of these subroutines are presumed to exist in the package denoted by the `Pkg` parameter. The parameters passed to these subroutines are the same as those passed to the `Start` and `End` handler routines.

Table A.3 `XML::Parser` **Styles (continued)**

Style name	Results
Tree	The `parse` method will return a parse tree representing the document. Each node is represented by a reference to a two-element array. The first element in the list is either the tag name or "0" if it is a text node. The second element is the content of the tag. The content is a reference to another array. The first element of this array is a reference to a (possibly empty) hash containing attribute/value pairs. The rest of this array is made up of pair of elements representing the type and content of the contained nodes. See section 9.2.3 for examples.
Objects	The `parse` method returns a parse tree representing the object. Each node in the tree is a hash which has been blessed into an object. The object type names are created by appending the type of each tag to the value of the `Pkg` parameter followed by ::. A text node is blessed into the class `::Characters`. Each node will have a `kids` attribute which will be a reference to an array containing each of the node's children.
Stream	This style works in a manner similar to the `Subs` style. Whenever the parser finds particular XML objects, it calls various subroutines. These subroutines are all assumed to exist in the package denoted by the `Pkg` parameter. The subroutines are called `StartDocument`, `StartTag`, `EndTag`, `Text`, `PI`, and `EndDocument`. The only one of these names which doesn't make it obvious when the subroutine is called is PI. This is called when the parser encounters a processing instruction in the document.

The `Handlers` parameter is a reference to a hash. The keys of this hash are the names of the events that the parser triggers while parsing the document and the values are references to subroutines which are called when the events are triggered. The subroutines are assumed to be in the package defined by the `Pkg` parameter. Table A.4 lists the various types of handlers. The first parameter to each of these handlers is a reference to the Expat object which `XML::Parser` creates to actually handle the parsing. This object has a number of its own methods which you can use to gain even more precise control over the parsing process. For details of these, see the manual page for `XML::Parser::Expat`.

Table A.4 `XML::Parser` **Handlers**

Handler	When called	Subroutine parameters
Init	Before the parser starts processing the document	Reference to the Expat object
Final	After the parser finishes processing the document	Reference to the Expat object
Start	When the parser finds the start of a tag	Reference to the Expat object Name of the tag found List of name/value pairs for the attributes

Table A.4 XML::Parser **Handlers (continued)**

Handler	When called	Subroutine parameters
End	When the parser finds the end of a tag	Reference to the Expat Object
Char	When the parser finds character data	Reference to the Expat Object The character string
Proc	When the parser finds a processing instruction	Reference to the Expat Object The name of the PI target The PI data
Comment	When the parser finds a comment	Reference to the Expat Object The comment data
CdataStart	When the parser finds the start of a CDATA section	Reference to the Expat Object
CdataEnd	When the parser finds the end of a CDATA section	Reference to the Expat Object
Default	When the parser finds any data that doesn't have an assigned handler	Reference to the Expat Object The data string
Unparsed	When the parser finds an unparsed entity declaration	Reference to the Expat Object Name of the Entity Base URL to use when resolving the address The system ID The public ID
Notation	When the parser finds a notation declaration	Reference to the Expat Object Name of the Notation Base URL to use when resolving the address The system ID The public ID
ExternEnt	When the parser finds an external entity declaration	Reference to the Expat Object Base URL to use when resolving the address The system ID The public ID
Entity	When the parser finds an entity declaration	Reference to the Expat Object Name of the Entity The value of the Entity The system ID The public ID The notation for the entity
Element	When the parser finds an element declaration	Reference to the Expat Object Name of the Element The Content Model

Table A.4 `XML::Parser` **Handlers (continued)**

Handler	When called	Subroutine parameters
Attlist	When the parser finds an attribute declaration	Reference to the Expat Object Name of the Element Name of the Attribute The Attribute Type Default Value String indicating whether the attribute is fixed
Doctype	When the parser finds a DocType declaration	Reference to the Expat Object Name of the Document Type System ID Public ID The Internal Subset
XMLDecl	When the parser finds an XML declaration	Reference to the Expat Object Version of XML Document Encoding String indicating whether or not the DTD is standalone

Pkg is the name of a package. All handlers are assumed to be in this package and all styles which rely on user-defined subroutines also search for them in this package. If this parameter is not given then the default package name is main.

This method also takes a number of other optional parameters, all of which are passed straight on to the Expat object. For details see the manual page for XML::Parser.

- `$parser->parse($source)`
  Parses the document. The `$source` parameter should either be the entire document in a scalar variable or a reference to an open `IO::Handle` object. The return value varies depending on the style chosen.

- `$parser->parse_file($filename)`
  Opens the given file and parses the contents. The return value varies according to the style chosen.

- `$parser->setHandlers(%handlers)`
  Overrides the current set of handlers with a new set. The parameters are interpreted as a hash in exactly the same format as the one passed to new. By including an empty string or undef, the associated handler can be switched off.

Essential Perl

Throughout this book I have assumed that you have a certain level of knowledge of Perl and have tried to explain everything that I have used beyond that level. In this appendix, I'll give a brief overview of the level of Perl that I've been aiming at. Note that this is not intended to be a complete introduction to Perl. For that you would be better looking at *Learning Perl* by Randal Schwartz and Tom Christiansen (O'Reilly); *Elements of Programming with Perl* by Andrew Johnson (Manning), or *Perl: The Programmer's Companion* by Nigel Chapman (Wiley).

B.1 *Running Perl*

There are a number of ways to achieve most things in Perl and running Perl scripts is no exception. In most cases you will write your Perl code using a text editor and save it to a file. Many people like to give Perl program files the extension `.pl`, but this usually isn't necessary.[1]

Under most modern operating systems the command interpreter works out how to run a script by parsing the first line of the script. If the first line looks like

```
#!/path/to/script/interpreter
```

then the program defined in this line will be called and your program file will be passed to it as input. In the case of Perl, this means that your Perl program files should usually start with the line

```
#!/usr/bin/perl
```

(although the exact path to the Perl interpreter will vary from system to system).

Having saved your program (and made the file executable if your operating system requires it) you can run it by typing the name of the file on your command line; e.g., if your script is in a file called `myscript.pl` you can run it by typing

```
myscript.pl
```

at the command line.

An alternative would be to call the Perl interpreter directly, passing it the name of your script like this:

```
perl myscript.pl
```

There are a number of command line options that you can either put on the command line or on the interpreter line in the program file. The most useful include:

---

[1] I say "usually" because Windows uses the extension of the file to determine how to run it. Therefore, if you're developing Perl under Windows, you'll need the .pl extension.

- -w Asks Perl to notify you when it comes across a number of unsafe programming practices in your program. These include using a variable before it is initialized and attempting to write to a file handle that is opened for reading. These warnings are usually very useful and there is no good reason not to use this option for every Perl program that you write.

- -T Turns on Perl's "taint" mode. In this mode all input from an external source is untrusted by default. You can make use of such input only by explicitly cleaning it first. This is particularly useful if you are writing a CGI script. For more details see the `perlsec` manual page.

- -c Checks a script for syntax errors without executing it.

- -d Runs the script using Perl's built-in debugger.

There is another way that you can pass Perl code to the Perl interpreter. This is to use the -e command line option. A text string following this option is assumed to be code to be executed, for example:

```
perl -e 'print "Hello World\n";'
```

will print the string "Hello World" to the console.

It may seem that this feature wouldn't be very useful as the only scripts that you can write like this would be very small; however, Perl has a number of other command line options that can combine with -e to create surprisingly complex scripts. Details of these options are given in chapter 3.

All of the information that you could ever need about running Perl can be found in the `perlrun` manual page.

B.2   Variables and data types

Perl supports a number of different data types. Each data type can be stored in its own type of variable. Unlike languages such as C or Pascal, Perl variables are not strongly typed. This means that a variable that contains a number can just as easily be used as a string without having to carry out any conversions.

The main data types that you will come across in Perl are scalars, arrays, and hashes. More complex data structures can be built using a combination of these types. The type of a Perl variable can be determined by the symbol that precedes the variable name. Scalars use $, arrays use @, and hashes use %.

B.2.1   Scalars

A scalar variable holds a single item of data. This data can be either a number or a string (or a reference, but we'll come to that later). Here are some examples of assigning values to a scalar variable:

```
$text = 'Hello World';
$count = 100;
$count = 'one hundred';
```

As you can see from the last two examples, the same scalar variable can contain both text and numbers. If a variable holds a number and you use it in a context where text is more useful, then Perl automatically makes the translation for you.

```
$number = 1;
$text = "$number ring to rule them all";
```

After running this code, $text would contain the string "1 ring to rule them all". This also works the other way around.[2]

```
$number = '100';
$big_number = $number * 2; # $big_number now contains the value 200.
```

Notice that we have used two different types of quotes to delimit strings in the previous examples. If a string is in double quotes and it contains variable names, then these variables are replaced by their values in the final string. If the string is in single quotes then variable expansion does not take place. There are also a number of character sequences which are expanded to special characters within double quotes. These include \n for a newline character, \t for a tab, and \x1F for a character whose ASCII code is 1F in hex. The full set of these escape sequences is in `perldoc perldata`.

B.2.2 *Arrays*

An array contains an ordered list of scalar values. Once again the scalar values can be of any type. Here are some examples of array assignment:

```
@empty = ();
@hobbits = ('Bilbo', 'Frodo', 'Merry');
@elves = ('Elrond', 'Legolas', 'Galadriel');
@people = (@hobbits, @elves);
($council, $fellow, $mirror) = @elves;
```

Notice that when assigning two arrays to a third (as in the fourth example above) the result array is an array consisting of six elements, not an array with two elements each of which is another array. Remember that the elements of an array can only be scalars. The final example shows how you can use list assignment to extract data from an array.

You can access the individual elements of an array using syntax like this:

```
$array[0]
```

---

[2] You can always turn a number into a string, but it's harder to turn most strings into numbers.

You can use this syntax to both get and set the value of an individual array element.

```
$hero = $hobbits[0];
$hobbits[2] = 'Pippin';
```

Notice that we use $ rather than @ to denote this value. This is because a single element of an array is a scalar value, not an array value.

If you assign a value to an element outside the current array index range, then the array is automatically extended.

```
$hobbits[3] = 'Merry';
$hobbits[100] = 'Sam';
```

In that last example, all of the elements between 4 and 99 also magically sprang into existence, and they all contain the value undef.

You can use negative index values to access array values from the end of the array.

```
$gardener = $hobbits[-1];  # $gardener now contains 'Sam'
```

You can use an *array slice* to access a number of elements of an array at once. In this case the result is another array.

```
@ring_holders = @hobbits[0, 1];
```

You can also use syntax indicating a range of values:

```
@ring_holders = @hobbits[0 .. 1];
```

or even another array which contains the indexes of the values that you need.

```
@index = (0, 1);
@ring_holders = @hobbits[@index];
```

You can combine different types of values within the same assignment.

```
@ring_holders = ('Smeagol', @hobbits[0, 1], 'Sam');
```

If you assign an array to a scalar value, you will get the number of elements in the array.

```
$count = @ring_holders;  # $count is now 4
```

There is a subtle difference between an array and a *list* (which is the set of values that an array contains). Notably, assigning a list to a scalar will give you the value of the rightmost element in the list. This often confuses newcomers to Perl.

```
$count = @ring_holders;     # As before, $count is 4
$last = ('Bilbo', 'Frodo'); # $last contains 'Frodo'
```

You can also get the index of the last element of an array using the syntax:

```
$#array
```

There are a number of functions that can be used to process a list.

- *push @array, list*—Adds the elements of `list` to the end of `@array`.
- *pop @array*—Removes and returns the last element of `@array`.
- *shift @array*—Removes and returns the first element of `@array`.
- *unshift @array, list*—Adds the elements of `list` to the front of `@array`.
- *splice @array, $offset, $length, list*—Removes and returns $length elements from `@array` starting at element $offset and replaces them with the elements of `list`. If `list` is omitted then the removed elements are simply deleted. If $length is omitted then everything from $offset to the end of `@array` is removed.

Two other very useful list processing functions are `map` and `grep`. `map` is passed a block of code and a list and returns the list created by running the given code on each element of the list in turn. Within the code block, the element being processed is stored in $_. For example, to create a list of squares, you could write code like this:

```
@squares = map { $_ * $_ } @numbers;
```

If `@numbers` contains the integers from 1 to 10, then `@square` will end up containing the squares of those integers from 1 to 100. It doesn't have to be true that each iteration only generates one element in the new list; for example, the code

```
@squares = map { $_, $_ * $_ } @numbers;
```

generates a list wherein each integer is followed by its square.

`grep` is also passed a block of code and a list. It executes the block of code for each element on the list in turn, and if the code returns a true value, then `grep` adds the original element to its return list. The list returned, therefore, contains all the elements wherein the code evaluated to true. For example, given a list containing random integers,

```
@odds = grep { $_ % 2 } @ints;
```

will put all of the odd values into the array `@odds`.

B.2.3 Hashes

Hashes (or, as they were previously known, associative arrays) provide a simple way to implement lookup tables in Perl. They associate a value with a text key. You assign values to a hash in much the same way as you do to an array. Here are some examples:

```
%rings = ();    # Creates an empty hash
%rings = ('elves', 3, 'dwarves', 7);
%rings = (elves => 3, dwarves => 7); # Another way to do the same thing
$rings{men} = 9;
$rings{great} = 1;
```

Notice that using the arrow operator (=>) has two advantages over the comma. It makes the assignment easier to understand and it automatically quotes the value to its left. Also notice that hashes use different brackets to access individual elements and because, like arrays, each element is a scalar, it is denoted with a $ rather than a %.

You can access the complete set of keys in a hash using the function keys, which returns a list of the hash keys.

```
@ring_types = keys %rings; # @ring_types is now ('men', 'great',
                                                 'dwarves', 'elves')
```

There is a similar function for values.

```
@ring_counts = values %rings; # @ring_counts is now (9, 1, 7, 3)
```

Notice that neither keys nor values is guaranteed to return the data in the same order as it was added to the hash. They are, however, guaranteed to return the data in the same order (assuming that you haven't changed the hash between the two calls).

There is a third function in this set called each which returns a two-element list containing one key from the hash together with its associated value. Subsequent calls to each will return another key/value pair until all pairs have been returned, at which point an empty array is returned. This allows you to write code like this:

```
while ( ($type, $count) = each %rings) {
  print "$count $type ring(s)\n";
}
```

You can also call each in a scalar context in which case it iterates over the keys in the hash.

The most efficient way to get the number of key/value pairs in a hash is to assign the return value from either keys or values to a scalar variable.[3]

```
$ring_types = keys %rings;  # $ring_types is now 4
```

You can access parts of a hash using a *hash slice* which is very similar to the array slice discussed earlier.

```
@minor_rings_types = ('elves', 'dwarves', 'men');
@minor_rings{@minor_rings_types} = @rings{@minor_rings_types};
         # creates a new hash called %minor_rings containing
         #    elves => 3
         #    dwarves => 7
         #    men => 9
```

---

[3] Note that this example also demonstrates that you can have variables of different types with the same name. The scalar $ring_types in this example has no connection at all with the array @ring_types in the earlier example.

Note, once again, that a hash slice returns a list and therefore is prefixed with @. The key list, however, is still delimited with { and }.

As a hash can be given values using a list, it is possible to use the map function to turn a list into a hash. For example, the following code creates a hash where the keys are numbers and the values are their squares.

```
%squares = map { $_, $_ * $_ } @numbers;
```

B.2.4 More information

For more information about Perl data types, see the perldata manual page.

B.3 Operators

Perl has all of the operators that you will be familiar with from other languages—and a few more besides. You can get a complete list of all of Perl's operators in the perlop manual page. Let's look at some of the operators in more detail.

B.3.1 Mathematical operators

The operators +, -, *, and / will add, subtract, multiply, and divide their two operands respectively. % will find the modulus of the two operands (that is the remainder when integer division is carried out).

Unary minus (-) reverses the sign of its single operand.

Unary increment (++) and decrement (--) operators will add or subtract one from their operands. These operators are available both in prefix and postfix versions. Both versions increment or decrement the operand, but the prefix versions return the result after the operation and the postfix versions return the results before the operation.

The exponentiation operator (**) raises its left-hand operand to the power given by its right operand.

All of the binary mathematical operators are available in an assignment version. For example,

```
$x += 5;
```

is exactly equivalent to writing

```
$x = $x + 5;
```

Similar to the mathematical operators, but working instead on strings, the concatenation operator (.) joins two strings and the string multiplication operator (x) returns a string made of its left operand repeated the number of times given by its right operand. For example,

```
$y = 'hello' x 3;
```

results in $y having the value "hellohellohello".

In an array context, if the left operand is a list, then this operator acts as a list repetition operator. For example,

```
@a = (0) x 100;
```

makes a list with 100 elements, each of which contains the number 0, and then assigns it to @a.

B.3.2 *Logical operators*

Perl distinguishes between logical operators for use on numbers and logical operators for use on strings. The former set uses the mathematical symbols <, <=, ==, !=, >=, and > for less than, less than or equal to, equal to, not equal to, greater than or equal to, and greater than, respectively, whereas the string logical operators use lt, le, eq, ne, ge, and gt for the same operations. All of these operators return 1 if their operands satisfy the relationship and 0 if they don't. In addition, there are two comparison operators <=> (for numbers) and cmp (for strings) which return –1, 0, or 1 depending on whether their first operand is less than, equal to, or greater than their second operand.

For joining logical comparisons, Perl has the usual set of operators, but once again it has two sets. The first set uses && for conjunction and || for disjunction. These operators have very high precedence. The second set uses the words and and or. This set has very low precedence. The difference is best explained with an example. When opening a file, it is very common in Perl to write something like this:

```
open DATA, 'file.dat' or die "Can't open file\n";
```

Notice that we have omitted the parentheses around the arguments to open. Because of the low precedence of or, this code is interpreted as if we had written

```
open (DATA, 'file.dat') or die "Can't open file\n";
```

which is what we wanted. If we had used the high precedence version of the operator instead, like this

```
open DATA, 'file.dat' || die "Can't open file\n";
```

it would have bound more tightly than the comma that builds up the list of arguments to open. Our code would, therefore, have been interpreted as though we had written

```
open DATA, ('file.dat' || die "Can't open file\n");
```

which doesn't achieve the correct result.

The previous example also demonstrates another feature of Perl's logical operators—they are *short-circuiting*. That is to say they only execute enough of the terms to know what the overall result will be. In the case of the open example, if the call to open is successful, then the left-hand side of the operator is true, which means that the whole expression is true (as an or operation is true if either of its operands is true). The right-hand side (the call to die) is therefore not called. If the call to open fails, then the left-hand side of the operator is false. The right-hand side must therefore be executed in order to ascertain what the result is. This leads to a very common idiom in Perl in which you will often see code like

```
execute_code() or handle_error();
```

Unusually, the logical operators are also available in assignment versions. The "or-equals" operator is the most commonly used of these. It is used in code like

```
$value ||= 'default';
```

This can be expanded into

```
$value = $value || 'default';
```

from which it is obvious that the code sets $value to a default value if it doesn't already have a value.

Perl also has *bitwise* logical operators for and ($\&$) or ($|$), exclusive or ($^$), and negation ($\sim$). These work on the binary representation of their two operands and, therefore, don't always give intuitively correct answers (for example $\sim$1 isn't equal to 0). There are also left (<<) and right (>>) shift operators for manipulating binary numbers. One use for these is to quickly multiply or divide numbers by a power of two.

B.4   Flow of control

Perl has all of the standard flow of control constructs that are familiar from other languages, but many of them have interesting variations.

B.4.1   Conditional execution

The if statement executes a piece of code only if an expression is true.

```
if ($location eq 'The Shire') {
  $safety = 1;
}
```

The statement can be extended with an else clause.

```
if ($location eq 'The Shire') {
  $safety++;
} else {
```

```
    $safety--;
}
```

And further extended with `elsif` clauses.

```
if ($location eq 'The Shire') {
  $safety++;
} elsif ($location eq 'Mordor') {
  $safety = 0;
} else {
  $safety--;
}
```

Perl also has an `unless` statement which is logically opposite the `if` statement—it executes unless the condition is true.

```
unless ($location eq 'The Shire') {
  $panic = 1;
}
```

Both the `if` and `unless` keywords can be used as *statement modifiers*. This can often make for more readable code.

```
$damage *= 2 if $name eq 'Aragorn';
$dexterity++ unless $name eq 'Sam';
```

B.4.2 Loops

Perl has a number of looping constructs to execute a piece of code a number of times.

for loop

The `for` loop has the syntax:

```
for (initialisation; test; increment) {
  statements;
}
```

For example,

```
for ($x = 1; $x <= 10; ++$x) {
  print "$x squared is ", $x * $x, "\n";
}
```

The loop will execute until the test returns a false value. It is probably true to say that this loop is very rarely used in Perl, as the `foreach` loop discussed in the next section is far more flexible.

foreach loop

The `foreach` loop has the syntax:

```
foreach var (list) {
  statements;
}
```

For example, the previous example can be rewritten as:

```
foreach my $x (1 .. 10) {
  print "$x squared is ", $x * $x, "\n";
}
```

which, to many people, is easier to understand as it is less complex. You can even omit the loop variable, in which case each element in the list in turn is accessible as $_.

```
foreach (1 .. 10) {
  print "$_ squared is ", $_ * $_, "\n";
}
```

This loop will execute until each element of the list has been processed. It is often used for iterating across the contents of an array like this:

```
foreach (@data) {
  process($_);
}
```

while loop

The `while` loop has the syntax:

```
while (condition) {
  statements;
}
```

For example,

```
while ($data = get_data()) {
  process($data);
}
```

This loop will execute until the condition evaluates to a false value.

Loop control

There are three keywords which can be used to alter the normal execution of a loop: `next`, `last`, and `redo`.

`next` immediately starts the next iteration of the loop, starting with the evaluation of any test which controls whether the loop should continue to be executed. For example, to ignore empty elements of an array you can write code like this:

```
foreach my $datum (@data) {
  next unless $datum;

  process($datum);
}
```

redo also returns to the start of the loop block, but does not execute any test or iteration code. Suppose you were prompting the user for ten pieces of data, none of which could be blank. You could write code like this:

```
foreach my $input (1 .. 10) {
  print "\n$input> ";
  $_ = <STDIN>;

  redo unless $_;
}
```

last immediately exits the loop and continues execution on the statement following the end of the loop. If you were processing data, but wanted to stop when you reached a number that was negative, you could write code like this:

```
foreach my $datum (@data) {
  last if $datum < 0;

  process($datum);
}
```

All of these keywords act on the innermost enclosing loop by default. If this isn't what you want then you can put a label in front of the loop keyword (for, foreach, or while) and refer to it in the next, redo, or last command. For example, if you were processing lines and words from a document, you could write something like this:

```
LINE:
  foreach my $line (getlines()) {
  WORD:
    foreach $word (getwords($line)) {
      last WORD if $word eq 'next';
      last LINE if $word eq 'end';

      process($word);
    }
  }
```

B.5   Subroutines

Subroutines are defined using the keyword sub like this:

```
sub gollum {
  print "We hatesss it forever!\n";
}
```

and are called like this:

```
&gollum;
```

or like this

```
gollum();
```

or (if the definition of the subroutine has already been seen by the compiler) like this:

```
gollum;
```

Within a subroutine, the parameters are available in the special array @_. These parameters are passed by reference, so changing this array will alter the values of the variables in the calling code.[4] To simulate parameter passing by value, it is usual to assign the parameters to local variables within the subroutine like this:

```
sub example {
  my ($arg1, $arg2, $arg4) = @_;

  # Do stuff with $arg1, $arg2 and $arg3
}
```

Any arrays or hashes that are passed into subroutines this way are flattened into one array. Therefore if you try to write code like this:

```
# Subroutine to print one element of an array
# N.B. This code doesn't work.
sub element {
  my (@arr, $x) = @_;

  print $arr[$x];
}

my @array = (1 .. 10);
element(@array, 4);
```

it won't work because, within the subroutine, the assignment to @arr doesn't know when to stop pulling elements from @_ and will, therefore, take all of @_, leaving nothing to go into $x which therefore ends up containing the undef value.

If you were to pass the parameters the other way round like this:

```
# Subroutine to print one element of an array
# N.B. Better than the previous version.
sub element {
  my ($x, @arr) = @_;

  print $arr[$x];
}

my @array = (1 .. 10);
element(4, @array);
```

---

[4] This isn't strictly true, but it's true enough to be a reasonable working hypothesis. For the full gory details see perldoc perlsub.

it would work, as the assignment to $x would pull one element off of @_ leaving the rest to go into @arr. An even better way, however, is to use references, as we'll see later.

A subroutine returns the value of the last statement that it executes, although you can also use the return function to explicitly return a value from any point in the subroutine. The return value can be a scalar or a list. Perl even supplies a function called wantarray which tells you whether your subroutine was called in scalar or array context so that you can adjust your return value accordingly.

More information about creating and calling subroutines can be found in the perlsub manual page.

B.6 References

References are the key to building complex data structures in Perl and, as such, are very important for data munging. They work somewhat like pointers in languages like C, but are more useful. They know, for example, the type of the object that they are pointing at. A reference is a scalar value and can, therefore, be stored in a standard scalar variable.

B.6.1 Creating references

You can create a reference to a variable in Perl by putting a backslash character (\) in front of the variable name. For example:

```
$scalar = 'A scalar';
@array = ('An', 'Array');
%hash = (type => 'Hash);

$scalar_ref = \$scalar;
$array_ref = \@array;
$hash_ref = \%hash;
```

Sometimes you'd like a reference to an array or a hash, but you don't wish to go to the bother of creating a variable. In these cases, you can create an *anonymous* array or hash like this:

```
$array_ref = ['An', 'Array'];
$hash_ref = {type => 'Hash'};
```

The references created in this manner are no different than the ones created from variables, and can be dereferenced in exactly the same ways.

B.6.2 Using references

To get back to the original object that the scalar points at, you simply put the object's type specifier character (i.e., $, @, or %) in front of the variable holding the reference. For example:

```
$orig_scalar = $$scalar_ref;
@orig_array = @$array_ref;
%orig_hash = %$hash_ref;
```

If you have a reference to an array or a hash, you can access the contained elements using the dereferencing operator (->). For example:

```
$array_element = $array_ref->[1];
$hash_element = $hash_ref->{type};
```

To find out what type of object a reference refers to, you can use the `ref` function. This function returns a string containing the name of the object type. For example:

```
print ref $scalar_ref; # prints 'SCALAR'
print ref $array_ref;  # prints 'ARRAY'
print ref $hash_ref;   # prints 'HASH'
```

B.6.3 References to subroutines

You can also take references to subroutines. The syntax is exactly equivalent for other object types. Remember that the type specifier character for a subroutine is &. You can therefore do things like this:

```
sub my_sub {
  print "I am a subroutine";
}

$sub_ref = \&my_sub;
&$sub_ref;   # executes &my_sub
$sub_ref->(); # another way to execute my_sub (allowing parameter passing)
```

You can use this to create references to anonymous subroutines (i.e., subroutines without names) like this:

```
$sub_ref = sub { print "I'm an anonymous subroutine" };
```

Now the only way to execute this subroutine is via the reference.

B.6.4 Complex data structures using references

I said at the start of this section that references were the key to creating complex data structures in Perl. Let's take a look at why this is.

Recall that each element of an array or a hash can only contain scalar values. If you tried to create a two-dimensional array with code like this:

```
# NOTE: This code doesn't work
@array_2d = ((1, 2, 3), (4, 5, 6), (7, ,8, 9));
```

the arrays would all be flattened and you would end up with a one-dimensional array containing the numbers from one to nine. However, with references we now have a way to refer to an array using a value which will fit into a scalar variable. We can, therefore, do something like this:

```
@arr1 = (1, 2, 3);
@arr2 = (4, 5, 6);
@arr3 = (7, 8, 9);

@array_2d = (\@arr1, \@arr2, \@arr3);
```

or (without the need for intermediate array variables):

```
@array_2d = ([1, 2, 3],
             [4, 5, 6],
             [7, 8, 9]);
```

Of course, having put our data into a two-dimensional array,[5] we need to know how we get the data back out again. It should be possible to work this out, given what we already know about arrays and references.

Suppose we want to access the central element of our 2-D array (the number 5). Actually, our array isn't a 2-D array at all, it is really an array which contains references to arrays in its elements. The element $array_2d[1] contains a reference to an anonymous array which contains the numbers 4, 5, and 6. One way to do it would, therefore, be to use an intermediate variable like this:

```
$row = $array_2d[1];
@row_arr = @$row;
$element = $row_arr[1];
```

While this will work, Perl gives us ways to write the same thing more efficiently. In particular, the notation for accessing an object given a reference to it has some extensions to it. Where previously we have seen syntax like @$arr_ref give us the array referred to by $arr_ref, there is a more general syntax which looks like:

```
@{block}
```

in which *block* is any piece of Perl code that returns a reference to an array (the same is true, incidentally, of hashes). In our case, we can, therefore, use this to our advantage and use

```
@{$array_2d[1]}
```

---

[5] Or, at least, something that simulates one rather well.

to get back the required array. As this is now the array in which we are interested, we can use standard array syntax to get back our required element, that is we replace the @ with a $ and put the required index in [..] on the end. Our required element is therefore given by the expression:

```
${$array_2d[1]}[1]
```

That does the job, but it looks a bit ugly and, if there were more than one level of indirection, it would just get worse. Surely there's another way? Remember when we were accessing elements of an array using the $arr_ref->[0] syntax? We can make use of that. We said that $array_2d[1] gives us a reference to the array that we need. We can, therefore, use the -> syntax to access the individual elements of that array. The element that we want is given by:

```
$array_2d[1]->[1];
```

which is much simpler. There is one further simplification that we can make. Because the only way to have multi-dimensional data structures like these is to use references, Perl knows that any multilevel accesses must involve references. Perl therefore assumes that there must be a dereferencing arrow (->) between any two successive sets of array or hash brackets and, if there isn't one there, it acts as though it were there anyway. This means that we can further simplify our expression to:

```
$array_2d[1][1];
```

This makes our structure look a lot like a traditional two-dimensional array in a language like C or BASIC.

In all of the examples of complex data structures we have used arrays that contain references to arrays; but it's just as simple to use arrays that contain hash references, hashes that contain hash references, or hashes that contain array references (or, indeed, any even more complex structures). Here are a few examples:

```
@hobbits = ({ fname => 'bilbo',
              lname => 'baggins' },
            { fname => 'frodo',
              lname => 'baggins' },
            { fname => 'Sam',
              lname => 'Gamgee' });

foreach (@hobbits) {
  print $_->{fname}, "\n";
}

%races = ( hobbits => [ 'Bilbo', 'Frodo', 'Sam'],
           men => ['Aragorn', 'Boromir', 'Theoden'],
           elves => ['Elrond', 'Galadriel', 'Legolas'],
           wizards => ['Gandalf', 'Saruman', 'Radagast'] );

foreach (keys %races) {
```

```
    print "Here are some $_\n";
    print "@{$races{$_}}\n\n";
}
```

B.6.5 More information on references and complex data structures

The manual page `perlref` contains a complete guide to references, but it can sometimes be a little terse for a beginner. The `perlreftut` manual page is a kinder, gentler introduction to references.

The `perllol` manual page contains an introduction to using Perl for the purpose of creating multi-dimensional arrays (or lists of lists—hence the name). The `perldsc` manual page is the data structures cookbook and contains information about building other kinds of data structures. It comes complete with a substantial number of detailed examples of creating and using such structures.

B.7   More information on Perl

Chapter 12 contains details of other places to obtain useful information about Perl. In general the best place to start is with the manual pages which come with your distribution of Perl. Typing `perldoc perl` on your command line will give you an overview of the various manual pages supplied and should help you decide which one to read for more detailed information.

index

Purchase of *Data Munging with Perl* includes free Author Online support. For more information on this feature, please refer to page xvi.